Anonymous

The evangelical succession: Third series

A course of lectures delivered in Free St. George's Church, Edinburgh, 1883-84

Anonymous

The evangelical succession: Third series
A course of lectures delivered in Free St. George's Church, Edinburgh, 1883-84

ISBN/EAN: 9783337283162

Printed in Europe, USA, Canada, Australia, Japan

Cover: Foto ©Lupo / pixelio.de

More available books at **www.hansebooks.com**

SUCCESSION

A Course of Lectures

*DELIVERED IN FREE ST. GEORGE'S CHURCH
EDINBURGH,* 1883-84

THIRD SERIES

EDINBURGH
MACNIVEN & WALLACE
1884

PREFATORY NOTE.

THE special object of these Lectures is, as the title indicates, to exhibit the genius of the Evangelical Principle, to trace its manifestation, development, and vicissitudes in various ages of the Church and human history, and to illustrate its ruling and moulding power over diverse types of national, intellectual, and spiritual character.

May 1884.

CONTENTS.

	PAGE
OWEN,	1
By the Rev. W. H. GOOLD, D.D.	
BUNYAN,	41
By the Rev. W. R. NICOLL, M.A.	
BOSTON,	73
By the Rev. W. SCRYMGEOUR.	
EDWARDS,	109
By the Rev. JAMES IVERACH, M.A.	
WESLEY,	145
By the Rev. J. H. WILSON, D.D.	
CAREY,	179
By GEORGE SMITH, Esq., LL.D.	
VINET,	219
By the Rev. R. J. SANDEMAN.	
CHALMERS,	255
By the Rev. W. C. SMITH, D.D.	
CHALMERS—A FRAGMENT,	291
By the late Rev. Sir H. WELLWOOD MONCREIFF, Bart., D.D.	

JOHN OWEN.

By the Rev. W. H. Goold, D.D., Edinburgh.

THERE is a spot, almost in the very heart of London, to which a peculiar and sacred interest attaches, in the estimation of those who have any sympathy with the struggles in which the religious freedom of our country had its birth. Streets upon streets surround it now, and, walking from one end of it to the other, you never lose the sound and din of busy traffic. Had we been standing near it almost exactly two centuries ago—in September 1683—our attention would have been arrested by a lengthened and solemn procession, winding upon our view from the west, and indicating by sable trappings and the usual insignia of death, that an interment was about to take place. It could be no common personage the open grave was about to receive. No fewer than sixty-seven carriages of noblemen and gentlemen—several mourning coaches,—and gentlemen on horseback follow the bier to the place of sepulture. The dark times of oppression had not passed away. Every form of Protestant dissent was under the ban of the Government, and yet this multitude, representative of all ranks in society, has gathered to pay the last tribute of respect and honour to the greatest of Dissenters—to commit dust to dust, ashes to ashes, all that remained on earth of JOHN OWEN.

He was worthy to whom this homage was rendered, and who thus sleeps in Bunhill Fields with other great and devout men, with Thomas Goodwin, associated with him in the most important official duties of his life, and with John Bunyan, whose sanctified genius was so warmly recognised by Owen, that he protested his willingness to part with all his learning if he could only preach the Gospel with the urgency and pathos of the tinker of Elstow—the dreamer of Bedford Jail. In the massive theological works which the great Puritan divine has bequeathed to posterity, ample reason will be found for the singular veneration in which he was held by his contemporaries; but, apart from his writings, there is much in his character, and in the course which he pursued in public life, that explains and justifies the grateful renown which embalms his memory. There are difficulties, however, besetting any attempt to sketch his career. No biography of him appeared till nearly forty years after his death. He has himself left on record nothing important, in regard either to his public conduct or private habits. Towering into a just pre-eminence among the leading men of his age, he allows his actions to speak for themselves and to find a record only so far as they belonged to the events of his time. Calm and self-possessed, with his faculties and affections uniformly under wise control, he favours us with no disclosure of the inward workings of his spirit, and no statement in regard to the incidents of his life, or the public movements with which his name was identified, beyond a few facts gleaned from some prefaces to his works. It is a marvellous instance of humility, when throughout twenty-four densely printed octavo volumes, so little of self-consciousness appears in his works, and hardly an egotistic reference can be found. There is but one exception to the truth of this remark. When the heart of Owen warms and opens under the influence of his love to Christ, his sentences sometimes glow with emotion, shedding a solemn light upon his secret principles of action and the real elements of his character. Otherwise we have no diary of religious experience, no details of domestic life, no glimpse behind the screen of his modest privacy. His biography, in the main, must be traced in the public events of his age,— his personal influence is seen in the extent to which his writings have moulded and consolidated the religious thought of his own and subsequent generations.

Born in 1616, and sprung from a Welsh family of distinction, he enjoyed certain advantages in his youth. His father was vicar of Stadham, a small parish in Oxfordshire, and distinguished himself by his zealous piety in the fulfilment of his duties. His son received from him for a time instruction in the ordinary branches of education, as well as a happy impulse in the direction of morality and religion. At a private academy in Oxford, he afterwards made good progress in his studies, under the care of an eminent tutor, Sylvester, till, at the early age of twelve, he entered the University. Resorting to physical exercises of a manly and even violent kind for the benefit of his health, and solacing himself with lessons in music from a teacher whom he afterwards, in the day of his power, made Professor of Music to the University, the young student devoted himself with ardour to the pursuit of learning, restricting himself to four hours of sleep in the day. For nine years, he thus toiled in study, correct in all his habits, but without the life of faith in his soul, and animated by no higher motive than ambition for preferment in Church or State.

It does not follow that a quiet season in the history of a nation, making no special demand on the higher energies of our nature, is the best for the origination and growth of the nobler virtues, or that absolute seclusion from public interests and affairs is most conducive to the real development of mind in a College. The breeze of political and ecclesiastical commotion visited Oxford, and Owen seems to have been awakened by it to the necessity for decision in regard to questions on which his conscience could not be silent. Laud sought to enforce his new ritualism on the University, and expulsion was the penalty which a refusal to comply with it entailed. Owen took the momentous step which committed him for life to the cause of the Reformation and of religious liberty. He had to leave the University, where his great attainments afforded every promise of office and honour in future years, and he lost besides the favour of an uncle, by whom he had been supported hitherto, and who so vehemently resented the conduct of his nephew as to cancel his will and bequeath to another the estate originally destined for Owen. But this outward change in his position and circumstances, while in part connected, is not to be confounded with a deeper change which about this time he experienced. He had been conscious of great spiritual perplexity and distress. It would seem that God fits his instruments for great work by a discipline of personal anxiety and concern. It was so with Paul, Augustine, and Luther. It was so with Owen. His vigorous intellect, competent to scale the utmost heights, and master all the details of sacred science, could not keep him from agony, when his soul awoke to consider the relation in which he stood to God. For three months, a peculiar tempest of spiritual anxiety raged within him. Oppressed with melancholy, he shunned all converse with his fellow-men, and when he spoke, the incoherency of his utterance betrayed the intensity of his convictions. By this time, he had received orders from Bishop Barlow, and yet his soul was a stranger to the peace of the Gospel. The long period of five years elapsed before he found it. Entering Aldermanbury Church in London, in order to hear the celebrated divine and preacher, Calamy, he experienced no small disappointment when an unknown minister officiated and preached from Matt. viii. 26.—"Why are ye fearful, O ye of little faith?" There are instances in which the Lord sends his people more than they sought. Owen sought the pleasure of hearing Calamy—the Lord sent him the peace that passeth all understanding. In spite of efforts to discover it, Owen never could learn the name of the man to whose simple preaching he owed under God his confirmation in the principles of grace, and to whom the whole Church of Christ owes so much in the rich tide of holy instruction with which Owen has refreshed and blessed it. The process of mental anxiety through which he had to pass,—anxiety in regard to the truths claiming reception from him, as well as to his own interest in Him in whom they all centred, and who is the Truth,—teaches an important lesson. How often is the modern agnostic prone to account for the faith entertained by the general body of Christians on the principle of facile acquiescence with traditional notions and impressions, as if there were a species of heredity in belief! Such a case as that of Owen,—belief cordially embraced and tenaciously held as the result of an agonising and prolonged conflict with difficulty and doubt—nor is the case unusual,—serves to prove that personal Christianity may be no dream of ignorance, but the conclusion attained by minds alert and awake in all their faculties to the legitimate demands of evidence.

It was important to dwell on the saving change which the great Puritan divine underwent, as it is in reality the key to the events of his life, and to the character of his whole theology. He believed, and therefore he spake. The whole Reformation of Europe had its germ in the cell of "the solitary monk who shook the world." Not an argument of the humble preacher, by whose discourse Owen's conversion was effected, but might have been familiar to him in his previous studies, and indeed his earliest biographer affirms as much. Brought home to him now, "in power and in the Holy Ghost and in much assurance," he felt the reality of grace in its actual influence and workings; and the essential distinction between nature and grace, upon which all evangelical theology proceeds, became henceforth not merely an article in his creed, but a fact in his experience. Need we wonder if his future years became a resolute consecration of his energies and resources to the exposition and defence of truths in believing which the storm within him had been changed into a calm? The precious discipline, while it gave him, amid all the waves of speculation and controversy, an anchor for his soul both sure and steadfast, taught him besides that pathetic tenderness in dealing with the awakened and the anxious which form a marked feature of several of his works.

Repairing to London, after having acted as chaplain in some noble families, he gave his first work to the press: *The Display of Arminianism*. So soon as Laud became Archbishop of Canterbury, he exerted himself in support of that theological system, between which and the ritualism he enjoined a natural affinity may be traced. A royal prohibition was issued against the discussion of the controverted points in the pulpit; and, in appointing to vacant benefices, patronage was extended specially to such men as evinced Arminian tendencies. Partly as the result of his new convictions as to the necessity of grace, partly in indignant protest against the arbitrary power which, to use his own phrase, "would beat poor naked Truth into a corner," Owen prepared this elaborate treatise against Arminian error. It is a remarkable production for a youth of twenty-four—replete with learning, acumen, some humour, and occasionally a spice of acerbity, with no tinge, however, of offensive personalities. It had the effect of drawing attention to his rare abilities, and he was presented to the living of Fordham, which, after a year and a half, he had to leave; but on the earnest request of the people of Coggeshall—a market town of Essex, five miles distant from Fordham—he consented to be their pastor under a presentation from the Earl of Warwick. Sometimes it has been affirmed that Owen could trace no spiritual results from his ministry. Asty, his biographer, writing under the eye and correction of Owen's personal and intimate friend, Sir John Hartipp, declares that at Fordham "great was the success of his labours in the reformation and conversion of many," and at Coggeshall equal success attended his ministry, a congregation of two thousand, Sabbath after Sabbath, hanging on the lips of the preacher. Engrossed with his work, he published on *The Duty of Pastor and People*, and catechisms also for the religious instruction of the young. His fame, however, began to spread beyond the limits of the district in which he laboured with such diligence, and, summoned in April 1646 to preach before Parliament, he delivered the "noble sermon from the cry of the man of Macedonia, entitled 'A Vision of Free Mercy.'" He seized the opportunity to urge upon Parliament the duty of providing the means of religious instruction for destitute districts in England, with a special reference to the country of his ancestors, Wales. To the sermon was appended a tract in which he deprecates appeals to the civil magistrate for the erection of an ecclesiastical polity, and yet he seems conscious of no inconsistency, when he insists before the great council of the nation upon the duty of sending the Gospel where it was needed, rising, in his ardent desire for this object, to a combination of argument and pathos,—the vehement logic of a holy enthusiasm —which John Howe or Richard Baxter never surpassed. Illustrating how much they want who are destitute of the Gospel, he proceeds:—

"They want Jesus Christ, for he is revealed only by the Gospel. Austin refused to delight in Cicero's 'Hortensius,' because there was not in it the name of Jesus Christ. Jesus Christ is all, and in all; and where he is wanting, there is no good. Hunger cannot truly be satisfied without manna, the bread of life, which is Jesus Christ;—and what shall a hungry man do that hath no bread? Thirst cannot be quenched without that water or living spring, which is Jesus Christ;—and what shall a thirsty soul do without water? A captive, as we are all, cannot be delivered without redemption, which is Jesus Christ;

—and what shall the prisoner do without his ransom? Fools, as we are all, cannot be instructed without wisdom, which is Jesus Christ;—without him we perish in our folly. All building without him is on sand, which will surely fall. All working without him is in the fire, where it will be consumed. All riches without him have wings or will away. 'Mallem ruere cum Christo, quam regnare cum Cæsare," said Luther. A dungeon with Christ, is a throne; and a throne without Christ, a hell. Nothing so ill, but Christ will compensate. The greatest evil in the world is sin, and the greatest sin was the first; and yet Gregory feared not to cry, 'O felix culpa, quæ talem meruit redemptorem!'—'O happy fault, which found such a Redeemer!' All mercies without Christ are bitter; and every cup is sweet that is seasoned but with a drop of his blood;—he truly is 'amor et deliciæ humani generis,'—the love and delight of the sons of men,—without whom they perish eternally; 'for there is no other name given unto them, whereby they may be saved,' Acts iv. 12. He is the Way; men without him are Cains, wanderers, vagabonds:—he is the Truth; men without him are liars, like the devil, who was so of old:—He is the Life; without him men are dead, dead in trespasses and sins:—He is the Light; without him men are in darkness, and go they know not whither:—He is the Vine; those that are not grafted in him are withered branches prepared for the fire:—He is the Rock; men not built on him are carried away with a flood:—He is Alpha and Omega, the first and the last, the author and the ender, the founder and the finisher of our Salvation. He that hath not him, hath neither beginning of good, nor shall have end of misery. O blessed Jesus! how much better were it not to be, than to be without thee!—never to be born, than not to die in thee!—A thousand hells come short of this, eternally to want Jesus Christ, as men do that want the Gospel."

Owen preached several times before the Parliament. In one of these sermons, delivered after his return from Ireland in 1649, while he admits the necessity of repressing such atrocities as the Irish massacre of 1641, he urges the adoption of remedial as well as coercive measures. If the Gospel had been sent to Ireland at that time, in the spirit of the Gospel,—in the spirit in which Owen would have sent it,—modern statesmen would not have had to complain of Ireland as their difficulty. It is thus he pleads:—

How is it that Jesus Christ is in Ireland only as a *lion staining all his garments with the blood of his enemies;* and none to hold him out as a *lamb sprinkled with his own blood to his friends?* Is it the sovereignty and interest of England that is alone to be there transacted? For my part, I see no further into the MYSTERY of these things but that I could heartily rejoice that, innocent blood being expiated, the Irish might enjoy Ireland so long as the moon endureth, so that Jesus Christ might possess the Irish. But God having suffered those sworn vassals of the man of sin to break out into such ways of villainy as render them obnoxious unto vengeance, upon such rules of government amongst men as he hath appointed; is there, therefore, nothing to be done but to give a *cup of blood* into their hands?

Listening to one of his sermons, Cromwell had formed such an estimate of Owen's gifts and abilities as led him to a conclusion which he carried out with his usual tenacity. Owen must accompany him to Ireland. He wrote himself to the church at Coggeshall, insisting that it was their duty to acquiesce in the loss of their pastor's services for a season. The congregation reclaimed against the proposal, but Cromwell was resolute, and, in the end, Owen proceeded with him to Ireland. Residing in Trinity College, he preached frequently to large audiences in the city of Dublin, not without the fruits of conversion and striking testimonies to the effects of his ministrations; on his return to England, under the influence of his appeals to Parliament, various Acts for the encouragement of religion and learning, and the extension of the University in Dublin, were immediately passed. Such had been the value of his counsels in Ireland, that when in 1650 Cromwell entered Scotland at the head of the army which may be said to have turned defeat into victory at Dunbar, by an order of the House of Commons, Owen was again enjoined to accompany him. He preached in Berwick and Edinburgh sermons afterwards printed, but beyond this publication, it is somewhat disappointing to Scotsmen to find no other authentic traces of the influence and proceedings of the great Puritan divine in their country.

The highest honour of his life was about to reach him. He had returned to his quiet and congenial work as a pastor in Coggeshall, when one morning he read, to his surprise, in some newspaper of the day, the following announcement—" On the 18th March

1651, the House, taking into consideration the worth and usefulness of John Owen, M.A., of Queen's College, ordered that he be settled in the Deanery of Christ's Church, in room of Dr. Reynolds." In the following year, Cromwell, having become Chancellor of the University of Oxford, nominated Owen Vice-Chancellor. His administration of its affairs is admitted, even by parties opposed to the policy of the Puritans, such as even Clarendon, to have done him the utmost credit. The University had been a scene of ruin and confusion. It settled down into order and peace when the firm hand of Owen controlled it, buildings shattered by the commotions of the times were repaired, its revenues were restored and increased, and a goodly crowd of eminent men, whether as professors or students, frequented it, adorning its history by the lustre of a reputation already achieved, or soon to be achieved, in various departments of learning. Incidents are on record, attesting the vigour and dignity with which he secured compliance with his rule. The natural benignity of the man, however, was not lost in the assertion of his authority. Cromwell, who generally is credited with larger and juster views on the subject of toleration than he really held, denied, in his "Instrument of Government," liberty to Episcopalians as well as Romanists, to "make profession of their faith and enjoy the exercise of their worship." Not far from the Vice-Chancellor's own door, however, Episcopalians held a meeting every Sabbath, and had worship according to their liturgy. Owen, though solicited to put the laws in force against them, would not suffer them to be disturbed. To the Presbyterians, though in respect of ecclesiastical polity he now differed from them, he was equally generous, consulting with them on important emergencies, and appointing their ablest men to vacant livings. When the Commission, called the Tryers', gave trouble to Pococke, the distinguished Arabic scholar, Owen wrote warmly against his threatened ejection, and hastened to the spot where the Commissioners met, to use his personal influence to the utmost in order to dissuade them from the step they proposed to take. In the end he was successful. Such actions, in unison with the tenor of his whole life, illustrate the consistent generosity of his nature—a generosity rare at any time—rarer still in those troublous times—to be ascribed, we cannot but believe, to that strength of religious principle which is the richest element in the character of Owen.

Owen, as we have seen, had left Oxford a friendless student, rather than violate conscience by compliance with the schemes of Laud. He had his reward, when he was recalled with honour to be its head as Vice-Chancellor. The circumstances under which he resigned the office, after he had held it for five years, reflect no honour upon Cromwell. Certain officers in the army—among them his own brother-in-law and son-in-law—had learned his design to assume royal dignity and prerogative, and resented it as inconsistent with the whole movement, the success of which they had purchased with their swords, and at the hazard of their lives. They resolved on a petition to Parliament, and got Owen to prepare it. How far he accorded with them in their opposition to Cromwell's project, it would be difficult to say, although at this time suspicion in regard to the ultimate designs of the Protector appears to have prevailed among the chief of the Puritan divines. Owen's share in this opposition to his aims was never forgiven by Cromwell. In 1656, changes were made through which Owen ceased to be Vice-Chancellor of the Oxford University, soon afterwards he was discharged from the Deanery of Christ Church, and his connection with Oxford thus terminated entirely. His address in demitting the former office is manly and dignified —reviewing in no boastful tone the services he had rendered the University, and without a syllable of resentment against the arbitrary and ungrateful spirit to which he owed his removal from it.

During the remainder of his life, Owen was busy with various controversies—preaching as often as he could find opportunity, though in the persecution to which dissenters during the reign of Charles II. were subjected, he could only officiate at times in secret assemblies, and sometimes was obliged to consult safety from arrest by flight. He exerted himself to procure the release of John Bunyan from prison. Availing himself of the connivance extended to the Puritans after the plague and the great fire of London, he preached in the "tabernacles,"—buildings, reared of wood, in which thousands gathered to hear messages of peace and consolation under these terrible visitations of Providence. A congregation afterwards gathered round him in Leadenhall Street. Several pious noblemen attended his ministrations. On one occasion he was summoned to an interview with the King and the Duke of York. Towards the close of his life, he suffered under painful maladies. But he was unwearied to the last in his efforts to commend the Divine Master whom he had served so well; on the very eve of death, he finished a treatise—his *Meditations on the Glory of Christ*. The seraphic elevation of Christian hope which the treatise breathes was soon to be fulfilled in the experience of its author. On the day of his death, when told by a friend to whom the publication of the work had been intrusted, that it was committed to the press, he expressed his satisfaction, "But, O brother," he exclaimed in an outburst of joy, "the long wished-for day is come at last in which I shall see that glory in another manner than I have ever done, or was capable of doing in this life." Dying saints have sometimes sighed for rest—for blessedness—for the presence of God, when the supreme moment has come to them. It was characteristic of Owen—the end and scope of his life-long toil, when his anticipations of heaven merge and centre in the vision of his Lord, glorious as John saw him in Patmos, "the brightness of the Father's glory and the express image of his person."

So much, briefly and imperfectly, have we given of the life of this great divine; for otherwise it would be difficult to estimate aright his writings generally on the religious views he specially espoused and advocated. It is a case in which a knowledge of the man sheds some light on the nature of his works. There is in his greater productions so little obtrusion of self, so little of the personal element, that some acquaintance with the public affairs and momentous interests which occupied the mind and time of Owen supplies a key at times to the prevailing turn of his thoughts, at times even to the precise conclusions which he is seeking to establish. He is indeed a voluminous author, no fewer than 80 treatises, that need twenty-four octavos to contain them, having issued from his pen; and he was only 67 years of age when he died. A large proportion of these treatises is controversial, though no great eagerness for controversy can be ascribed to him, most of his publications in this department having been enjoined upon him by authority, or elicited by request, or provoked by assaults. He has occasion to be firm at times even to severity; but it may be claimed for him that, on the whole, he is singularly free from acrimonious invective and personalities.

His place and rank, however, in the "Evangelical Succession" must be determined by his doctrinal and exegetical works, though some reference is due to his writings on the subject of toleration and church-government, all the more that the peculiar tendencies of Owen on these subjects spring undoubtedly from the intensity of his Evangelical convictions. It is when clear views and a vivid grasp of the doctrines of grace take hold of the mind, that a spirit of wise consideration and forbearance will manifest itself.

Under an outer shell of character, hard, rigid, unyielding, where faith in salvation by grace notwithstanding really exists and reigns, the heart is most likely to be amenable to the kindlier and nobler influences under which the Gospel trains us to fulfil the duties of life. It is in this school—the school of Evangelical belief and training,—that the grandest benevolence of our age has been developed—on a scale wide as the vast field of missionary enterprise.

So far as relates to TOLERATION, the honour has been claimed for Owen of first announcing and advocating the principle on which Governments should proceed in allowing the free expression of thought in a community. He would be a bold man who would assert that to this hour all the difficulties encumbering this question have been removed and solved. Owen did much to extricate it from prejudice and misconception. On the one hand, it may be admitted that he was by no means the first to assert and vindicate the great principle of religious liberty. The right to the free expression of conscientious belief, when not abused to the purposes of public disorder or impious blasphemy, had been often affirmed. The essential principle on which the right is founded is clearly stated by the early Christian Father Lactantius, has been traced in mediæval writings, was vehemently asserted by Luther, was enunciated by Zuingle, and embodied in authoritative documents by divines in Holland. Nor should it be forgotten that two years before the the treatise on toleration from the pen of Owen appeared, the Westminster Confession of Faith had been finished and published, containing the noblest assertion of the true principle by which legitimate freedom of thought and utterance is secured,—" God alone is Lord of the conscience." On the other hand, while we cannot concede to Owen the merit of any originality or priority in asserting the genuine principles of religious liberty, we are not disposed to involve him in the condemnation to which he has sometimes been subjected in connection with the Sixteen Fundamentals. These were a summary of the essential truths of Christianity, prepared by a number of divines who had been called upon by a Committee of Parliament to undertake the duty Cromwell had presented to the House his Instrument of Government, granting protection to all " in the profession of their faith and the exercise of their religion,"—"provided" (it is significantly added) "this liberty be not extended to Popery or Prelacy." In dealing with this document, Parliament went into a discussion as to what were the fundamentals of religion, and ultimately appointed the Committee, in answer to which the divines consulted submitted a list of Sixteen Fundamentals. Nothing appears from which it can be directly concluded that these divines, of whom Owen was one, held that no toleration should be extended beyond the tenets specified, and the title of the paper rather suggests a different object in view—"The principles of faith presented to the Committee of Parliament for Religion, by way of explanation to the proposals for *propagating* the Gospel."

The value of Owen's treatise on the subject of

toleration lies in the fact that, not content with a mere incidental expression of his views, he enters frankly on a full and formal discussion of the whole question. He commits himself, moreover, to the advocacy of toleration, when the political party to which he belonged was in power; for under the fires of persecution or when but a weak minority, most parties can plead for liberty, and, as the elder M'Crie has shown, even Roman Catholics, so early as the reign of Elizabeth, could talk of "the inestimable blessing of toleration." The chief merit of Owen, however, is that he places the liberty for which he pleads, on the true ground—on a principle much deeper and safer than Jeremy Taylor and John Locke have done—not the difficulty of arriving at certainty in regard to any truth, but on the incompetence of the civil magistrate to act as a judge of spiritual offences, and on the prohibition by the Gospel itself of any resort to external force for its propagation. It is true that he admits the warrantableness of civil penalties against blasphemy and errors directly published in order to promote rebellion and disturbance, and these are to this day civil offences in the British Statute Book. He would lay some restraint on Popery, for in his time the friends of liberty had to deal with it, not simply as a system of theological error, but as a political conspiracy. But while he holds the magistrate bound to ascertain the truth for himself, and even to take measures for the spread of it in his dominions, he "is bold positively to assert" that, saving the qualifications just referred to, "the magistrate hath no warrant from the Word of God to force persons to submit unto the truth as by him established, or to molest them with any civil penalty in case of refusal." Simple words these may seem in the light of modern opinion! But had the principle embodied in them swayed the rulers of this country in Owen's day and after it, what a world of strife and anguish and suffering had been saved to England—what torrents of blood to Scotland!

The truth is that, in wading through the discussions which took place in the time of the Commonwealth and subsequently, it must be admitted that no party, as such, was altogether consistent with itself. As to the Independents, passages have been quoted from John Cotton against John Owen; as to Presbyterians, Samuel Rutherfurd has been quoted against Robert Baillie. It is well, accordingly, in the long struggle from the early times of Puritanism to grasp the essential principle at stake, and, to judge of all the parties who, by their heroism in doing or suffering, had an honourable share in that struggle, we must be guided in the main by the general scope of their policy and conduct. To be on the right line is much, though we may not have reached the station. No man questions the debt which the cause of civil and religious liberty owes to the Long Parliament, and yet from that Parliament emanated the terrible Ordinance of 1648, enacting death without benefit of clergy as the penalty due to certain heresies. Men are often better than their principles, as principles too are often better than the men who advocate them. The Ordinance was never carried into effect, and it must be remembered that the real conflict of the nation was with a system embodying royal and hierarchical despotism, and which had for a century resorted to the worst extremes of persecution. The attempt to suppress Puritanism was an attempt to suppress the doctrine so admirably asserted and unfolded by Calvin in his *Institutes*, that the Church of Christ must not, in the maintenance of discipline, resort to civil penalties or external force. Hooker himself, representing moderate Anglicanism, in his elaborate argument against the views of the Puritans, thus states the question as between him and his opponents: "Their judgment is that the Church of Christ should admit of no law-makers but the Evangelists, no courts but Presbyteries, no punishments but ecclesiastical censures." There can be no difficulty in drawing by legitimate evolution from these words such principles as the exclusive Headship of Christ over His Church, the supreme authority of the Word, the spiritual independence of the Church, the rights of the Laity in the administration of its affairs, and religious liberty to all beyond the Church who dissent from it conscientiously. How many generations of effort and of sacrifice has it cost us to get these simple principles, so essential to civil and religious liberty, understood simply, not to say established in paramount influence and ascendency—effort and sacrifice as yet in some measure in vain. Once admit, in the rites and tenets of the faith, an authority beyond the Word, and the result is spiritual despotism on the one hand, and bondage on the other.

The only fragment of autobiography which Owen gives will be found in his *Vindication of the Treatise on Schism*. It is so remarkable that we could wish to have had more of such allusions to his personal history. It is a defence of himself against the charge of inconsistency in the change his sentiments underwent on the subject of CHURCH GOVERNMENT. He intimates that if his opponent conceived any advantage to accrue from thus charging him with inconstancy, "I shall not labour," he meekly replies in allusion to a greater change, "to divest him of this apprehension, having abundant cause to rejoice in the rich grace of a merciful and tender Father, that, men seeking occasion to speak evil of so poor a worm, tossed up and down in the midst of innumerable temptations, I should be found to fix on that which I know will be found my rejoicing in the day of the Lord Jesus."

It is a poor and narrow spirit which affects indifference to the question how the living resources of Christianity are best to be marshalled and organised for its support, and defence, and spread. Under an honourable eagerness to get men to embrace and act upon the principles of the Gospel —in other words, directly to save souls,—some may feel unable, even averse, to occupy their thoughts with what they deem subordinate questions, such as the proper government of the Church or its legitimate independence. Let all justice be done to the predominant motive by which they are influenced; but an enlightened anxiety to secure the most effective organisation for the Christian Church may spring from a zeal for conversion quite as great, if not indeed even greater. To set the battle in array may be as great a service as to fight in the ranks. If we could place ourselves for a moment in the circumstances of Owen and realise the exigencies of the Church in his age, we would feel the need of earnest inquiry how it was to be guided and governed. He had broken utterly with the hierarchical system, to which the miseries of the nation must be ascribed. Virtually to all intents and purposes a Presbyterian, he might be convinced that the great majority of the nation could not be won to Presbyterianism all at once, and that to establish it by the mere authority of the State would render it still more unacceptable. Above all, Owen had a strong yearning for a higher measure of godliness and spirituality, as requisite to membership in the Church. A vast national system, the sudden creation of the State, would foster tendencies at variance with his most cherished convictions of what a church should be. He falls back upon Scripture; "impartially examining," he tells us, "all things by the Word, comparing causes with causes and things with things." The attempt to confute a work by Cotton, in favour of Independency, led him into this careful examination and ultimately into the adoption of that system. The perusal of all he has written on the subject, however, leaves the impression that beneath the argument on the surface, honestly felt and stated, there was the desire as honest for a system which could most directly sustain and deepen religious life in the Church. It was his belief and hope that not in a vast system, the result of parliamentary enactment, but in separate communities of the faithful, piety, deep and true, might grow and prosper.

As the result of his examination into Scripture, the views of Owen on the polity of the Church were in the first place settled and abiding, and they were at the same time somewhat fresh and peculiar. He could plead for them a *divine right*, in the proper sense of these words, as implying merely that they were "founded upon and agreeable to the Word of God," not in the sense in which they have sometimes been used, and with which they are often confounded,—to the denial that any association of Christians under a different polity could be a Church of Christ. Holding that his principles on this question had the sanction of Scripture, he adhered to them steadily. With Owen, however, it was not the mere change from one denomination into another, when he became a Congregationalist. There was a specialty in the conclusions at which, in the exercise of his own free inquiry and judgment, he arrived, on the footing of which it has been contended that he was still in a measure Presbyterian. It seems no easy task to discriminate from Presbyterianism his views on the subjects of the Ruling Elder and of Synodical authority; and perhaps on this ground he was led in one of his treatises to remark, "For my part, so we could once agree practically in the matter of our Churches, I am under some apprehension that it were no impossible thing to reconcile the whole difference as to a Presbyterian Church and a single congregation." These words deserve consideration as indicating his pacific disposition, or, as one of his contemporaries calls it, "his healing temper," and as confirming the view given of his chief aim in all his researches and writings on church-government—his paramount desire for purity and spiritual life in the Churches. It will be noticed that the one thing on which he insists as essential to the reconciliation, which he deemed not impossible, is practical agreement as to "the matter of the Churches,"—in other words, the character of their membership. Free from bigotry, sanctimoniousness, or any tinge of sectarian bitterness, Owen stands honourably distinguished in Christian authorship, for his fervent yearnings after a devout, pure, holy, and spiritual Church.

It is, however, on his character and work as a THEOLOGIAN that his claim to the reverence and gratitude of posterity chiefly depends. The very number of his works in this department—the profound and comprehensive nature of the discussions embraced in them—the extent to which they influenced religious thought, not in Britain only, but in other countries—the revived demand for them in our own times, as attested by the sale of five thousand copies of the complete edition of his works, are reasons which surely warrant and constrain inquiry into the leading features and principles of an author whose productions in size and number almost form a literature of themselves. They vary in style; in some instances, rare enough we admit, vigorous, effective, beautiful, blending a heroic manliness with tender pathos, they are for the most part heavy and diffuse, the result of the haste and urgency in which they were commonly written, and perhaps of a certain proud disregard for minor graces, if only he had ascertained the truth and honestly stated it. Nevertheless there is a sonorous majesty in his lumbering sentences, which, when they were uttered by himself, helps to explain the effect his speaking produced; for it is the testimony of Wood, who had heard him at Oxford, and was bitterly opposed to the cause of the Puritans, that "he could by the persuasion of his oratory move and wind the affections of his admiring auditory almost as he pleased."

To discuss the wide range of sacred learning which he traversed would be impossible. In order to a proper estimate of the nature and tendency of his theological views, the standard by which he tested them, the system into which they were reduced, the scope contemplated in them, and the application made of them, may in succession be considered.

1. With Owen, *the standard of truth*, as revealed, was Scripture exclusively, Scripture supremely. It is needful to bear this fact in mind to distinguish him from one class of theologians, such as Hooker, who, in the external administration of the Church, contended for a certain measure of deference to reason, apart from revelation, and from another school which, even in the highest articles of faith, leaned to the former, as in some sense a co-ordinate revelation of the Divine Mind. According to Owen, reason had its own function and province in re-

ligion, but so far as truth was the substance of a revelation, it could not emanate from our mental faculties, nor could these be in any sense a test and criterion of it. Their limits were reached, their function was exhausted, when they had determined its character, as an essential part of revelation. Hence in Puritan theology—in the writings specially of Owen—the authority of Scripture is supreme, not merely as regards the doctrines to be believed, but in the regulation of the discipline, government, and worship of the Church. He manifests a stringent, but, at the same time, a discriminating jealousy in defence of the supreme authority of Scripture; he dwells on the principle with peculiar fulness and urgency, not merely from a profound insight into the limits of the human understanding in matters of faith, but from a conviction that any departure from this ground—any recognition of another authority in revealed religion beyond the Word of God—would, as history had proved, be fatal to the spiritual liberties of the Church.

Take a brief illustration of his views from the subject of Christian worship. To use almost his own words—certain things "without worship, but about it," such as the fit time and place for publicly observing it, "may be left to common prudence;" but he objects to "the imposition of uncommanded rites," and holds that "instituted worship . . . depends on supernatural revelation," and therefore that Divine revelation must be "the sole rule" in regard to the proper observance of it.

Impressed with a deep conviction of the paramount importance of this principle, he was naturally led to defend with peculiar fervour what he called "the perfectness of the standard." Hence arose what has been represented as "the only blunder of Owen," and a grievous blot upon his memory. He is supposed to have denounced sacred criticism by writing against the Polyglott of Walton, and objecting to the collection of discrepancies in the manuscripts of the sacred text. That Owen, in common with eminent scholars of his day, erred on some questions of Biblical criticism, such as Hebrew punctuation, cannot be denied; and that he shared in the panic created by the publication of the various readings existing in the manuscripts is also to some extent true. His fear, however, was occasioned by the use actually made of them by Romanists and sceptics, to whom he refers,—the former exalting, in consequence, the authority of the Church to the disparagement of Scripture,— and the latter maintaining, on the same ground, that no confidence could be reposed on the sacred text. So far, however, from Owen evincing "the outrageous violence" imputed to him, it was his desire, according to his own profession, to conduct the dispute "with Christian candour and moderation of spirit." His work on the subject is in existence, and it will take sharp eyes to discover any sentence inconsistent with this profession of its author. So far from assailing Walton or his Polyglott with unseemly invective, he declares that "he would never fail to commend the usefulness of the work, and the learning, diligence, and pains of the worthy persons that have brought it forth." It will even be a greater surprise to many, when they are told that, instead of condemning the cultivation of sacred science, he admitted the existence of various readings in the New Testament, and held that if others, from a collation of manuscripts, could be discovered, they " deserved to be considered." He assigns rules by which worthless errata could be discriminated from more important discrepancies entitled to such consideration. His chief object was a just and noble one, specially needed when the existence of various readings was almost a new disclosure to the mass of Christian readers ;—it was to vindicate the text from such uncertainty as to afford an excuse for disdaining its authority. Conscious at the same time that his own learning, vast as it was, great even in relation to the very subject discussed, did not lie in the line of Biblical criticism, he says, with a humility which should be remembered to his credit, and which might have saved him from some bitter epithets of reproach, " Those who have more wisdom and learning, I hope will rather take pains to instruct me, and such as I am, than be angry or offended with us, that we are not so wise and learned as themselves."

In relation to the Word of God as the standard of faith, the merits of Owen as an exegete cannot be overlooked. Here too he was in advance of his times. Apart from minor works in this department, such as his delightful treatise *On the 130th Psalm*, his *Commentary on the Epistle to the Hebrews*—in a sense his dying bequest to the Church of Christ—

constitutes the noblest monument to his memory, discussing, with exhaustive fulness and a spiritual tact which is unrivalled, the meaning of the sacred writer, the doctrine to be evolved from his statements, and the application to be made of it. Refraining from any attempt to describe his rare qualities as an expositor, as beyond our limits, we content ourselves with one remark. The principles on which he constructed his commentary, as well as special solutions of difficulties in the course of it, are singularly anticipative of the light which modern research has brought to bear on the subject. For instances of the latter, his work itself may be consulted; as to the former, the principle on which he conducts the exposition, he recognises the value of what is now termed the historical method of interpretation, and holds it essential for the discovery of the real scope and bearing of the Scripture expounded that it should be studied in relation to the circumstances of the age when it was written, and specially to the condition of the Church to which it might be addressed.

Another important principle in regard to Scripture Owen has the merit, if not of discovering, at least of first placing in a clear light. It is known as "the self-evidencing power of the Word." He was at pains, and wrote indeed a particular treatise, to discriminate the principle from any taint of mysticism. He illustrates this self-evidencing efficacy by the analogy of two influences, light and power. As light manifests itself, and otherwise would be no light, and as power would be no power unless it made itself felt, so with Scripture. In its necessary effect on the awakened mind, when its truths are brought home to it by the Holy Spirit, there is a source of internal evidence commending the Word to the conscience, and investing it with the qualities divinely claimed for it as "quick and powerful." Prejudice may resist this evidence, but, as he quaintly remarks, "the light is not the eye," and unwillingness to appreciate the truth of God, either in its own nature or in its claims to our belief, may be due to causes independent of both.

2. Advancing from the *standard* by which he regulates his faith, to the *system* of theological truth which he deduced from it, we are confronted with a series of massive treatises on some of the weightiest truths of revelation, such as the Divinity of Christ, the Person and Work of the Spirit, the Extent of Redemption, Justification by Faith, and the Perseverance of the Saints. The general character of his theology may be described as Evangelical rather than Calvinistic; for, though he embraces the Calvinistic system, he reaches his conclusions so directly in the light of Scripture, that there is a freshness all his own in his presentation of Divine truth. He has stamped the impress of his religious thinking so deeply on the generations that followed him in the same school, that the originality of Owen in the sense just indicated is not discerned, because his views have become so familiar to us. Dr. James Hamilton draws attention to the fact, and states that the "Evangelical theology of the last hundred years has been chiefly alluvial," and that the element

in it "which we chiefly recognise is a detritus from Mount Owen." The great Puritan thought out his conclusions for himself, differing on some points from Calvin, from Twisse, from Rutherfurd, and others. His comprehensive learning enabled him to take stock of the theology of ages. But he is never encumbered with all he knows; far less does he quit his hold of Scripture to drift on the current of human opinions. Unlike his great contemporary, Jeremy Taylor, not certainly his inferior in learning, he does not, simply to clench an argument or point a moral, surprise us with a curious felicity of quotation or with incidents selected from some dark recess of ancient literature. The whole field lies open to him, and the ease with which he accumulates facts to bear upon the question on hand with him is wonderful. There are two schools of Evangelical divines: such as travel upward from the ruin of man to the redemption by God; others who travel downward from the Divine purpose of redemption to our actual deliverance in all its process and results. Both methods have their advantages and disadvantages. Owen belonged to the latter class. His very first publication—*The Display of Arminianism* —led him to unfold the sovereignty of the Divine will in salvation, and his mind kept throughout life to this line of contemplation, in expounding the mystery of the faith. It had its disadvantages, for we have no such direct dealing with sinners, as in Baxter's *Call to the Unconverted*, in any treatise from Owen specially devoted to such a purpose; and at times he may be conceived to press his argument to conclusions unduly rigid. There is compensation for these defects, as we shall afterwards see. Meanwhile it is not to be supposed that there are not, interspersed with his hardest argumentations, arousing appeals to the conscience and the most urgent commendation of Christ. There are passages, even in the work in which he contends for definite and particular redemption, asserting in the noblest terms the duty not merely of tendering a free and universal offer of the Gospel, but of urging upon every sinner individually his responsibility under the call thus addressed to him. This much must be said, on the other hand, that from his standpoint in viewing the system of Divine truth, he was brought to realise and cherish a vivid apprehension of God, as the source and substance of all truth. Revealed truth was of value to him as it gave him, to borrow words from the title of one of his own treatises, "an understanding of the mind of God." He wrote for the same purpose for which he lived. Nor did he either write or live in vain. "In the treatises of Owen," says Dr. Hamilton, "there is many a sentence which, set in a sermon, would shine like a brilliant, and there is bullion enough to make the fortune of a theological faculty." If any man is under the delusion that the exhibition and enforcement of dogma, even though it bear the seal of inspiration, are necessarily inconsistent with depth of thought, warmth of emotion, and originality of genius, let him peruse Owen *On Communion with God*, in which he expounds the relationship of the saint to all the persons in the Trinity. He has occasion, for example, to insist on the holiness of the Saviour: "Adam," he tells us, "had this spotless purity, so had the angels, but they came immediately from the hand of God, without concurrence of any secondary cause. Jesus Christ is a plant and root out of a dry ground, a blossom from the stem of Jesse, a bud from the loins of sinful man,—born of a sinner, after there had been no innocent flesh in the world for four thousand years, every one on the roll of his genealogy being infected therewith. To have a flower of wonderful rarity to grow in Paradise, a garden of God's own planting, not sullied in the least, is not so strange; but, as the Psalmist speaks, to hear of it in a wood, to find it in a forest, to have a spotless bud brought forth in the wilderness of corrupted nature, is a thing which angels may desire to look into."

3. It would be injustice to Owen if we overlooked the *scope* of his theology. There is a noble consecration in it to a special end. The greatest name in infidel literature of our day, Strauss, in his New Confession, remarks, as if it were a discovery of his own, that the controversy between faith and unbelief turns mainly on the Person of Christ. Had he read Owen, he would have found that it was no discovery. So convinced was Owen of the fact, that he wrote a treatise specially on this very point— *On the Person of Christ*—a treatise of which the elder M'Crie does not hesitate to say that " of all the theological works published since the Reformation, next to Calvin's *Institutes*, he would have deemed it his highest honour to have produced." Dr. M'Crie

was not accustomed to speak from ignorance, or without weighing his words. To exhibit Christ in the strength of His claims is the design of the work, and he brings out, with rare fulness and felicity, how in the whole contendings of the Church, directly or indirectly, the momentous claim embodied in the doctrine of His Person has been the design and scope of its testimony. The settlement of it so far, in the happy issue of the Arian controversy, committed the Church, in the elucidation of Scripture, to lines of development and progress, necessarily resulting in evangelical theology, for to assert the divinity of the Redeemer was, in other words, to assert that redemption was not human, but Divine, and this obviously is the essence of evangelical teaching. But the profound discussions of Owen on the Person of Christ must be taken into connection with another of his works, published in the year after his death,— his *Meditations on the Glory of Christ.* In these two works will be found the prevailing aim of his life, the scope of all he taught and wrote. In Christ he found the rock and foundation of all theology, as a revelation of mercy and pardon for a fallen world—the basis of the Divine administration in the moral universe—the bond that unites heaven with earth in the experience and hopes of the saint —the source of life to the Church as well as the central doctrine of its beliefs. In the former treatise, rising above the irritation of controversy, the great Puritan casts his eye in profound and pensive thoughtfulness over the Christian Church in its past history as well as its present condition. He finds it in a woful state. The world itself in its opposition to Christ had been filled "with blood and confusion." To terminate "these woful conflicts," he would "re-enthrone," to use the words expressive of his own grand design, "the Person, Spirit, Grace, and Authority of Christ in the hearts and consciences of men." All prophecy is a fable, if his conviction is a fallacy and his hope a dream. Not that he would commit himself in the least to any mood of despondency under the present disorder around him. The faith he breathes in all he wrote on this theme comes like a refreshing breeze over the mind, imparting new invigoration to our spiritual nature; and towards the close of the latter treatise, when he anticipates the recognition of his Lord in glory, there is such a gathering up of all the elements of that glory revealed in Scripture that the day seems to break and the shadows to flee away under the dawn of a Sun of righteousness, not merely with healing under its wings for all the miseries of time, but with the brightness of a joy that gives to heaven itself all its savour and its zest.

Finally, small space has been left, we fear, to dwell on what is really the cardinal and distinctive honour of Owen as a great divine,—the *spiritual application or bearing* of Divine truth on human character generally, on the experience of the saint in particular. No divine excels him in this department. Profound insight into human nature is needed for it,—human nature as renewed and wrought upon by grace. To discover and trace the relation of Divine truth to the human conscience requires no common skill, is indeed a holy art learned only in the school of the ripest experience, and taught only through a special gift of the Holy Ghost. In this field of religious thought and inquiry,—the field in which the truest originality in preaching the gospel may be evinced,—it would be impossible to name a Christian author who surpasses Owen, difficult to name another who ranks on the same level. It is not with him morbid speculations in casuistry, such as some divines have indulged in. It is the calm, faithful, lucid, searching investigation into the workings of grace,—analysis keen and penetrating into the motives of human action, with a view to separate the precious from the vile, the genuine from the counterfeit, thought and feeling as the result of grace from thought and feeling which, under the veneering and varnish of seeming piety, may be nothing better than the old corruption in disguise. In most of his purely religious treatises this skill in spiritual diagnosis may be noticed, as in his *Communion with God*, when he distinguishes between the dying of sin as to the habit, and the dying of sin as to the root; but he has special treatises of this character *On Temptation*, *On Indwelling Sin*, *On Spiritual-mindedness*, and others. Amongst all these some of the ablest men I have met with, who have made a study of Owen, give the palm to his work *On the Mortification of Sin*.

To such lectures as have now been resumed on

the Evangelical Succession, objection has been taken that "the great biography"—the life of our Lord alone—should be unfolded in the pulpit, and constituted the subject of meditation on the day of God. The holy feeling from which the objection springs is worthy of the deepest respect. Christ, however, is to be seen, and it is his glory that he is seen, not merely in the page of Scripture, but in the persons of all who truly love and follow him; and so far as they have done Christ's work, reflected Christ's image, advanced Christ's cause, our faith surely can rise from the servant to the Master, and give Him all the praise. You remember the scene in the south of Scotland, as recorded in faithful history. One aged martyr struggles amid the rising waters, soon to engulf her, and her companion, in the sweet years of tender girlhood, tied to a stake nearer the shore, is made to notice the death with which her friend was threatened, and asked what she thought of her, and her terrible situation. She answers in calm heroism, "What do I see, but Christ in one of his members suffering there?" If in the history of the Church, in the individual lives of martyrs, confessors, and reformers, while making due acknowledgment of the human error and frailties which abound in the best of them, we recognise what grace has wrought in them, and wrought by them, and see Christ in them, as the dying martyr saw in her companion, we are but reading a new chapter in the great biography and erecting new trophies to the praise of Him who is its theme; and if I have succeeded in inspiring any minds with the desire to study the writings of him who has been styled " the prince of Puritan divines," it is my humble belief that they will be brought nearer the truth of Christ, nearer Christ Himself.

JOHN BUNYAN.

By the Rev. W. Robertson Nicoll, M.A., Kelso.

GREAT as is the place occupied by John Bunyan in English literature and theology, many points in his life are still obscure, and many incorrect and incomplete statements appear to this day even in books by writers of authority. A brief sketch of his life may therefore not be superfluous. I have to acknowledge my indebtedness, in preparing it, to the kindness of the chief living authority on John Bunyan, Dr. John Brown, his accomplished successor at Bedford, from whom we expect what will doubtless be the standard biography of Bunyan.[1]

He was born at the village of Elstowe, about a mile from Bedford, in 1628. At that time, the disparity of Bedford and the village beside it was by no means so great as it is now. It seems probable that then the population of Bedford was about four times the population of Elstowe; by the census of the present year it is thirty-five times. Few places in England have been less changed in the eventful years that have passed since Bunyan's time than

[1] See *Personal Relics and Recent Memorials of Bunyan*, and Wylie's indispensable *Book of the Bunyan Festival*.

Elstowe. The old half-timber cottages, with overhanging storeys, gabled porches, and peaked dormers, covered with roses and honeysuckles, must be much the same as in the days of the Commonwealth. It is only recently that we have been able to identify with precision the exact place of Bunyan's birth. The tradition held for many years by the oldest inhabitants was that the cottage where he was born was about a mile from the Church, at a place called Bunyan's End. About a year ago Dr. Brown was fortunate enough to verify this tradition by a discovery in the Record Office, which shows that Bunyan's ancestors were living there in 1542, nearly one hundred years before his birth, and that the place was then called Bunyan's End, and had probably been in the possession of his family long before that. Bunyan's father was a tinker—the first in the family—what we should now call a white-smith or brazier; indeed he describes himself in his will by the latter name. His son says: "My father's house was of that rank which is meanest and most despised of all the families in the land." The fact that the family were so long living in the same cottage and cultivating the same ground is quite fatal to the utterly baseless theory that Bunyan was of gipsy blood; nor is it in the least more probable that he was, as has been recently asserted, of Scotch descent. There is the clearest evidence that more than 400 years before his birth there were Bunyans living in the neighbourhood. Dr. Brown is inclined to consider the name Norman in its origin, and derived from some ancient Norman town or village. The name of

Bunyan's mother has been discovered very recently; it was Margaret Bentley. We have always known that he was born in 1628, and now it has been discovered that it was on the last of the chill November days of that year that his mother carried out the son, who was afterwards to be so famous, from the tinker's cottage to Elstowe Church for baptism. His father was able to send him to school, and it was perhaps neither his fault nor his son's that what the boy learned there he forgot afterwards almost utterly, being driven by poverty soon to bear a hand at the anvil.

The years of Bunyan's boyhood were those when the Puritan spirit culminated in England, and especially in Bedfordshire; and from the very beginning the young mind, so full of undeveloped forces, was exercised by religious terrors. As he grew older these increased, and his vivid description of his own youth has led to the most varying inferences. Ryland says: "No man of common sense and common integrity can deny that Bunyan was a practical atheist, a worthless contemptible infidel, a vile rebel to God and goodness, a common profligate, a soul-despising, a soul-murdering, a soul-damning thoughtless wretch, as could exist on the face of the earth. Now be astonished, O heavens! to eternity, and wonder, O earth and hell! while time endures. Behold this very man become a miracle of mercy, a mirror of wisdom, goodness, holiness, truth, and love." On this Lord Macaulay observes: "Whoever takes the trouble to examine the evidence will find that the good man who wrote this had been deceived by a phraseology which he ought to have understood better. It is quite certain that Bunyan was at eighteen what in any but the most austerely Puritanical circles would have been considered as a young man of singular gravity and innocence." He points out that when Bunyan was accused of impurity he broke into vehement and passionate protest; that there is no evidence that he was ever drunk, and that the worst that can be said of him was that he had a great liking for some diversions, harmless in themselves, but condemned by the rigid precisians among whom he lived. In this opinion Lord Macaulay has almost been universally followed, and yet those who read with attention his own writings and the contemporary biographies may hesitate in affirming that the whole truth has been told. He says himself that "he did still let loose the reins of his lust, and delighted in all transgressions against the law of God, so that until he came to the state of marriage he was the very ringleader in all manner of vice and ungodliness." Nor do other utterances, fairly interpreted, recall this confession. Besides, in him the text was illustrated, "When the commandment came, sin revived." "One day," he says, "I was standing at a neighbour's shop window, and there cursing and swearing and playing the madman with my wonted manner. There sat within the woman of the house and heard me, who, though she was a very loose and ungodly wretch, yet protested that I swore and cursed at that most fearful rate, that she was made to tremble to hear me, and told me further that I was the ungodliest fellow for swearing that ever she heard in all her life, and that

I, by thus doing, was able to spoil all the youth in the whole town if they came in my company." Besides, we can see that his associates were amongst the wildest, and that when outward reformation came it excited the great astonishment of his neighbours. His sins, however, we may hope, were sins done against God rather than against man—sins for which he received a complete forgiveness. We may hope that he never fell into those transgressions which disable and darken the whole life, even after they have been forgiven by God, by their irretrievable results in others.

However this may be, when he was about seventeen he became a soldier, and here we approach one of the most controverted points of his life— viz., on which side he took up arms. Lord Macaulay pronounces, without hesitation, that he was a soldier in the Parliamentary army. His most recent biographers are strongly of opinion that he was a Royalist, and Mr. Froude holds this view, supporting it with somewhat doubtful arguments. For example, one of the reasons he gives for saying that Bunyan was probably on the side of the Royalists is that John Gifford, afterwards his pastor, had been a Royalist. It is scarcely necessary to point out that Gifford and Bunyan could not have known of each other's existence for at least four years after Bunyan's soldiering experiences were all over. The evidence on the other side seems very strong. At the time when Bunyan was a soldier, Bedfordshire declared unmistakeably that the Parliament and not the King was the lawfully constituted authority of the realm, and it does not seem likely, as Dr. Brown remarks, that he, a mere lad of sixteen or seventeen, listening to a Puritan preacher, and living in a county intensely Puritan, should have come to different conclusions from the majority of his neighbours on the great question then agitating the nation. Next, even if this were the case, it is very improbable that he would be able to make his way to the King's quarters through strong lines of Parliamentary forces, and long roads jealously guarded. The only reference made by himself to his military experience is the well-known passage: "When I was a soldier, I with others were drawn out to go to such a place to besiege it, but when I was just ready to go one of the company desired to go in my room, to which when I had consented, he took my place, and going to the siege, as he stood sentinel, he was shot into the head with a musket bullet, and died." It has been unhesitatingly taken for granted that this passage refers to the siege of Leicester, but against this view there are very strong arguments. More probably it refers to some sudden call made upon the garrison at Newport, for men to assist in the Parliamentary operations in the west. The significant fact is that it should be possible to have any doubt upon which side Bunyan served. Lord Macaulay remarks that "his brief glimpse of the pomp of war strongly impressed his imagination, and to the last he loved to draw his illustrations of sacred things from camps and fortresses, from guns, drums, flags of truce, and regiments arrayed each under his own banner."

After a few months he returned home. His first biographer, a personal acquaintance, says: "The few friends he had thought that changing his condition to the married state might reform him, and therefore urged him to marry as a sensible and comfortable advantage; but his poverty and irregular course of life made it very difficult for him to get a wife suitable to his inclination." His mercy, however, was to light upon a wife whose father was counted godly. "This woman and I," he says, "though we came together as poor as poor might be, not having so much household stuff as a dish or spoon betwixt us both, yet this she had for her part—*The Plain Man's Pathway to Heaven* and *The Practice of Piety* which her father had left her when he died. In these two books I should sometimes read with her, wherein I also found some things that were somewhat pleasing to me; but all this while I met with no conviction. She also would be often telling of me what a godly man her father was, and how he would reprove and correct vice, both in his house and among his neighbours; what a strict and holy life he lived in his days, both in word and deed." Soon there commenced the tremendous spiritual conflict described in his *Grace Abounding*. A mighty external reformation took place in his character. He abandoned one sin after another, and astonished his neighbours by his conversion from "prodigious profaneness" to moral life. With all this he found no real peace. One day in the streets of Bedford he came to where there were three or four poor women sitting at a door in the sun, and talking about the things of God. He heard, but hardly understood, for their themes were out of his reach. They talked of the new birth, their miserable state by nature, God's love in Christ, the suggestions and temptations of Satan, their own wretchedness of heart and unbelief; and they spoke, he thought, as if joy did make them speak. They were like people that dwelt alone in a new-found world. He saw himself then in a forlorn and sad condition, and yet was provoked by a vehement, hungering desire to be one of the number that did sit in the sunshine. At home or abroad, in house or field, he lifted up his heart in prayer, "O Lord, consider my distress!" But peace was far off, and difficulties were endless. Was he elected? Was the day of grace past and gone? He broke his mind to these poor people in Bedford, but all was for a time in vain. Though his conscience was very tender, and he shrank from sin, whole floods of blasphemies were poured upon his spirit. He doubted the Scriptures. He was tempted to think that the Turks had as good Scriptures to prove Mahomet their Saviour, as we had to prove our Jesus is. His heart was very hard. He would have given a thousand pounds for a tear, and, although he was not without brief glimpses of comfort, they were, like Peter's sheet, suddenly caught up to heaven again. At last he began to find rest. He saw, with great evidence from the relation of the four Evangelists, the wonderful work of God in giving Jesus Christ to save us, both from His conception and birth, even to His second coming to judgment. "Methought," he says, "I saw as if I had seen Him born, as if I had seen Him grow up, as if I had seen Him walk through this world from the cradle to His cross, to which also when he came I saw how gently He gave Himself to be hanged and nailed on it for my sins and wicked doings; and as I was musing on this His progress that dropped on my spirit, *He was ordained for the slaughter.*" As he gazed on the thorn-crowned head, he often longed that the end were come. "Oh! thought I, that I was fourscore years old now, that I might die quickly, and that my soul might be gone to rest." About this time he earnestly longed to read the experience of another soul, and he found it in an old tattered copy of Martin Luther's *Comment on the Galatians.* Luther had himself ploughed through like seas of terror and blasphemy, and it is pathetic to see these mighty spirits meet—deep calling unto deep, heart answering to heart. "I found my condition in his experience so largely and profoundly handled as if his book had been written out of my heart. I do prefer this book of Martin Luther before all the books that ever I have seen as most fit for a wounded conscience." But the end was not yet. He was tempted to sell and part with Christ; and, though he answered, "I will not, I will not; no, not for thousands, thousands, thousands of worlds," one day he felt the thought pass through his heart, "Let Him go, if He will," and that terrible Scripture seized him, "He found no place of repentance, though he sought it carefully with tears." For two years together nothing would abide with him but damnation and the expectation of damnation. Thoughts like these make the soul like a sword of fire, wearing its way through its sheath. His body was racked with such pains that he expected to burst asunder like Judas. He trembled for whole days together with fear of death and judgment. At last light came. He heard the assurance, "I have loved thee with an everlasting love," and after, with grateful heart and watchful eye, turning over with great seriousness every leaf, and considering every sentence of the promises, he had amazing experience of the grace of God. Once he saw himself within the arms of grace and mercy, and though he was afraid before to think of a dying hour, yet now he cried, "Let me die." Death was lovely and beautiful in his sight, for he saw that we shall never live indeed until we be gone into the other world. "Oh! methought, this life is a slumber in comparison with that above." He joined himself to the little society of Baptists at Bedford, consisting of "twelve ancient and grave persons," including the women whom he had heard speaking in the sun, and presided over by John Gifford, a man with a strange history. He had been a major in the King's army, a desperate profligate, but, by God's mercy, a new life entered into him, and the little society at Bedford—one amongst them being Harrington, whom Gifford in old days purposed to kill on account of his religious principles—made him their pastor. He was baptized in the river Ouse. Although a Baptist, he never attached great importance to the distinguishing principle of that sect. "The Gospel," he said, "may be effectually preached, and yet baptism neither administered nor mentioned. Paul made no such matter of baptism as some in these days do. No; he made no matter at all thereof with respect to Church communion. When Satan abuseth it and wrencheth it out of its place, making that which was ordained of God for the edification of believers the only weapon to break in pieces the love, the unity, the concord of saints, then what is baptism? Then neither is baptism anything."

How are we to regard these awful and prolonged agonies? Were his troubles a mere series of phantasies? Was he, as a recent writer has said, led astray by failing to understand the use of the Bible? "The cause," says Canon Venables, "of this protracted agony was his regarding the Bible as a bundle of isolated texts instead of a comprehensive revelation of God's loving and holy will." The very simplicity of these explanations suggests a doubt of their completeness. It is true, indeed, that Bunyan had that deep and even mystical faith in the letter of Scripture which unites men so far apart as, for example, Milton, Newman, and Maurice. And, if we are to set aside the personal agency of the Tempter as an exploded fable, if we are satisfied to label as morbid fancies the similar experience of so many other souls that have sought the face of God; if we see in the revelation of Christ nothing but sunshine, and are able to get rid of all the deep shadows of sin and judgment, then, indeed, such solutions may suffice. But if not, we may see in the record of Bunyan's experience a frequent understanding of Scripture not given to the mere scholar, an insight into the real, piercing, and tremendous significance of words too familiar to our dull eyes, and a record of the Divine preparation and training of a great soul for a high and singular service. By and by, Bunyan began to preach. He tells us that after he had been about five or six years awakened he was desired by some "to take in hand to speak a word of exhortation unto them, and did twice, at two several assemblies and in private, though with much weakness and infirmity, discover my gift amongst them, at which they not only seemed to be, but did solemnly protest as in the sight of the great God, they were both affected and converted, and gave thanks to the Father of mercies for the grace bestowed on me." At last he was more particularly called forth and appointed to the preaching of the Word, and soon gained great popularity. "They came in," he says, "to hear the Word by hundreds, and that from all parts, though on sundry and divers accounts." His profound experience, deep conviction, thorough knowledge of the Scriptures, and vigorous genius, gave him great and immediate influence. After he had been about five years a preacher, he was thrown into the jail at Bedford. Under an unrepealed Act of Parliament, and within six months of the King's arrival, he was arrested for preaching at Samsell, and sent on to Bedford jail. He would have to walk through Elstowe in the custody of the constable. Past the cottage door where he had lived with the gentle companion of his youth, past the scene of his early sports and struggles, "along the road where he had once thought of putting his faith to the test of miracle, but where it was now to be put to a nobler test than that," he makes his way to the grim structure of the county jail, long since thrown down, where he was to lie for twelve years. He had seen what was coming, and had had two considerations especially warm upon his heart. The first was how to be able to endure the long tedious imprisonment, and the next was how, if need be, he might glorify God in dying. He was not afraid that he would shrink from death, but his terror was that he should die with a pale face and tottering knees for such a cause as this. He was wonderfully comforted—enabled to see that the best way to go through suffering was to trust in God through Christ for the world to come, and, as for this world, to count all things dead. But still he was a man compassed with infirmities. "The parting with my wife and poor children have often been to me in this place as the pulling the flesh from my bones, and that not only because I am somewhat too fond of these great mercies, but also because I should have often brought to my mind the many hardships, miseries, and wants that my poor family were like to meet with should I be taken from them —especially my poor blind child, who lay nearer my heart than all I had besides. O, the thought of the hardship I thought my blind one might go under would break my heart to pieces! Poor child, thought I, what sorrow art thou like to have for thy portion in this world! Thou must be beaten, must beg, suffer hunger, cold, nakedness, and a thousand calamities, though I cannot now endure the wind should blow upon thee. But yet, recalling myself, thought I, I must venture you all with God, though it goeth to the quick to leave you. O, I saw in this condition I was as a man who was pulling down his house upon the head of his wife and children; yet, thought I, I must do it, I must do it."

Of late years it has been maintained that Bunyan's imprisonment was by no means irksome, and Mr. Froude goes so far as to say that it was little more than formal. This view is supported by the remarkable argument that "the church in Bedford would never have abandoned to want its most distinguished pastor." But Bunyan was not chosen to be pastor at all till his imprisonment had been ended, and his distinction had all of it yet to be won. It is true that Bunyan was too high-hearted to whine over his afflictions, and that there were mitigations. He had a friend in the under-jailer, John White, who in 1668 was brought before the Archdeacon's Court for refusing to pay the church rates of his parish. It is also true that he was several times out of prison during the twelve years of his imprisonment. "I had," he says, "some liberty granted me more than at the first, and, following my wonted course of preaching, did go to see Christians at London, taking all occasions that were put into my hand to visit the people of God." All this freedom, however, he expressly says, was granted between the two assizes of August 1661 and April 1662, when he was seeking in vain to get his name on the calendar for trial. He also tells us that his enemies were so enraged by the clemency of his jailer, that they almost cast him out of his place. We may be sure his confinement was hard enough. A man of the name of John Bubb, who was in jail along with him for about nine months, sent up a most plaintive petition to the King, still extant in the Record Office, in which he says that during his imprisonment he "hath suffered as much misery as soe dismall a place could be capable to inflict, and so is likely to perish without your Majestie's further compassion and mercie towards him." John Bubb evidently would not have agreed with Mr. Froude; he knew what imprisonment in Bedford jail meant. Not being able to carry on his old trade in prison, Bunyan learned to make long tagged thread laces for the hawkers, and thus supported his family. He formed a little church out of his fellow-prisoners, and, as he tells us himself, "I was never out of the Bible," words which are the key to a true understanding of his life and work. He had also Foxe's *Book of Martyrs*, and on the margin of his copy are still legible "the ill-spelt lines of doggerel in which he expressed his reverence for the brave sufferers, and his implacable enmity to the mystical Babylon."

An application for release failing, Bunyan resolutely set himself to writing. The first book he published while in prison, *Christian Behaviour*, is dated "From my place of confinement at Bedford, this 17th of the 4th month, 1663,"[1] that is, in the third

[1] See Brown's *Personal Relics*, etc., p. 8. Offor erroneously gives the date as 1674.

year of his imprisonment. His writings were at first mainly controversies against the Quakers, the liturgy, and Church of England, and the Close Communion Baptists. At last, however, he commenced the work that was to make him immortal—*The Pilgrim's Progress*. It was begun, he tells us, *before he was aware*, and carried on to its completion in silence. For while he made his fellow-prisoners free of all his other writings as they went on, this he kept secret, as if there were about it something separate. A great critic of our own day, writing on Dante, uses words that may well be applied to Bunyan : " We approach the history of such works, in which genius seems to have pushed its achievements to a new limit, with a kind of awe. The beginnings of all things, their bursting out from nothing, and gradual evolution into substance and shape, cast upon the mind a solemn influence. They come too near the fount of being to be followed up without our feeling the shadows which surround it. We cannot but fear, cannot but feel ourselves cut off from this visible and familiar world as we enter into the cloud. And as with the processes of nature, so it is with those offsprings of man's mind by which he has added permanently one more great feature to the world, and created a new power which is to act on mankind to the end. The mystery the invention and creation presents, the subtle and incalculable combinations by which it was led to its work, and carried through it, are out of the reach of investigating thought. Often the idea recurs of the precariousness of the result : by how little the world might have lost one of its ornaments—by one sharp pang, or one chance meeting, or any other among the countless accidents among which man runs his course. And then the solemn recollection supervenes that powers were formed, and life preserved, and circumstances arranged, and actions controlled, that thus it should be; and the work which man has brooded over, and at last created, is the foster-child too of that Wisdom which 'reaches from end to end, strongly and sweetly disposing all things.'"[1]

Something was no doubt due to the circumstances in which the book was written. He had, what is so hard now-a-days, to gain the stillness and leisure needful for a great and worthy expression of his genius. We can see how his mind gradually worked itself clear of all partial and impairing elements; how the petty interests of the world outside cease at last to torment. His mind attained the calmness needful for the healthy activity of the imagination, and, if the controversialist was silenced for the time, the poet's mouth was opened. The prison became a large place, as he took counsel with himself, and gradually brought to perfection an undying product of the imagination. Some of the most famous studies of that period were prison cells, and it is impossible not to speculate how many preachers and publicists of our time might save their souls alive if they were provided with another such opportunity as Bunyan's.

When he had finished the manuscript of the first

[1] Church's *Dante*, pp. 2, 3.

part, he, if we may trust what seems a good tradition,[1] read it to his fellow-prisoners in jail:

"Some said, John, print it; others said, Not so;
Some said, It might do good; others said, No."

The author concluded not to publish it in the meantime, and the first part did not appear till 1678, six years after his release from prison.

As to how that release was obtained, there is considerable controversy. In 1672 there was a lull in the storm which had raged so long, and, either from weariness in the cruel and fruitless work of suppression, or from a policy meant to favour Rome, a Declaration of Indulgence was issued, under which more than 3000 licences to preach were granted, Bunyan's being one of the first. Thus came to an end the long bondage so devoutly borne, so nobly used. He had been elected in January of the same year pastor of the Baptist Church at Bedford, "after much seeking of God by prayer and sober conference," and for the next seventeen years there, and over all the neighbouring country, he laboured in season and out of season.

The *Pilgrim's Progress* in a very short time caught the popular mind. Its circulation among religious families of the lower and middle classes in England was immense, and was even greater in Scotland and New England. In Holland and in France he had numerous admirers. It was Bunyan's fate as an author to be scourged by his own laurels; but in 1682 he published the *Holy War*, which, says Lord

[1] See Birrell, *Book of the Bunyan Festival*, p. 102.

Macaulay, if the *Pilgrim's Progress* did not exist, would be the best allegory that ever was written. *Grace Abounding* was first published in 1666, and six editions were called for in that year. In 1684 appeared the second part of the *Pilgrim's Progress*, the *Odyssey* of Christiana to the *Iliad* of Christian —unaccountably depreciated by recent critics, but delightful for the tenderness of its pervading spirit and the exquisiteness of many separate touches.

It is not wonderful that his incessant labours and great literary reputation, gained for him paramount authority amongst his co-religionists. His large place of worship in Bedford was usually crowded with a devout auditory. When he preached in London an immense concourse assembled to hear him in the coldest winter weather, and before daylight in the morning. From London he went through the country animating the zeal of his brethren, distributing alms, and settling disputes. With all this his literary activity never relaxed.

In the year 1685, on the accession of James II., an advanced Papist, scarcely one eminent dissenting minister remained unmolested. Feeling the uncertainty of his position, Bunyan that year made over by deed of gift to his wife, all his worldly possessions. In this, with a characteristic touch of his grand simplicity, he describes himself as John Bunyan of the parish of St. Cuthbert's, *brazier*.

The end was not far away. In 1688 he suffered from the sweating sickness, but, in addition to his other labours, published six considerable volumes, and left twelve more ready for the press. In the August he rode on horseback to Reading, to reconcile a father and son who were at variance. His mission was successful, but on his return he had to ride through heavy rain to the house of his friend John Strudwick, on Snow Hill, London. Not old in years, but worn with the stress of life, he was stricken for death. Before the worst symptoms of his fever showed themselves, he sent out a short treatise, *The Acceptable Sacrifice, or the Excellence of a Broken Heart*. He was able to revise some of the proof-sheets, but that was all. His last words, it is said, were: "Take me, for I come to Thee," and therewith the pilgrim ended his journey. He died, as he had desired, at the feet of Christ in prayer.

He was buried in Bunhill, in the great city which is the centre of the national life. I may mention that his great-granddaughter, Mrs. Bithrey of Carlton, died in 1802. His will, whose existence was unknown to his wife, was found in a recess of his house in St. Cuthbert's. His estate was of the value of £42, 19s.

It remains that something should be said of Bunyan as a man, as an author, as a preacher, and as one of the Evangelical Succession.

As a man, it is natural to compare him with his great contemporary Milton. While it is too much to say that the personality of Milton repels all commentators, it is certainly true that Bunyan is much more strongly attractive. His human sarcasm, penetration, and poetry are never far away from a deep and constant tenderness. "He appeared," says Charles Doe, "in countenance to be of a stern and rough temper, but in his conversation mild and affable; not given to loquacity or much discourse in company, unless some urgent occasion required it, observing never to boast of himself or his parts, but rather seem low in his own eyes, and submit himself to the judgment of others, abhorring lying and swearing; being just in all that lay in his power to his word; not seeming to revenge injuries; longing to reconcile differences, and to make friendship with all. He had a sharp quick eye, accompanied with an excellent discerning of persons, being of good judgment and quick wit. As for his person he was tall of stature, strong-boned though not corpulent, somewhat of a ruddy face with sparkling eyes, wearing his hair on his upper lip in old British fashion; his hair reddish, but in his latter days time had sprinkled it with grey; his nose well set, but not declining or bending, and his mouth moderate large, his forehead something high, and his habit always plain and modest." It has been assumed that he was an ascetic, but he understood Christianity too well for that. He knew that earthly good is possessed only when surrendered. And so he had his own simple and modest tastes, and sunned himself in the love of his home. From all records we get the same impression of a character sometimes playful, sometimes stern, sometimes using the weapons of war unsparingly, sometimes striving to heal wounded hearts, but always simple, and unselfish, and loving, because always submitting itself completely to the truth and will of God.

In determining his place as an author, many things are more needful than to pile up testimonies to the supremacy of his genius. It is only in comparatively recent times, however, that it has been fully allowed. Scarcely a century ago Cowper shrank from naming him,

> "Lest so despised a name
> Should move a sneer at thy deservèd fame."

It is mainly due to Southey and Macaulay that the *Pilgrim's Progress* is now recognised as one of the glories of our literature. "Bunyan," says Macaulay, "is as decidedly the first of allegorists as Demosthenes is the first of orators or Shakespeare the first of dramatists." "I have always," says Arnold of Rugby, "been struck by its piety. I am now equally struck, and even more, by its profound wisdom." The catholicity of its spirit, the raciness of its style, its kindly undeceivable insight into life and character, the strong and effortless freedom with which the writer's imagination works, and, perhaps above all, the human interest of the book, which makes it so enthralling to those who see nothing of its deeper meaning,—all these have been sufficiently dwelt upon. It is a true judgment which sees as much of the novelist as of the allegorist in Bunyan, and makes him, much rather than his follower Defoe, the parent of English prose fiction. But I may say something of the place he held among his literary contemporaries. The whole literary bent of the generation was towards borrowing foreign elements and style. When he grew up the influence of the "spacious times of great Elizabeth," in which Milton shared, was exhausted, and the age was correctly represented by such men as Butler and Dryden. Cynical, satirical, faithless, the spirit of such a time was not for him. His genius would have died in it. Hence it was in all respects fortunate that he owed so little either to predecessors or contemporaries. "I was never out of the Bible"—that is the explanation of his literary activity, so far as it can be explained. His royal genius not only worked on the biblical vocabulary and style, but shared to an unexampled degree in the new imaginative force and direction which has been given to the common life of Englishmen by their study of the Bible. And thus alongside of the purely literary developments of the Augustan age, there was kept alive a fashion of writing and speech which presents the historical continuity of the English language, and which was both literary and popular. It is needless to slay again the thrice-dead fables which accuse Bunyan of plagiarism:

"It came from mine own heart, so to my head,
And thence into my *fingers* trickled."

He practised, without knowing it, Sidney's complete *Ars Poetica:* "Foole, saide my Muse to mee, look in thine heart and write."

He explains in a singularly interesting part of his *Grace Abounding*, his experiences as a minister of the Gospel.

Notwithstanding great natural diffidence, he was

brought to see that his gifts should not be buried but stirred up; he began to preach, and did not preach long before hearts were touched, and he recognised with a strange incredulous joy that God "had owned in his work such a foolish one as I." Next he preached the terrors of the law, "what I smartingly did feel, even that under which my poor soul did groan and tremble to astonishment." Next he much laboured "to hold forth Jesus Christ in all his offices, relations, and benefits, unto the world, and did strive also to discern, to condemn, and remove those false supports and props on which the world doth both lean and by them fall and perish." After that God led him into something of the mystery of the union with Christ. Wherefore that he discoursed and showed to them also. He never cared to meddle with controverted subjects, "yet it pleased me much to contend with great earnestness for the Word of truth, and the remission of sins by the death and sufferings of Jesus." He knew the unspeakable depressions of the Christian ministry. To see his converts go back, as many did, was more than to lay his own children in the grave. Yet there were hours when the work drew itself up to its true grandeur; and he counted himself more blessed in his labour than if he had been lord of all the glory in the earth without it. Always he was in pains to win souls; if he were fruitless, it mattered not who commended; if he were fruitful, he cared not who condemned. He was sometimes tempted to pride, and yet not greatly. All gifts, he knew, would cease and vanish, "so I concluded a little grace, a little love, a little of the true fear of

God is better than all these gifts." So it continued to the end, and if, in the later part of his life, his unparalleled popularity was a temptation to pride, it was met and vanquished. For, as we are told, by the friend that closed his eyes, to the very last God " was still hewing and hammering him by His word and sometimes also by more than ordinary temptations and desertions." His ministry was also steadily carried on by his pen. No doubt he wrote too much for his reputation, if reputation was his aim. But an author whose books are messengers of the most high God, sent to declare the way of salvation, is not much moved by considerations such as these. Perhaps no writer has ever yet done justice to the enormous self-forgetting toil which Bunyan and others of the Puritans, in their high and true estimate of the power of the press, went through, that the Gospel might be spread in the land. In short, this was a ministry which sought, above all things, to grave deeply on the minds of men the abiding distinction between saint and sinner.

In conclusion, Bunyan's place in the Evangelical Succession suggests two lessons for those who hold his creed in these anxious days when the ground of religious controversy is strewn with ruins; when all who can think are in some measure saddened and sobered; when we are loudly told that we have exhausted the legacy of the past, and must now strike out a new path for ourselves and our children.

1. He teaches the priceless value of a true spiritual

experience. He preached and wrote what he himself had gone through. He was never out of the Bible, but then he had proved the Bible; he had taken the guide with him through all the devious and difficult paths of his experience, and his heart and the Word answered each unfailingly to the other. He tells us that he made no use of other men's lines; he spoke what was taught him by the Word and Spirit of Christ and his own experience. Thus he speaks of spiritual things as a witness; he has seen with his own eyes the glories and terrors of the spiritual universe. He has been tempted by Satan, crucified with Christ; with Christ he has risen from the grave, and now Christ liveth in him.

If Evangelical preaching is to retain and increase its power, it also must rest on an original and definite experience on the part of the preacher. This is the only way in which we can speak freshly even on the most worn themes. A witness does not weary. Let him describe the roads with which we have been familiar all our days—the hills that have almost become friends; and still it is new. Some aspect, colour, flower, cloud he has seen which we have always missed. How different if the description is compiled from a guide-book! And so men are very weary of permutations and combinations of theological phrases and words with a pious sound. They will not grow any less weary. Once it may be such phrases were stained through with soul-colour and filled as it were with the very blood of life. Now they seem faded and worn, and only living souls can renew their youth.

And it is this experience alone which will give us security and wisdom in controversy. The strength of Evangelicalism lies in its accordance with the teaching of Scripture, now growingly admitted by fair-minded scholars of all schools, and its correspondence with the experience of the exercised human heart—the inner facts of the world of consciousness. If we are to be calm and bold in the face of the tremendous onslaught now made upon our creed, we must plant ourselves firmly there. So long as we look upon faith as merely intellectual, we shall always be liable to panic; afraid of the ideas of the age, or, what is scarcely less humiliating, dependent upon them. This experience also will teach us wisdom. Bunyan has been much applauded by certain writers for his breadth of mind in not dwelling upon controverted points. But it should be almost superfluous to say that in his days unbelief was comparatively a rare and distant enemy, and men were agreed, as they are not now, on what was fundamental to faith. No one with any real knowledge of Bunyan's writings will deny that he held a large, fixed, and exacting creed. No doubt, if his beliefs as to his lifelong conflict with principalities and powers, the infinite evil of sin, the justice and judgment of God, the straitness of the gate, and the narrowness of the way, were mere morbid fancies, much of his creed must go, and they who care will fight for the rest. But if the human heart and its needs are deeper than some judge them, it will turn from those who would heal its hurt slightly and cry, "Peace, peace," when there is no peace, and pray again—

> "Rock of Ages! cleft for me,
> Let me hide myself in thee."

How securely Bunyan kept by his foundation is illustrated by the almost forgotten attempt of John Mason Neale—the simplicity of whose sternly self-denying career demands a charity he could never give to others—to turn the *Pilgrim's Progress* into a Tractarian manual. With stupendous crassitude Neale not only tampered with the masterpiece of one of the great lords of the imagination, but made the two sacraments the most conspicuous part of the allegory. Here the ground of experience was forsaken, and it is not wonderful that the audacity was received with universal derision.

Once more: it is only as we are possessors of this experience that we have the true temper in which religious questions should be discussed. Of the two indispensable requisites for treating properly the questions and issues brought before us—accuracy and elevation—we have the first abundantly, the second scantily. Yet surely elevation is as needful as cleverness, accuracy, knowledge of facts, and the day will be evil when it is not counted so. "A due sense of what these questions mean and involve; a power of looking at things from a height; a sufficient taking into account of possibilities, of our ignorance, of the real proportions of things,"—these we shall need more and more.

2. A consideration of Bunyan's life and work shows us how we are to meet the reproach that associates Evangelicalism with meanness in conduct and in thought. In conduct, because men are often repelled by its high pretensions, unctuous boasts, and pitiful performances; in thought, because it frowns upon the development of the intellect and imagination. There has doubtless been ground for both charges, but they cannot successfully be brought against Bunyan.

As regards the first—meanness of conduct—it must be confessed that the complacent, censorious, selfish life of many Evangelicals is perhaps the most unlovely and repellent of all types of the religious life. Nor is it less so because it is connected with such a creed. For Evangelicalism, which insists on the soul's direct approach to Christ, its everlasting union with Him, the awful hazards of the future, and the terrible needs of perishing man, ought to issue in lives high, simple, heroic, unworldly, and devoted. So it issued in Bunyan. The heroism of the simple unconscious kind that accepts peril and suffering without effort, and as a matter of course, was conspicuously his. The "holy hope and high humility" with which his imprisonment was endured, the clear and delicate conscience never moved by menace—ready, if need be, not only to confront opponents, but to disappoint friends—compelled belief in the reality of his professions. Evangelicalism has been most powerful in days of adversity. When it was associated, as in the early part of this century, with an unselfish war against such evils as slavery; when it issued in the sacrifice of the Disruption, men owned its power. Somehow it seems to become enervated in days of prosperity, and it perhaps needs again to be associated with some heroic struggle, some great sacrifice, to rekindle its dying fires.

A word on the charge of meanness of thought—which also is not undeserved. For it cannot fairly be denied that many Evangelicals have looked with suspicion upon many legitimate developments of the God-given faculties of intellect and imagination. Many were scandalised in Bunyan's time at a minister of the gospel copying the evil fashions of the world by writing an allegory like the *Pilgrim's Progress*. In our own day the comparative inferiority of distinctively Evangelical literature is too painfully apparent, and Bunyan's critics have living representatives. Such join hands with unexpected allies—those who would separate religion and imagination, and speak as if poetry were something high, distant, and far apart from the realities of life and the everlasting conflict of our Lord with Satan. Bunyan followed in the footsteps of his Master when he showed that the highest truths can be conveyed in the noblest forms of imaginative speech.

Christianity claims the ministry of the beautiful in the whole field of life. It seeks to present the truth of things under the aspect of beauty, while at the same time the firmest stress is laid upon all the aspects of duty. This ministry is the privilege of the redeemed soul, as is said so profoundly in *The Palace of Art*—

"'Make me a cottage in the vale,' she said,
'Where I may mourn and pray.
Yet pull not down my palace towers, that are
So lightly, beautifully built:
Perchance I may return with others there,
When I have purged my guilt.'"

THOMAS BOSTON.

By the REV. W. SCRYMGEOUR, Glasgow.

THOMAS BOSTON was born at Dunse[1] on the 17th March 1676, " of honest parents of good reputation among their neighbours," as he has a justifiable pride in telling us. His lot was cast on troublous times. Charles II., then on the throne, had abolished Presbyterianism and set up Episcopacy in its place, casting forth from their charges about 400 ministers who refused to submit to the change. But, as the great mass of the people espoused the cause of the ejected ministers, and gathered around them wherever they found it possible to preach, the holding of such conventicles was forbidden, and those who disregarded the prohibition were subjected to severe punishment. Armed resistance to such measures followed, and was treated as rebellion. After the disastrous battle of Bothwell Bridge, the persecution waxed hotter, till five years afterwards it reached its climax in "the killing-time," when Graham of Claverhouse and his troopers hunted to death the adherents of the Covenanted Reformation, and the best blood of Scotland's sons was shed with-

[1] The house in which he was born is still to be seen, with a tablet on it bearing this inscription: " Thomas Boston was born in this house March 17th, 1676; ordained minister at Simprin Sept. 21st, 1705; minister of Ettrick July 1707 ; died May 20th, 1732."

out mercy and without stint. The death of Charles, and the accession of his brother, James VII., did nothing to mitigate the severity of this treatment, till dread of the consequences likely to follow on it imposed a check upon the persecutors. It was only, however, when James Renwick, on the 11th of February 1688, sealed his testimony with his blood, that the martyr roll of our native land could be declared complete. The Revolution, accomplished by the aid of William of Orange, towards the end of that year, effaced the Stewart dynasty, and put both England and Scotland once more in possession of civil and religious freedom.

Within a year after the Revolution, Presbyterianism had been re-established, all of the ejected ministers who survived, sixty in number, restored to their parishes, and a General Assembly of the Church held amid the rejoicings of the nation. Not, however, till five years after this (A.D. 1694) could the Church be regarded as settled on a permanent basis; when, in compliance with the wish of the Sovereign, and with an Act of the National Parliament, the General Assembly consented to recognise the ministerial status of as many of the Episcopal clergy as were willing to conform to Presbyterian rule. But, though this measure seemed to be dictated by expediency, the adoption of it could not contribute to the true well-being of the Church. The admission to the ranks of the ministry of a considerable body of men but little influenced by conscientious conviction did much to lead onward to that general laxity both in life and in doctrine which now made itself painfully manifest.

At the time of Boston's birth Charles II. was still on the throne, and the persecution of Nonconformists, though far from having reached its most sanguinary stage, was being carried on with rigour. While he was yet a little boy his father, whether for attending a conventicle or for failing to appear at the parish church, was thrown into prison, and had his son beside him for a time to keep him company. After this, however, he "kept the kirk punctually," he tells us, and "heard those of the episcopal way, that being then the national establishment." Attending at first a dame's school, he made such progress that, at seven years of age, he could read the Bible. A course of five years at the grammar-school followed, at the close of which he was a good Latinist and knew the rudiments of Greek. But the great event of his boyhood was his spiritual awakening. This occurred in the twelfth year of his age under the preaching of Henry Erskine, one of the outed Presbyterian ministers, and the father of Ebenezer and Ralph Erskine, who, availing himself of a proclamation of indulgence issued by James VII., was conducting a meeting at the village of Revelaw. "After that," says he, "I went back to the kirk no more till the Episcopalians were turned out; and it was the common observation in those days that, whenever one turned serious about his soul's state and case, he left them." The first effect of the earnest preaching of the gospel by this honoured servant of God was that his youthful hearer was "like one amazed with some new and strange thing." His lost state by nature and his need of Christ being disclosed to him, he began to pray in earnest, to attend carefully on the preaching of the Word, and to hold meetings for the study of Scripture, and for converse on Divine truth with some of his school-fellows whose hearts the Lord had also touched. "Sure I am," says he long afterwards, "I was in good earnest concerned for a saving interest in Jesus; my soul went out after Him, and the place of His feet was glorious in mine eyes." At one time the doctrine of election threatened to turn him aside from further pursuit of what he felt to be the one thing needful, and he was tempted to come to the conclusion that, since the number of those destined to be saved was already made up, there was no room for him. But this and other stumbling-blocks were happily taken out of his way, and he was enabled to take Christ as his own Saviour.

Before his school course reached its close, Prelacy had passed away and the Presbyterian Church had regained its rightful place. And now his father's wish and his own choice pointed toward the Gospel ministry as the employment for which he should seek to prepare himself. Two years, however, intervened ere the means requisite for accomplishing this could be provided. It was in the fifteenth year of his age that he set out for Edinburgh to enter college. After attending the literary and philosophical classes for three sessions, he had the satisfaction of taking his degree, or (as it was then termed) laureating. And it gives us some idea of the stern resolution required to carry him through the work of these three winters, and of the rigorous self-denial which he had to practise, when we learn that the entire cost of his maintenance and college education amounted to the sum of £128, 15s. 8d. Scots, or about £11 sterling. A bursary given him by the Presbytery of Dunse enabled him next winter to attend the Hebrew class at college, taught by Mr. Alexander Rule, from which he obtained no great advantage, and the theological class taught by Mr. George Campbell, "a man of great learning, but excessively modest, undervaluing himself, and much valuing the tolerable performances of his students." This single session, supplemented by a month's attendance at the Divinity Hall two years afterwards, constituted the whole of his formal training for the ministry. Much against his own will, his theological studies were interrupted by several unavoidable engagements, and particularly by a tutorship which took him away to Kennet in Clackmannanshire, and detained him there for a year. "It was heavy to me," says he, "that I was taken from the school of divinity and sent to Kennet; yet I am convinced God sent me to another school there, in order to prepare me for the work of the Gospel for which He designed me." At this period of his life he passed through spiritual experiences of a very decided kind, at once evidencing the genuineness of his piety, and stimulating him to seek still higher attainments. "I had some Bethels there," says he, "where I met with God, the remembrance whereof hath many times been useful and refreshful to me, particularly a place under a tree in Kennet orchard where, Jan. 21, 1697, I vowed the vow and anointed the pillar."

Yet though for years he had been looking forward to the ministry, a sense of unfitness for it for a long time kept him back from seeking Presbyterial licence. But at last his scruples were overcome, and on the 15th June 1697 he was licensed by the Presbytery of Dunse and Chirnside as a preacher of the Gospel. His first sermon was on the words, "Consider this, ye that forget God, lest I tear you in pieces, and there be none to deliver" (Ps. L. 22), and his second on the words, "Not every one that saith unto me, Lord, Lord, shall enter into the kingdom of heaven" (Matt. vii. 21). "I began my preaching of the word," says he, "in a rousing strain, and would fain have set fire to the devil's nest." Yet it was with a trembling heart that he delivered his message. At first, indeed, he could scarcely look on the people whom he was called to address. But in course of time he attained such confidence that, when once the pulpit door was closed on him, fear was shut out. The quiet hint, however, dropped by a minister whom he deeply esteemed, "If you were entered on the preaching of Christ, you would find it very pleasant," led to a great change in the general strain of his preaching. But how was he to speak to his fellow-men of a Saviour whom he knew but imperfectly? This question caused him great distress. At last, however, he was able to put on record such an experience as this: "I conversed with Christ, and it was a Bethel to me. Long-looked-for came at last. If ever poor I had communion with God, it was in that place."

It may seem strange that at a time when, throughout the land, there was a famine of the Word, a preacher so devoted and so gifted should have remained for more than two years without a call to any congregation. But the character of Boston and the circumstances of the times go far to account for this. Though patronage had been abolished, the initiative in the settlement of a minister was not in the hands of the congregation. The heritors and elders proposed to a congregation the one who seemed to them fitted to be its pastor, and the people simply intimated their approval or disapproval of the proposal made to them. Now, though it might be said of Boston that "the common people heard him gladly," it very often happened that those representing the landed interest in a parish objected to his preaching as being bold and severe. Sometimes also, when he was assured that a visit from him to the leading heritor was all that was required to secure his support, he declined to have recourse to any such expedient. "This," says he, "was the ungospel-like way that then much prevailed in the case of planting of churches; a way which I ever abhorred." Only if there should occur a case in which heritors and elders and congregation should all unite in electing him, could there be presented to him a call to the pastorate which it was possible for him to accept. These indispensable terms were first of all fulfilled in an invitation given to him to become minister of Simprin, a small parish in Berwickshire, since absorbed into that of Swinton. But still the question remained, Was the call addressed to him one that could be recognised as coming from God? The population was very sparse; the parish only containing, as he afterwards found, 88 examinable persons. And he could have wished for a larger and more important sphere of labour. Yet an attentive and prayerful consideration of all the circumstances of the case seemed to him to show that this was the place providentially marked out for him. And very specially he tells us, "It contributed not a little to the clearing of me, that if I was at all to be admitted to the holy ministry, it should be at Simprin, as being unfit for a more considerable post." Accordingly he was ordained as minister there on the 21st September 1699, and on the following Sabbath entered on his work by preaching from Heb. xiii. 17, "They watch for your souls, as they that must give account."

From the day on which he became minister of Simprin, he threw himself with his whole soul into his work. He preached twice every Sabbath, giving the evening service a character of its own by entering on the systematic exposition of the Shorter Catechism. He began a week-day sermon also on Thursdays. Occasionally too he held diets of catechising, for the purpose of ascertaining to what extent his people were really acquainted with Divine truth. And his visiting of the families of his congregation was no formality, as he endeavoured to acquaint himself with the spiritual state of old and young, and pressed on them the necessity of attending to secret and family prayer, and to the discharge of their relative duties.

For some years after entering on his ministry, he did not write out his sermons, but took somewhat copious notes of the thoughts suggested by the text, and then trusted to Divine help to enable him to present to the people what he had thus prepared. But by-and-by he came to feel that, in dealing with important subjects, greater exactness of expression was desirable than could be attained by this mode of pulpit preparation; and this led him to write out his sermons at large,—"a yoke," says he, "which often I would have been glad to have shaken off, but could not get it done."

While busily fulfilling the duties of his quiet rural charge, Boston was also an ardent seeker after truth. While believing all that the Bible tells both regarding God and man, and specially all that it states concerning Redemption by the work and sacrifice of Christ, there was not a little in God's plan of salvation which he failed to understand. There were important truths also which it was difficult to reconcile with other truths quite as clearly revealed. Some of these hard questions he felt himself under not merely an intellectual, but a practical necessity of looking at and grappling with. As a Christian man, he met with difficulties which he must endeavour to get solved. And as a minister of Christ, called on to deal with his fellow-men in regard to their spiritual interests, he could not be satisfied till he had got light on some things which were dark to him. It was mainly under a spiritual pressure of this kind that Boston became an earnest thinker. And he got little help from others in prosecuting his inquiries. Books were for a long time almost beyond his reach. He tells us that a brother minister, who happened to look into his book-press shortly after his settlement at Simprin, could not refrain from smiling at the contents of it. Being anxious to read the famous work of Witsius on the Covenants, he had to borrow a copy of it. It was a great event in his history, when he was able to possess himself of Luther on the Galatians, of Beza's Confession of Faith, and of the works of Zanchius. Another parcel of books which he succeeded afterwards in purchasing, and which included the works of Lightfoot, seemed to have gone amissing when on the way to him; and with touching simplicity he tells us of his distress on this account, and of the joy to which it gave place when the treasure was at length delivered to him safe. For many a day his only commentary on the whole of Scripture consisted of the Westminster Assembly's Annotations. And it was not till years after his removal from Simprin that he became the happy possessor of a Hebrew Bible, and addressed himself to the earnest study of it.

There was, however, one book which he met with at an early stage in his ministry, and which proved invaluable to him. He was sitting in the house of one of his parishioners, when he got sight of a little old book above the window-head, which he took down and began to read. It was entitled

The Marrow of Modern Divinity, and was from the pen of Edward Fisher, a graduate of Oxford. Published in the year 1646, it had been brought to Scotland by one who had been engaged as a soldier in the wars of the Commonwealth. Its object was to set forth the freeness and fulness of the Gospel salvation, so that every sinner might feel himself warranted to come at once to Christ, and that the believer might be assured that in Christ he had an all-sufficient Saviour. Boston became so deeply interested in the book that he got it away with him and at length purchased it. "I found it," says he, "to come close to the points I was in quest of, and to show the consistency of those which I could not reconcile before; so that I rejoiced in it, as a light which the Lord had seasonably struck up to me in my darkness." By the end of the year 1700 he had not only digested the doctrine of the book, but had begun to preach it. The extent to which its teachings influenced him can be seen in his discussions in *Miscellany Questions in Divinity*, written for the most part during his ministry at Simprin. And it can be seen still more clearly in events which afterwards gave a distinctive stamp to the theology and the religious life of Scotland.

After a ministry of about eight years at Simprin, Boston was called to Ettrick in Selkirkshire, and, having accepted the call, was inducted to his new charge on the 1st of May 1707, a day ever memorable as that in which the Legislative Union between England and Scotland was consummated. In making this change "I parted," says he, "with a people whose hearts were knit to me, and mine to them; nothing but the sense of God's command making me to part with them." But for many a day it seemed as if the translation were little likely to be of any advantage either to himself or to those who had obtained him as their minister. With deep disappointment he says, "Being settled here, I soon found I was come from home." The people he describes as being "naturally smart, and of an uncommon assurance, self-conceited, and censorious to a pitch, using an indecent freedom both with Church and State." His chief difficulty arose from the Society-men or Cameronians, many of whom were scattered throughout his parish, and who, instead of attending on his ministry, held separatist meetings of their own. He felt constrained in the most public manner to condemn all such as guilty of schism; maintaining that those who separate themselves from a true Church because of corruptions in her, which they are not called on to approve or take part in, or because they have got hold of some truth which that Church does not oblige them to renounce, act wrongly and sinfully. But such sermons as that on "The evil and danger of Schism," though they might be of some use in preventing the spread of dissent, could not but exasperate conscientious dissenters. Another matter which excited much dissatisfaction in Ettrick and the south of Scotland generally was the willingness of the great majority of the ministers to take the Oath of Abjuration, which, while designed to secure the Protestant Succession, was so framed as apparently to exclude

Presbyterians equally with Papists from the throne. Boston, indeed, was one of the non-jurants; but, since he refused to break off from ministerial communion with the jurants, even he was regarded with suspicion. So thoroughly alienated did his people at length become both from the Church and the Government, that, on occasion of the Jacobite insurrection in 1715, Ettrick was the only parish within the Synod that could not be induced to raise a company of volunteers to aid in suppressing the movement. It is open to doubt whether the attitude assumed by Boston toward his parishioners was fitted to win for him their favour. Moved as he was in all his public actings by a high and stern sense of duty, he tried with all his might to prove to others that it was incumbent on them to adopt his views and to apply them to the guidance of their conduct; but, if his reasonings had no influence over them, he was apt to think of their case as hopeless, and either to leave them out of account, or to meet them with resolute resistance. On the first occasion on which there appeared any serious difference of opinion between him and his congregation, though he might have gone some way to humour their prejudices, he refused to do so. "Considering the temper of the people," says he, "I thought, if I should have yielded to them in this, I would teach them to dictate ever after unto me." Had he sought to conciliate opponents, rather than to subdue opposition, he would often have gained his end more effectually, and would have escaped much that not only saddened his heart, but militated against his usefulness. And

no one was better aware of this deficiency than himself,—as appears from his ingenuous confession:—
"I am very little serviceable with regard to public management, being exceedingly defective in ecclesiastical prudence,—and very little useful in converse, being naturally silent." From the first, indeed, there were some in Ettrick to whom Boston's ministry was precious. His devoted life and powerful preaching and unceasing labours in course of time obtained for him general esteem. But it was not till ten years had come and gone and his worth had been discovered for them by others, that they came fully to understand what a treasure they possessed.

From the time of his settlement at Ettrick, the great aim of his preaching was to impress the people with a sense of their need of Christ, and to bring them to consider the foundations of practical religion. With this view he delivered a series of discourses on "Human Nature in its fourfold state;" the four states being:—the state of innocence or primitive integrity, the state of nature or of entire depravation, the state of grace or of begun recovery, and the eternal state. These discourses made such an impression on his hearers as to convince him that they had not been preached in vain. And when, some years afterwards, it was suggested to him, that outside of his own parish there were many who would fain get some benefit from his ministry, it seemed to him as if there were no theme on which he could so fitly address that larger audience, as the one handled in these sermons. It was not, however, easy at that time for a country minister to become an author. It was difficult to find any one willing to take the risk of publishing a volume which might fail to repay him. And when, through the kindness of a friend, who held the office of treasurer to the City of Edinburgh, this difficulty had been overcome, another quite as formidable presented itself. For to this friend it seemed as if the work which he had undertaken to introduce to the reading world were, notwithstanding its great merits, written in a style uncouth and harsh. What has been termed the Augustan æra of our literature had just passed by, and the polished diction and flowing periods of Addison and the other English essayists had come into favour. Boston's patron, earnest Christian man as he was, was smitten with the prevailing admiration of this ornate style of writing, and wished that even such subjects as the depravity of the human heart should be treated with "true spirit and elegancy of expression." Accordingly, setting to work with the best intentions on the manuscript transmitted to him, with the view of removing whatever appeared likely to be unpleasing to men of refined taste, he made so many and such material changes on it, that the author had at length to interfere and to insist on his being allowed to speak in words of his own choosing. For this "modish style," as he termed it, Boston would have none of. But at last, after much experience of hope deferred, a bound copy of the *Fourfold State* was put into his hands on the 6th November 1720, and he was able to make this entry in his memoir: "I did, on the morrow after, spread it before the Lord in prayer, for His blessing to go out with it, and to be entailed on it while I live, and when I am gone, and that it might be accepted." And most abundantly was this earnest prayer answered. A few years afterwards he could record that he had received "a comfortable account of the acceptance and usefulness of the *Fourfold State* in remote places, particularly in the Highlands." A second edition of the work, carefully revised by himself, was issued during his lifetime. Within half a century after his death, about thirty impressions of it had been published. Indeed, there was a time when, throughout the homes of our Scottish peasantry, wherever a little library was to be found, Boston's *Fourfold State* was one of the volumes sure to have a place in it. It was read and prized, not only by the poor, but by pious people of all ranks. More perhaps than any other uninspired book, not excepting the *Pilgrim's Progress*, was it the means of leavening the community with the knowledge of Gospel truth. Nor, among the many treatises on Practical Divinity that have appeared in more recent times, would it be easy to point out one in which the whole teaching of Scripture with regard to man, is so clearly, and fully, and impressively set forth.

But certain views of truth, to which Boston had been led to attach great importance, and which on this account obtained a prominent place in his preaching, seemed likely to be not only called in question, but condemned by the Church of which he was a minister. He had brought under the notice of several of his brethren the book which had been mainly instrumental in leading him to the adoption of these views. One of their number, Mr. Hog, minister of Carnock, thought so highly of it as to republish it, and to preface it with some words of earnest recommendation. *The Marrow of Modern Divinity* thus found its way into the hands of a large circle of readers, and obtained for itself a measure of attention which had never been given to it before. Principal Haddow of St. Andrews, in particular, passed some severe strictures on it in a sermon preached before the Synod of Fife, in April 1719; and in consequence of this and similar manifestations of opinion, the Assembly, which met in the following month, instructed its Commission to inquire into the publishing of books inconsistent with the Confession of Faith, and to call the recommenders of such books to account for their conduct. The issue of this inquiry was, that the Assembly of 1720 condemned certain doctrines alleged to be taught in *The Marrow*, and prohibited " all the ministers of this Church, either by preaching, writing, or printing, to recommend the said book, or, in discourse to say anything in favour of it," but enjoined them rather " to warn and exhort their people, in whose hands the said book is, or may come, not to read or use the same."

This decision could not but deeply disquiet those against whom it was levelled. They would have had no difficulty in admitting that some expressions occurring in *The Marrow*, and condemned by the Assembly, were objectionable. Certain of the doctrines attributed to the author of the book they could in the most explicit manner disavow, while stating that in their opinion his words, fairly interpreted, did not bear the meaning attached to them. But what caused them most concern was, that the Assembly had singled out and denounced, as contrary to the Church's Confession, views which they believed to be in harmony with it, and which they held to be essential to a clear and full exhibition of Gospel truth. Such being their convictions as to the import of this Act of Assembly, they could not in silence submit to it. They could not, out of deference to Church authority, be unfaithful to the commission received from their Master, or refrain from proclaiming to their fellow-men the whole counsel of God. Accordingly, after anxious consultation with each other, it was resolved that they should join in making a representation to the next Assembly, complaining of the Act that had been passed, and asking for its repeal. A draught of the representation, prepared by Boston, was revised by Ebenezer Erskine, and, having been put into a form acceptable to those ready to take part in the movement, was signed by twelve ministers in all, who on this account came to be spoken of as the Marrowmen. The Representation, however, though brought before the Assembly, was remitted to the Commission, which, after several meetings with the Representers, handed them certain questions on the matters of doctrine in dispute, with a demand that written answers should be given to them. These answers, prepared by a man singularly fitted to undertake such a task, Mr. Gabriel Wilson of Maxton, were in due time presented, and the case was finally adjudicated on by the Assembly of 1722. The judgment was a long and elaborate one, formally confirming the decision of 1720, but giving important explanations of it, with a view to meeting weighty objections that had been taken to it, and sentencing the Representers to receive a solemn rebuke from the Moderator's chair. And rebuked accordingly they were, though protesting against the sentence passed on them, and intimating that they meant to continue to preach the doctrines that had been condemned, whatever the consequences. Nor did they shrink from carrying out their intentions. They preached the Gospel of the grace of God with the same fulness as before. Boston went so far as to write full explanatory notes on *The Marrow*, which were published a few years afterwards. And painful as the controversy had been, he was able to say of it:—"That struggle hath been, through the mercy of God, turned to the great advantage of truth in our Church, both among some ministers and people; having obliged both to think of these things and inquire into them more closely and nicely than before; insomuch that it has been owned that few public differences have had such good effects."

The Marrow Controversy and the preaching and writings of the Marrow-men had undoubtedly the effect of bringing clearly out certain important Gospel truths.

1. The truth which, in the view of Boston and his friends, held the foremost place among all that they were called on to contend for, was this,—that

the Saviour and the salvation provided by Him are offered to all men without distinction. This truth is expressed in *The Marrow* in such words as these :— "God the Father, moved with His free love to mankind lost, hath made a deed of gift and grant unto them all, that whosoever of them shall believe in this His Son, shall not perish, but have eternal life. And hence it was that Jesus Christ Himself said unto His disciples, 'Go and preach the Gospel to every creature under heaven;' *i.e.* Go and tell every man without exception, that here is good news, Christ is dead for him, and, if he will take Him and accept of His righteousness, he shall have Him." Nothing, however, was further from the mind of the writer who used such language than to hint that it was the intention of God, or the effect of the work of Christ, to save all men, or even to bring all men into a condition of salvability. It is true that he said, "Christ hath taken upon Him the sins of all men," and even "God hath, for the obedience and desert of our good brother Jesus Christ, pardoned all our sins." And it is true that such expressions were interpreted by the Assembly as showing that he taught "Universal atonement and Pardon" or "A Universal redemption as to purchase." Yet, in point of fact, he was a thorough predestinarian, and taught that Christ "had all the elect included in Him," that He came "to deliver believers," and "put Himself in the room and place of all the faithful."

But, whatever the opinions of the author of *The Marrow*, certainly his Scottish followers put it beyond a doubt that they, for their part, held no theory of Universal Redemption. "Although we believe," said they, "the purchase and application of redemption to be peculiar to the elect, who were given by the Father to Christ in the counsel of peace; yet the warrant to receive Him is common to all; ministers, by virtue of the commission they have received from their great Lord and Master, are authorised and instructed to go to preach the Gospel to every creature,—*i.e.* to make a full, free, and unhampered offer of Him, His grace, and righteousness, and salvation, to every rational soul to whom they may in providence have access to speak." To the same effect Boston, in his notes on *The Marrow*, remarks regarding the statement that "Christ hath taken upon Him the sins of all men,"—"Our Lord Jesus Christ died not for, nor took upon Him the sins of, every individual man; but He died for, and took upon Him the sins of, all the elect; and no other doctrine is here taught by our author." So, in explaining in what sense God can be said to have "pardoned all our sins," and to have ordered proclamation of this to be made throughout the whole world, he distinguishes between the "general pardon," of which offer is made to all, and the "formal personal pardon" that comes only to those by whom the offer is embraced.

The Marrow-men, therefore, had little in common with universalism. They did not think of God as having, out of love to the whole world, provided a salvation in which all men might share. They believed Him to have out of His mere good-pleasure elected some to everlasting life, to have sent His Son to be a Saviour to these, and to have provided for and secured the salvation of these, and of these alone. But they saw also that salvation, ere it could be enjoyed, must be accepted, and that in order to its being accepted by any, it must be offered to all. All men equally, elect and non-elect, stood in need of a Saviour, because all were sinners. The Saviour of whom all had need must therefore be set before all, and pressed on the acceptance of all, that those whose hearts the Divine Spirit touched and influenced might be led to embrace Him as their own. With all the greater confidence could Christ be offered as a Saviour to sinners of mankind generally, since as their kinsman He stood related most intimately to them all, and since His work and sacrifice were of such intrinsic worth as to suffice for the salvation of them all. "He died," says Boston, "in the room and stead of the elect only; but, being offered up for them, and being of sufficiency for the needs of all, He is made the ordinance of God for taking away the sin of the world of mankind, and as such is gifted to them of the Father." "Christ," says he, "is given to mankind sinners indefinitely. It is not to the elect only, but to sinners indefinitely, elect or not elect, sinners of the race of Adam without exception. If Christ were not given to mankind sinners indefinitely, but there were some in the world who have no part in the gift of Christ, then the ministers of the Gospel might not offer Him to all, nor might all receive Him."

This is far from being the doctrine of a Universal

Redemption, but it contains some of the elements that contribute to give to the creed of the Universalist its attractiveness. In the weighty words of Dr. M‘Crie (himself, like Boston, a native of Dunse): " The Marrow doctrine, while it holds forth a complete salvation, presents a revealed ground—call it an offer, a promise, or a deed of gift, or grant, from God—warranting sinners, as such, irrespective of any decree, or any qualification connected with the decree, to believe in, receive, and rest upon Christ for all they need for their recovery and happiness."

2. Only second in importance to God's *giving* of salvation is man's *receiving* of it. By *grace* are we saved through *faith*. Hence, as the author of *The Marrow*, and those who indorsed his teachings represented God as graciously making over Jesus Christ to men to be their Saviour, they strove to show how each man for himself may become possessor of God's unspeakable gift. What Scripture itself says on this point is, " Believe on the Lord Jesus Christ and thou shalt be saved," and this charge to the earnest inquirer after salvation was interpreted thus: " Be verily persuaded in your heart that Jesus Christ is yours, and that you shall have life and salvation by Him,—that whatever Christ did for the redemption of mankind, He did it for you."

To this definition of saving faith, however, it was objected that it represents assurance of personal acceptance with God as an essential element in it, and, in doing so, contradicts the statement of the Confession, that " this infallible assurance doth not so belong to the essence of faith, but that a true believer may wait long and conflict with many difficulties before he be made a partaker of it," and the still stronger statement of the Larger Catechism that such an assurance of salvation is "not of the essence of faith." But it was easy for Boston and the other Marrow-men to show that this objection arose from a misapprehension of the definition complained of. For when it was said to one earnestly seeking salvation, "Be persuaded that Jesus Christ is yours," the meaning was not that Christ was his *in possession*, but that He was his *in offer;* and, when such an one was exhorted to be confident that he should have "life and salvation by Him," he was simply told to entertain the confidence with regard to Christ which every one must have who would "receive and rest on Him alone for salvation." Nor could it be denied that one who thus believed in the offered Saviour and appropriated Him as his own, would be entitled to say that whatever Christ did for man's redemption He did it *for him*. It was easy also to show that faith in Christ had never been understood by the Scottish Church or by any of the Churches of the Reformation as being merely an assent to certain doctrinal statements in regard to Christ, but had always been considered as combining with this assent a personal appropriation of Him and confidence in Him as an all-sufficient Saviour. But how could there be trust in Christ without some accompanying feeling of comfort and peace?

At the same time Boston and his friends freely admitted that it is not essential to faith that the believer should have a clear and settled conviction that he is Christ's and that Christ is his. They distinguished between the assurance that springs up in the heart simultaneously with the exercise of faith, and the assurance derived from reflection on the facts of Christian experience. The former they called the assurance of faith, the latter the assurance of sense or evidence. "The assurance of faith," they said, "looks to Christ, the promise and covenant of God," and says, "This is all my salvation; God has spoken in His holiness; I will rejoice." But the assurance of sense looks inward at the works of God, such as the person's own graces, attainments, experiences. The one says, "I take Christ for mine;" the other says, "I feel He is mine." The one says, "My God will hear me;" the other, "My God has heard me." The one says, "He will bring me forth to the light, and I shall behold His righteousness;" the other, "He has brought me forth to the light, and I do behold His righteousness."

3. Another point on which the Marrow theology laid much stress was the believer's freedom from subjection to the Law. Its favourite statement was, that the believer had been set free "both from the Law's condemning and commanding power." But this was simply another way of stating that "true believers are not under the Law as a covenant of works, to be thereby justified or condemned." It was never meant to convey the idea that believers are under no obligation to accept the moral law as the rule of their life. Yet the teaching of the Marrow-men on this point had something distinc-

tive in it and intensely practical. If, said they, Christ as the representative of all the believing came under the Law to bear the penalty due to their transgressions, the condemning power of the Law has, so far as they are concerned, been put forth and exhausted. There is no reason therefore why believing men, when they are conscious of having committed any sin, should be overcome with terror, and should implore forgiveness as if it were possible for them to be doomed to the punishment which their sin has merited. And if Christ, in the room of His people, rendered to the Divine Law a perfect obedience and earned for them the reward of eternal life, there is no fear of their losing the prize, and no reason for their thinking of any work of theirs as indispensable to their gaining it. The believer should not be deterred from sin by any slavish dread of the consequences of it, or drawn to a life of holiness by any mercenary hope of reward. His salvation is secured by Christ, and by the faith which laid hold and keeps hold of Christ. And it is the love which a sense of his unspeakable indebtedness to Christ awakens within him, that should repel him from everything displeasing, and draw him toward everything pleasing, to his Redeemer. The Law that should govern his life is the Law of Christ. That Law is not, indeed, different from the Law of God, the Creator, engraven at first on the human heart, and republished in its main requirements in the Decalogue. It is the same Law; but it comes to the believer as the expression of his Saviour's will with regard to him, and he yields to it the submission due from one whom Christ has redeemed with His blood.

This view of the believer's relation to the Law was at the time condemned as Antinomian. But it was welcome to many who longed to be animated by the spirit of adoption, and to live a loving and childlike and holy life.

In the year 1729 Boston finished a treatise on the Covenant of Grace, the substance of which had been previously preached to his people. It was published shortly after his death, and is in several respects the most important contribution made by him to theology. It treats of the parties in the Covenant, of the making of the Covenant, of the conditionary and promissory parts of the Covenant, of the administration of the Covenant; and it gives practical directions as to the trial of a personal saving inbeing in the Covenant, and the way of instating sinners personally and savingly in it. The parties in the Covenant are, on Heaven's side, God the Father, and, on man's side, God the Son, *as representing the elect of mankind.* In the description of the parts or contents of the Covenant also, the elect alone are taken into account: Christ fulfils all righteousness *for them,* and, as the reward of this, He obtains the blessings of salvation *for them.* But, when we come to the administration of the Covenant, it is not the elect only, but *all mankind,* that are viewed as coming within its scope. Christ is the administrator of the Covenant, and those to whom He administers it are sinners of mankind. His commission clothes Him with ample powers to administer the Covenant to all ; and from this fulness of power He issues forth the general offer of the Gospel. And He executes this commission *in an unhampered manner*, saying to His apostles, "Go ye into all the world, and preach the Gospel to every creature," *i.e.* "Be they what they will, if ye can but know them to be *men*, ask no questions about them on this head, what *sort* of men they are: being *men*, preach the Gospel to them, offer them the Covenant; and, if they receive it, give them the seals thereof; my Father *made* them, I will *save* them." It is admitted, indeed, that Christ, considered as an *actual* Saviour, saves only the elect ones who are led to believe in Him; but, considered as an *official* Saviour, He is the Saviour of the world: —by the authority of His Father He is invested with that office, and, wherever the Gospel comes, His patent to that effect is intimated. It belongs also to the office of Christ as administrator of the Covenant to be the trustee and the testator of it, and to be the executor appointed to carry His own testament into effect. As the sole executor of the testament, He is called on to dispense the legacies to those to whom they are bequeathed. But who are the legatees? "Not *actual believers:* for actual believing is the legatees' *claiming* of the legacies left them, which claim must of necessity have a foundation in the testament *prior* unto it." "Neither are the legatees *the elect;* for, though in them only is the testament effectual, yet it is not to them only that the legacies *are left:* election, being a secret, not to be known by us until once we *believe*, cannot be the *ground and warrant* of believing, or embracing the testament and claiming the legacies." But the legatees are *mankind sinners* indefinitely: "to those of the family of Adam are the legacies left, to be claimed and possessed of them by faith." Whosoever therefore would have any saving benefit by Christ's testament, or would partake of the legacies therein bequeathed, must come to Himself to receive them. "Thus it is left open to mankind sinners to come into the Covenant, taking place therein under Christ the head, and to become personally confederate with Heaven to their eternal salvation. And there is room enough within the compass of the infinite name of the Second Adam for all of us to subscribe our little names."

It must be admitted that, in this treatise on the Covenant of Grace, Boston has succeeded in showing that a salvation intended only for some may be presented for acceptance to all, and that, consistently with the strictest Calvinism, the fullest proclamation may be made of the Gospel offer. And to have done this is to have done much. But the question remains, Is this all that is meant, when we are told that God has no pleasure in the death of the wicked, that He is not willing that any should perish, and that He so loved the world as to give His only-begotten Son, that whosoever believeth in Him should have everlasting life? Is it enough to say, that the salvation provided is sufficient for all, and is offered to all, if we cannot also say that it is intended for all? Does not Scripture represent God as yearning to save, not some men merely, but all men,—as with all the earnestness of tenderest love pressing salvation on their acceptance,—as rejoicing when they close with, and grieved when they reject His gracious offer? It is true that Scripture speaks as decidedly of those who are "ordained to eternal life," and tells us that "many are called, but few are chosen." But why should we follow one of these lines of Scripture representation, to the exclusion of the other? Though we cannot see it to be possible that the two lines should meet and harmonise, is it therefore impossible? Surely the Church should find it possible to give a place in its creed to such a statement as this: "We trust in the living God, who is the Saviour of all men, specially of those that believe." Boston did not go so far as this, but he prepared the way for others doing so. And he did noble service to the cause of the Gospel, when he addressed to his fellow-men such words as these: "*None of us shall perish for want of a Saviour;* Jesus Christ is the Saviour of the world; He is *your* Saviour, and *my* Saviour, be our case what it will."

Of other well-known works of Boston, such as *The Crook in the Lot*, great as their value is, we have not time to speak. Nor can we do more than name a few of his sermons, such as those on "Gospel compulsion," "The necessity and foundations of a throne of grace," "The everlasting espousals," "The worm Jacob threshing the mountains,"—sermons of rare doctrinal richness and spiritual power. It cheers us, as we read such sermons, to think that, a century and a half ago, they formed the daily bread set on the Father's table for His children in a secluded Scottish parish. We are not surprised to learn that strangers, hearing of the fare provided for the people of Ettrick, often joined them on Sabbath-days, and sat down with them to partake of it. At Communion seasons especially, the influx of visitors was very great,—so great, that on one occasion the number of tokens distributed was 777. And many of these occasional hearers of Boston's carried away with them precious truth, which became seed to the sower as well as bread to the eater.

There was work of another kind also done at Ettrick, which few would have thought of. For Boston was a hard student, and his chosen study was Hebrew, and especially the Hebrew Bible. His attention was at an early period directed to the somewhat recondite subject of Hebrew accentuation. As the result of earnest consideration of it, he came to the conclusion "that the accents are the true key to the genuine version and sense of the Hebrew text, and that they are divine." He was led also to regard all previous theories concerning the use of the accents as defective, and to form one of his own, to which he attached all the greater value, as the application of it to several obscure texts seemed to irradiate them with meaning. His views on this subject were at length thrown into the form of a treatise on Hebrew accentuation, a Latin translation of which, made by himself, was brought under the notice of some of the leading scholars in Europe, and drew forth the expression of their warm approbation.[1] With much

---

[1] This treatise was published at Amsterdam in 1738, with a recommendatory preface by David Mill. It forms a quarto volume of 220 pages. The title is curious:—"Thomae Boston, Ecclesiae

earnestness also he addressed himself to the work of rendering into English the Book of Genesis, but had only got to the end of the 23d chapter, when an arrest was laid on his labours by the illness that soon afterwards terminated in death.

Boston never enjoyed robust health. From his student days onwards, he was subject to fainting fits and other symptoms of constitutional weakness. But the last seven years of his life brought with them a succession of serious ailments, often causing him acute pain, and producing growing enfeeblement. He speaks of this as "the groaning period" of his life; and, during it, he is to be found employed at one time in settling his worldly affairs, at another, in keeping a secret fast to aid him in preparing for death; and at another, in "gathering some evidences for heaven." Yet, during all that time, the work of studying, preaching, visiting his parishioners, and assisting brethren on Communion occasions, went on very much as before; Divine help being graciously given him after the fashion which he himself thus describes: "Perceiving myself overcharged with necessary business, I prayed for strength for it, trusted I would get it, and accordingly I did get it." Nor did the bodily infirmity that pressed so sorely on him, keep him from discharging a most painful public duty, and rising up in the General Assembly when it seemed to him that in an important case faithfulness to truth was about to be sacrificed for

---

Atricensis apud Scotos Pastoris Tractatus Stigmologicus Hebræo-Biblicus, quo accentuum Hebræorum doctrina traditur, variusque eorum in explananda Sancta Scriptura usus exponitur."

the sake of peace, and saying, "I dissent in my own name, and in name of all that shall adhere to me,— and for myself alone, if nobody shall adhere."

Distress and debility, however, gradually gained on him, till he was no longer able to stand when preaching. Then it became impossible for him to leave his room; but from the window of the Manse for several Sabbaths he spoke, as he was able, to the people standing outside. And at length, on the 20th May 1732, he entered into the joy of his Lord.

The story of his life cannot be better summed up than in his own words, penned when the end of it was coming into view: "I bless my God in Jesus Christ that ever He made me a Christian, and took an early dealing with my soul; that ever He made me a minister of the Gospel, and gave me some insight into the doctrine of His grace; and that ever he gave me the blessed Bible, and brought me acquainted with the originals, and especially with the Hebrew text. The world hath all along been a step-dame to me; and, wherever I would have attempted to nestle in it, there was a thorn of uneasiness laid for me. Man is born crying, lives complaining, and dies disappointed from that quarter. 'All is vanity and vexation of spirit:' 'I have waited for thy salvation, O Lord.'"

The full extent of the influence exercised by Boston over the religious thought and life of Scotland could not be estimated during his lifetime. He lived and laboured, not merely for his contemporaries, but for posterity. The works that he left behind him soon found thousands of appreciative readers.

And, within half a century of his death, his name was a household word all over the land, and the free and full Gospel that he proclaimed was as sunshine streaming into many a soul that would otherwise have been in darkness.

Nor should we, in estimating Boston's influence, leave out of account the work done by his chosen friends, Ebenezer and Ralph Erskine, and the other fathers of the Secession. It was fully as much on grounds of doctrine as of ecclesiastical policy that they were led to leave the National Church, as may be seen from the Act concerning the Doctrine of Grace passed by the Associate Presbytery in 1742. Indeed the favourite phraseology of Boston and the Marrow-men regarding the grant of Christ in the Word to mankind sinners as such is perpetually recurring in the writings of the first seceders. And the doctrine of "The open door" (as it was familiarly called), or of the free access that sinners have to the Saviour, has from the beginning down to our own time been the leading characteristic of the theological teaching of the Secession.

It deserves to be remembered, too, that Boston's youngest son, Thomas, who succeeded him in the pastorate of Ettrick, after a ministry of more than twenty years in the Established Church, left it and became one of three who formed the first Presbytery of the Relief, and that he contributed materially to leaven that important Denomination with his father's teachings and spirit.

By far the greater part, however, of Boston's personal friends, though grieved with the dead orthodoxy on the one hand, and the laxity of doctrine on the other, which prevailed in the Church of their fathers, did not feel it to be their duty to leave it. Though but a small minority and in disrepute with the leaders of their Church, they kept bravely on their way, preaching the Gospel of the grace of God with all earnestness, and hoping and praying for the advent of a brighter day. And, long after they had been called from their field of labour, the seed which they had sown in tears yielded its rich fruit in the triumph of Evangelism, and in an outburst of missionary zeal and effort worthy of the best days of the Church of Christ.

JONATHAN EDWARDS.

By the REV. JAMES IVERACH, M.A., Aberdeen.

TO-NIGHT we follow the Evangelical Succession into new lines, and see it at work under new conditions. In former lectures it has been shown that Evangelical principles were equal to the task of reforming a nation, of pouring new life into institutions grown old and effete, and of lifting an old nation to a great height of purity, charity, and self-sacrifice. In America a new historical test is applied to the efficacy and power of Evangelical principle. Is it equal to the task of laying the foundations of a national life? Has it strength enough to mould the character, influence the life, and to give a moral aim and purpose to a people struggling with special circumstances, and trying to solve an historical problem untried before in the whole history of the world? To New England the Evangelical Succession was handed over at one of the greatest eras in its history. In Scotland, in England, and in many parts of Europe, Evangelical principles had come into the clear consciousness of the Church, and were held by the people with a full view of their causes and their consequences. Debate and discussion, and practical application of Evangelical principles, had combined to set them forth in detailed and reasoned order and method, so that the Evangelical Churches had come into full possession of their birthright.

It was when this was accomplished, when the question of principle had been fully discussed in the Old World, that the foundations of New England life were laid. The founders of New England were men in every way worthy of the great future which lay before that English-speaking people on the other side of the Atlantic. We sometimes speculate with some curiosity on what would have happened in England and in America, had Oliver Cromwell been able to carry out his purpose of setting sail for America, and of settling in the New World. Or perhaps we ask ourselves what would have been the result if Dr. John Owen, "who had given orders for his passage in a vessel bound for Boston," had carried over to America his vast learning, his wise counsel, and his earnestness of purpose. A greater theologian than Dr. John Owen, —namely, Dr. Ames, better known as Amesius, the greatest Calvinistic theologian since Calvin, almost the only English theologian who has permanently influenced the thought of Europe,—was on the eve of departure for America when death took him. These great names are mentioned because of the conviction, which some reading has forced on my mind, that the leaders of New England thought and life were men of the same bulk and mental stature as Amesius and John Owen. Some of the men mentioned in Mather's *Magnalia* were the foremost in their time at the English Universities,—men of widest culture, and richest learning, and of great spiritual strength. One testimony I quote. Amesius says of one of them, Mr. Thomas Hooker, "though he had been acquainted with many scholars of divers nations, yet he never met with Mr. Hooker's equal, either for preaching or for disputing." What old England had to give, in the way of scholarship, of culture, of religious earnestness, and strength of mind, body, spirit, she gave, whether willingly or unwillingly, to the New England on the other side of the Atlantic.

It is true, indeed, that the outcome in the form of theological literature we have received is not great. Their work was of another kind. They were pioneers, and they had to plant the people in the wilderness, to impress on them the stamp of an earnest, serious purpose in life. In short, their lives were spent in living contact with men, and their influence was not of the kind transmitted through books, but of the kind more personal and quite as lasting. So powerful was that influence, that the New England type of thought and life is the dominant one among the fifty millions who people the United States to-day.

New England society had been founded by men to whom Evangelical principles were so precious that they had not hesitated to expatriate themselves for their sake. They were earnest, zealous, and godly people, to whom life was full of seriousness, and on whom the responsibilities of life pressed with great weight. They had a great ideal before their minds, and they set themselves with all their strength to live up to it. Amid the roughness of their outward circumstances, and amid the unloveliness of speech and form which clung to them, they sought to live a true, godly life on the earth. Notwithstanding all that has been written on the narrowness and unloveliness of the life lived by the descendants of the Pilgrim Fathers, it is still true that no people ever lived in more conscious nearness to God, in no people did belief and conduct correspond more closely, and no people ever tried more sincerely to shape their personal, family, social, and public life according to the pattern revealed to them in the Scriptures.

The more immediate ancestors of Jonathan Edwards were in full sympathy with the prevailing tone and tendency of the time. His father, the Rev. Timothy Edwards, was minister of Windsor on the banks of the Connecticut, and his mother was herself the daughter of a minister, to whom Jonathan Edwards was, in after years, colleague for a lengthened period. Born on the 5th October 1703, at Windsor, one of a family of eleven children, he was from his infancy surrounded with influences of a grave and serious kind. From the accounts we have of the family life in the midst of which he grew up, we gather that the influence of his parents was steadily directed to one great end. They were people of high intellectual power, and of great religious decision, and they made it one of the great aims of their life to make their children realise their relation to God. Thus it came to pass that when a child he was "familiarly conversant with God and Christ, with his own character and duty, with the way of salvation, and with the nature of that eternal life which, begun on earth, is perfected in heaven." The life of the family was shaped in consistency with the views of truth and duty taught by the parents. "There was nothing in the example of those who taught to diminish the force of instruction; there was nothing in social habits which counteracted the lessons of wisdom." Both in precept and practice the parents of Jonathan Edwards showed him that the aim of human life was to walk with God, and its reward to be for ever with the Lord.

It was to be expected that a boy brought up amid such surroundings should soon come to have religious experiences of his own. Passing by some earlier thoughts, we come to these experiences which were personal and characteristic of the man. It is characteristic that his entrance upon the settled peace of religious conviction came to him through the apprehension of the absolute sovereignty of God. He had been earnest and sincere in seeking salvation through Jesus Christ, and in seeking to share the rapture of others who believed in Christ. But no settled peace or gladness came until one day he read the words, "Unto the King, eternal, immortal, invisible, the only wise God, be honour and glory for ever and ever" (1 Tim. i. 17). "As I read these words, there came upon my soul, and was as it were diffused through it, a sense of the glory of the Divine Being; a new sense quite different from anything I ever experienced before." It was the decisive moment of his life, and gave colour to all his thinking and acting from that time forth. With earnestness and sobriety of resolution, he henceforth made the glory of the Divine Being, whose glory was thus flashed upon him, the guiding purpose of his life. The absolute sovereignty of God satisfied the need of his speculative intelligence, the need of his moral nature, and the need of his affections. His thought, his acting, and his love were all evoked, and were all satisfied by the thought of the gracious sovereignty of God.

The rapture of this man of such logical understanding, the language of whose affections ever was set forth in abstract terms, resembled the raptures of the mystics, who seemed to have lost the sense of self in the sense of God. For instance, read the following, and think that it is written by him who wrote the treatise on the *Freedom of the Will* :—

"I walked abroad alone, in a solitary place in my father's pasture, for contemplation. As I was walking there, and looking upon the sky and clouds, there came into my mind so sweet a sense of the glorious majesty and grace of God, as I know not how to express. I seemed to see them both in a sweet conjunction, majesty and meekness joined together. It was a sweet, a gentle, and holy majesty, and also a majestic meekness, an awful sweetness, a high and great and holy gentleness. After this, my sense of Divine things gradually increased, and became more and more lively, and had more of that inward sweetness. The appearance of everything was altered, there seemed to be, as it were, a calm sweet cast or appearance of divine glory in almost everything. God's excellency, His wisdom, His purity, and love seemed to appear in everything; in the sun, moon, and stars, in the clouds and blue sky, in the grass, flowers, trees, in the water and all nature, which used greatly to fix my mind. I often used to sit and view the moon for a long time, and in the day spent much time in viewing the clouds and sky, to behold the sweet joy of God in these things; in the meantime singing forth with a loud voice my contemplations of the Creator and Redeemer. And scarce anything among all the works of nature was so sweet to me as thunder and lightning; formerly nothing had been so terrible to me. Before, I used to be uncommonly terrified with thunder, and to be struck with terror when I saw a thunderstorm rising; but now, on the contrary, it rejoiced me. I felt God, if I may so speak, at the first appearance of a thunder-storm; and used to take the opportunity at such times to fix myself in order to view the clouds and see the lightnings play, to hear the majestic and awful voice of God's thunders, which oftentimes was exceedingly entertaining, leading me to sweet contemplations of my great and glorious God."—(*Works*, Tegg's Edition, p. lv.)

I have quoted this paragraph at length, because of the light it casts on Edwards' character, and the insight we get from it into his religious life. His delight in nature is not that of the man of science, who is bent on seeking into the causes of things, and the laws of their working, nor is his pleasure that of the artist, who delights in form and colour, and stands enraptured before the beautiful effects, visible before him on earth, and sea, and sky. His delight is more akin to that of the Hebrew prophet and psalmist to whom the heavens declared the glory of God, and had much in common with the mystic sentiment, in which all finite being and second causes are swallowed up in the mysterious life which seems to pervade the universe. Edwards touches at points not a few that mysticism which has so great a fascination for the greatest spirits of our race. Religion, in its fundamental principle, is fellowship and communion between the Infinite and the finite, between the Eternal Spirit and the creatures He has made; and therefore, in its very nature, it is a mystery. In common with Paul, and Augustine, and Calvin, Edwards felt the profound mystery which pervades all existence. He has the feeling of dependence, and an exalted conception of the glory of the Supreme Being. So great was this apprehension of the glory of God, that we note a tendency in Edwards to lose sight of the finite in the Infinite, to realise but feebly the reality and the working of second causes, and to see in nature nothing but the manifestation of the power of the First Great Cause. To see God in everything, and everything in God, to regard the thunder as the voice of God, and the light as His garment, and to look at the laws of nature as embodied Divine thoughts, has been the tendency of the greatest spirits of the race. They have felt themselves to be encompassed behind and before, and to be pervaded through and through with a presence from which they could not escape. The presence, the power, the glory of the Divine was the starting-point of all their thought; to know the divine, to be united with the divine, was also the goal of all their efforts. It was emphatically so with Edwards, to whom the glory of God was purpose and desire, aim and goal of life.

It is a habit of mind, quite consistent with the most fervent faith in a personal God, and with the most devoted attachment to practical duty. When a man's apprehension of the majesty, glory, and grace of God is intense and vivid, and, at the same time, is accompanied by a firm conviction of the character of God as personal, we find the elements of religion present in a powerful degree. In almost any other person, the language often used by Edwards would have come perilously near to the view which regards God as "the thought or self-consciousness which is beyond all individual selves, which is the unity of all thinkers, and of all objects of thought." From this view Edwards was saved by the firm persuasion he had of the living God, not only as "He in whom we live, and move, and have our being," but also as the supreme Judge, Ruler, and Governor of the world, of whose personal character, holiness, justice, and love, he had no doubt. Sometimes indeed Edwards speaks of God, as the all-comprehensive existence; but to the interpretation of these statements we must bring the other conviction which he ever felt, that the God he worshipped was the living God, who is truth, light, and love, who could exercise justice and show mercy to His creatures. If at times we find expressions which, strictly interpreted, would logically lead to a modified pantheism, we must remember to place alongside of them the profound persuasion of Edwards, that God is a person with whom we can have personal dealings,—not the Supreme Being, or the sum of existence, or the self-consciousness in which all distinctions and differences are lost.

At this point, however, let us seek to obtain some knowledge of the man, of his way of work, ere we seek to inquire what place he fills in the Evangelical Succession. The life we have to consider was one of singular purity. No stain rests upon it. From his childhood he responded to the loving care and anxious guidance of his parents, and in early youth manifested the intensity of purpose and the decision in the search after truth, which were characteristic of him while life lasted. The intellectual fare supplied to him was of the severest kind. The graces and charms of literature were not likely at that time to visit him in his New England home, nor were there any of those more kindly ways of communicating knowledge, and arousing the attention of young people, to which we have now grown accustomed. We find Edwards at the age of fourteen reading Locke's Essay, pen in hand, not merely to find out what Locke had to teach him, but reading as a critic, whose business it was to weigh arguments, to notice weak points, and to form an estimate of the value of the system of philosophy contained in the work of Locke. The results he recorded in writing, which appears in his works. In his College days his chief delight was to study philosophy. To it he gave his strength. But he was too conscientious a student to neglect any part of his work, and he so bore himself, that when he quitted college at the age of eighteen he left with the highest honours.

He was appointed to be colleague to his maternal grandfather, February 15, 1727, and there he continued to labour until 1750, and he makes the following business-like entry in his Family Bible: "I was dismissed from my pastoral relation to the first church in Northampton, June 22d, 1750." For the next few years he labours among the Indians, was elected President of New Jersey College, 1758, and died, March 22, 1758.

The greater part of Edwards' life was spent in the work of a preacher of the Gospel and the pastor of a congregation. Any view of his work which did not notice how he bore himself in both relations would be inadequate. Most of us know his sermons, —those closely-reasoned, massive, thoughtful structures of theological thinking and close-searching practical application. His mode of preparation varied: some sermons were written out, and read word for word; others, and these by far the greater number, were simply jottings, written down on any scrap of paper which came to hand; and having thus traced out the line of thought, he trusted to the moment to find suitable language. But whether the sermons were fully written out or partly extemporised they were always solemn and impressive. With Edwards preaching was business, by means of which work was to be done. Men must be persuaded to surrender themselves to God, and for this end all the resources, mental, physical, spiritual, which Edwards possessed were used to the utmost.

By his preaching work was really done, and during his ministry there was a great revival of religion. Some recent writers, who agree with the views of Edwards on the freedom of the will, and who admire beyond measure his intellectual and dialectic vigour, hardly know what to say when they come to speak of these revivals which took place under his ministry at Northampton. They do not give any earnest consideration to the phenomenon, or they speak of it as an "excitement," or they coldly pass it by with a sneer. Leslie Stephen says of it:

"When the angel of the Lord comes down to trouble the waters, one would expect rather to see oceans upheaved than a trifling ripple in an insignificant pond," and he affects to speak with deep pity of Edwards' delusion, and smiles at the "simplicity with which he traces distinct proofs of the Divine hand in the familiar phenomena of religious conversion." Edwards' reputation will no doubt survive the pity and the smile. For here Mr. Stephen is dealing with magnitudes for which he has no measure. He could understand the upheaving of an ocean, which he thinks a task worthy of an angel of the Lord; he is unable to conceive the magnitude of an event which we have reason to believe causes joy among the angels in heaven. The repentance of a sinner is an event of greater magnitude, and has more lasting consequences, than the upheaving of an ocean. But those who have learned to regard the birth of the Child who was born at Bethlehem as the greatest event of the world's history have learned a new way of measuring the comparative magnitude of events, and think of the conversion of the three hundred souls who, in the course of six months, were "savings brought home to Christ" under the ministry of Edwards, as a greater triumph in itself, and in its consequences, than any victory won through blood and iron.

Into that work Edwards cast himself without reserve, and gave to it all his strength, and his ministry went prosperously on. At length he seemed somehow to lose touch of his people. Perhaps this may have been owing in some measure to the fact that he was not much in the habit of social intercourse with them. He deliberately came to the conclusion that the most profitable way of discharging his ministerial duty was not to visit his people from house to house. He had not much readiness of speech, nor could he enter easily into conversation on any of the chance topics of the time and place. He was ready always to see them when they called, and would freely converse with them on matters connected with their religious life and experience. But he held that pastoral visitation was for him, though not for others who were ready of speech, waste of time and of strength. Thus the solitary student became even more solitary, and went his way apart. We need not trace the steps of the process which issued in the severance of the pastoral tie, nor need we dwell in detail on the work he did and the difficulties he overcame in his mission to the Indians. Our interest mainly lies in the life as a thinker and theologian. He was a loving husband, a kind father, a great preacher, a man who always did his duty, yet his eminence lies in his strength as a thinker.

In this connection therefore the following account will be of interest :—

"Owing to his constant watchfulness and self-denial in food and sleep, and his regular attention to bodily exercise, notwithstanding the feebleness of his constitution, few students are capable of more close or long-continued attention than he was. He commonly spent thirteen hours every day in his study; and these hours were passed, not in perusing or treasuring up the thoughts of others, but in employments far more exhausting—in the investigation of difficult subjects, in the origination and arrangement of thought, in the invention of arguments, and in the discovery of truths and principles. Nor was his exact method in the distribution of his time of less essential service. In consequence of his uniform regularity and self-denial, and the force of habit, the powers of his mind were always at his command, and would do their prescribed work in the time appointed. This enabled him to assign the preparation of his sermons each week to given days, and specific subjects of investigation to other given days, and, except in cases of sickness, or journeying, or some other extraordinary interruption, it was rare indeed that he failed of accomplishing every part of his weekly task, or that he was pressed for time in the accomplishment."—(*Works*, vol. i. p. lxxxi.)

He was thus a solitary thinker, and pursued solitary trains of thought, sometimes indeed to issues which were fruitful, and sometimes to issues which were barren. As with Reformed theology in general, so also with respect to the theology of Edwards, the bearing of his system is most clearly seen when we group his works in their relation to one central thought. The ruling idea of Edwards is the sovereign grace of God ; and man in his relation to divine grace. When we inquire into the state of man apart from divine grace, and ask what in the view of Edwards is the state of a man without grace, we have his answer in the great treatise on *Original Sin*. When we ask, What is the relation of Divine sovereignty to human agency? in other words, What is the mode of God's government of the world? we find Edwards' answer fully set forth in the treatise on *The Freedom of the Will*. When we ask what is the relation of the Sovereign God to the bestowal of grace on man, we have Edwards' answer in the treatise on *Grace*.[1]

[1] Published in *Selections from the Unpublished Writings of Jonathan Edwards*, by the Rev. A. B. Grosart. Printed for private circulation. 1865.

If we ask further, What is the behaviour of those on whom grace has been bestowed? there we find an adequate description of their dispositions and desires in the work on the *Religious Affections*, and the great outcome of grace working in man, we find in the treatise on the *Nature of Virtue*. The manifestation of divine grace in actual human history we find delineated by Edwards in the *History of Redemption* ; and lastly, the supreme justification of the ways of God to man, the result which vindicates the power, wisdom, and glory of God, is set forth by Edwards in the work *The End of God in Creation*.[1] Unless we have some such guiding clue in our hands, we shall certainly lose ourselves amidst the many mazes of his profound and intricate reasoning; with this clue in hand, we shall gradually find his system fall into order, and every part become luminous. Had he lived to complete his great work, he would no doubt have set forth in detailed order the main thought of his system, and have shown the mutual dependence and internal consistency of all the related parts, and their logical connection with the central thought. The student of Jonathan Edwards has to do this for himself, and has to deal with a number of detached treatises, written at different times and with different aims, most of them controversial, and bearing the local marks of their origin.

In our endeavour to set forth the system of Edwards, we shall follow the order given above.

---

[1] This classification is largely due to Dr. H. B. Smith, of New York. See *Faith and Philosophy*, by H. B. Smith, D.D., p. 151, *et passim*.

What is the state of man apart from Divine grace? The treatise on *Original Sin* sets forth the common view of the Reformed Churches on this subject, and also some modifications of the view made by him, which has had important consequences in more recent New England theology. In seeking to establish the doctrine of original sin, Edwards draws his arguments from the actual experience of man, and from the Holy Scriptures. He proves with great and characteristic elaboration, that all men tend to sin and ruin, that such a universal tendency must have a cause—a cause not to be found in the freedom of every one to sin. The cause lies in a universal sinful propensity; men are stupid and wicked, and men are mortal, therefore sin is as universal as death is. The Scripture testimony to the fact is set forth with patient elaboration, and the conclusion is drawn afresh, both from the fact of redemption and from its application. Then objections to these doctrines are stated and answered, but the question arises, What is the explanation of this state of universal sin and misery? Edwards gives the usual answer, that all sinned in Adam, and all died in Adam. Adam is the federal head of the race. He is not content merely to give the general answer of the Covenant theology. He seeks unconsciously to find a real basis for imputation, and finds it in the assumption that the relation between Adam and his posterity is not merely federal but real. He did not merely represent them. He was one with them as the tree is one with its germ, and the man is one with the child:—

" Indeed the derivation of the evil disposition to Adam's posterity, or rather the co-existence of the evil disposition, implied in Adam's first rebellion, in the root and branches, is a consequence of the union that the wise Author of the world established between Adam and his posterity; but not properly a consequence of the imputation of his sin, nay rather antecedent to it, as it was in Adam himself. The first depravity of heart, and the imputation of that sin, are both the consequences of that established union; but yet in such order that the evil disposition is first and the charge of guilt consequent, as it was in the case of Adam himself."
—(*Original Sin*, iv. 3.)

Edwards thus inverts the order of terms in the imputation of the guilt of Adam's first sin to all mankind. The charge of guilt follows on the contraction of guilt, and in his hands the basis of imputation is real. Along with this, and to justify it on grounds of reason, he propounds a thing which is far-reaching. Identity does not lie in things themselves, but in the fact that " God treats them as one, by communicating to them like properties, relations, and circumstances; and so leads us to regard and treat them as one." " When I call this an arbitrary constitution, I mean that it is a constitution which depends on nothing but the Divine will; which will depends on nothing but the Divine wisdom. In this sense the whole course of nature, with all that belongs to it, all its laws and methods, constancy and regularity, continuance and proceeding, is an arbitrary constitution. In this sense, the continuance of the very being of the world and all its parts, as well as the manner of continued being, depends entirely on an arbitrary constitution." Preservation thus becomes a continued creation, and the identity even of a personal being is possible, because it depends on "God's sovereign constitution." His argument shortly is, that if personal identity depends solely on the constitution given to consciousness by God, then such a constitution may have been given by God to the whole human race, as may establish a real organic unity between Adam and his posterity. The metaphysical foundation established by Edwards is precarious, and the theory of an "arbitrary constitution" has far-reaching consequences, which must cause us to hesitate ere we commit ourselves to it.

It is not necessary to accept the metaphysical foundation, in order to test the results attained by Edwards in this relation. For the tendency of philosophy and theology has been in the direction of establishing a closer unity of the human race. A new series of facts has been discovered, and a new way of regarding these facts has arisen, so that we now have a new word, "solidarity," to express what Edwards has expressed in a round-about way. The main thing in the doctrine is conserved, on the view of Edwards as on the other, and this thing is, that there is a proper imputation, that certain penal consequences of the great apostasy are reckoned to Adam's posterity, in virtue of their union with him, and from these evils no one can be delivered save by Divine grace. Our own Dr. Duncan, that great and subtile thinker, near of kin in speculative insight to Edwards, puts Edwards' view in these striking words: "My Theanthropology has only two texts: 'God made man in His own image, in the image of God created He him,' and 'God sent forth His Son, made of a woman, made under the law, to redeem those who are under the law,' therefore theologically there are only two men, Adam and Christ." This last sentence sums up what is characteristic in the theory of Edwards, and, so stated, it enables us to solve problems, and to answer questions, which press somewhat heavy on us when we make what is legal the basis of what is real in this matter.

Unfortunately Edwards approached the great question of the relation of Divine sovereignty to human agency from the philosophical side. In his treatment of the subject there is no reference to the bondage of sin under which man lies as a sinful creature. It is only incidentally, and in answer to objections, that sin comes into view, and then it is discussed to obviate the charge brought against his system that it makes God the author of sin. As Principal Cunningham has shown, the question of the freedom of the will in man, considered simply as a creature, is a different question altogether from the freedom of man considered as a sinful fallen creature. Reformed theology has a definite opinion on the theological question : it has left the other an open question on which men may take different sides according to their view of the evidence.

It is unfortunate also that, while Edwards establishes his system of determinism by abstract arguments, drawn from reason and experience, in the second part, when he seeks to prove that men are subjects of moral obligation, his arguments are drawn from Scripture. In the case of those readers who do not care for argument drawn from Scripture, the natural consequence was that they accepted the first part of the treatise, which proves the will to be determined, and rejected the second part, which held man to be responsible notwithstanding. As a matter of fact, Edwards' peculiar theory is now held mainly by Agnostics. But it is held with a difference. It seems somehow to be forgotten by almost all people that Edwards' theory is of a most refined order. He is very careful to show that there are different kinds of necessity, according to the different natures and conditions of the beings with which, or whom, the necessity deals. His favourite illustration of the kind of necessity which determines the will to action, is that set forth in the relation of subject and predicate in a sentence. Obviously the necessity here spoken of is rational and not mechanical. In truth, Edwards' illustration may be used for another purpose, and may go far to establish freedom as the very essence of intelligence. He can reach the connection between the subject and predicate only by the exercise of our rational freedom. Let me seek to make this plain. You may test the matter for yourselves easily. For you have only to sit quietly down in your chair at the fireside, let your mind free to wander where it will, make no effort to check the flow of idle fancy, and you will at once learn what kind of world that would be in which there was no rational order. There, in your idle reverie, you let your mind drift, and you speedily enough know the result of the association of ideas, which knows no higher order. On the other hand, when you desire to find out the full and fixed connection between the subject and predicate of a proposition, you pause, you control yourself, you cause the aimless flood of ideas to cease, you choose, select, and try again, until you reach what seems to be the rational order of thought. It is strange that the most rigid determinists are those who also most strongly advocate freedom of thought.

It is only bare justice to Edwards to say that he anxiously disclaimed fatalism of all sorts, that he did assign to every one the power of doing as he pleases. It is also fair to say that in the particular conflict, which was the occasion of his elaborating his view, he was victorious all along the line. The forces of the opponent were routed everywhere. The question is too large to be fully reasoned here; but I may remark that the strength of Edwards' argumentation lies in the abstractness of his terms, and in the way in which he isolates the faculty of the will from the other faculties of the human spirit. His argument becomes meaningless when you substitute for the action of the will the action of the person, and when you get away from abstractness to the concrete realities of life.

At all events, we do not need Edwards' particular view of the will, in order to vindicate the main conclusions of Reformed theology. The Westminster divines have said, "Although, in relation to the foreknowledge and decree of God, the First Cause, all things come to pass immutably and infallibly, yet by the same providence He ordereth them to fall out according to the nature of second causes, either necessarily, freely, or contingently." Edwards first eliminated freedom from the number of second causes, and, when the issue was raised between necessity and contingency, he had no difficulty in showing that the idea of contingency in relation to human action was quite irrational. But the issue is not so plain when we introduce between necessity and contingency a third thing—freedom. We may then, with Kant, regard freedom as the transcendent correlative of the categorical imperative, or, to keep on lower ground, we may regard freedom as the fundamental quality of a rational being, whose conduct is not shaped by pressure from behind, or kept in position by pressure from without, but who can guide his conduct by a foresight of the future, and strive onwards and upwards to an ideal end. In either event, we overthrow the pre-supposition of those who recognise only one kind of necessity, and who regard the present as the outcome of the past, and that alone. When we place Edwards' theory of determinism alongside his view of preservation as a continued creation, we obtain some strange and curious results. Taken by itself, his determinism, which has regard to the nature of will in itself, and not merely to the human will, logically leads to the conclusion that God acts necessarily, and the creation of the world was an act which God could not but do; on the other hand, his statement about an arbitrary constitution already quoted is a tremendous assertion of the freedom of God, not only that He is free to create or not to create, but that at any moment He is free to sustain or not to sustain the universe. The one view leads to the pantheistic assertion, that the world is the necessary evolution of the Divine; the other view tends to regard the world and man as unreal, and only the shadowy manifestation of the mysterious life that lies beyond. Edwards seems to have held both views, and some of the most strange of the peculiarities of New England theology arose out of them.

But theology has not followed Edwards' steps in either direction. On the contrary, while affirming strongly the freedom of God to make the world or not to make, it recognises that, when once creation began to be, the course of it did not proceed on arbitrary lines; God graciously bound Himself to have respect to the nature of the creatures He had made. As in revelation the first promise included all the others, so in creation the first work was a pledge that the outline thus begun would be filled up. Predestination is not to be taken by itself in an abstract manner, nor is there any arbitrariness in the method of nature or providence. Predestination is ethical, it is the action of the highest wisdom in the service of the greatest goodness, working for the blessedness of created life in harmony with the infinite perfections of God. How great soever be the difficulty of harmonising some speculative views of Edwards with this conclusion, it is abundantly evident that this, or something like this, is his fundamental principle :—

"If there be any such doctrine of fate as is inconsistent with the world being in all things subject to the disposal of an intelligent wise agent, that presides—not as the soul of the universe, but—as the sovereign Lord of the universe, governing all things by proper will, choice, and design, in the exercise of the most perfect liberty conceivable, without subjection to any constraint, or being properly under the power or influence of anything before, above, or without Himself, I wholly disclaim any such doctrine."—(*Will*, iv. 6.)

We pass to his treatises on the doctrines of grace. In addition to many sermons, Edwards has devoted three of his greater works to this great subject. In the treatise on *Grace* we find how grace is bestowed, in the treatise on *Religious Affections*, we see how the regenerated man behaves under the influence of Divine grace, and in the treatise on *The Nature of True Virtue* we are shown grace in its triumph over the weakness and selfishness of man. In speaking of these treatises, I cannot help saying that here the results of Edwards agree, in a remarkable manner, with the conclusions reached by modern exegetes. "We have thus found," says Dr. Dickson in his work on St. Paul's use of the terms Flesh and Spirit, "from an induction of the leading fact presented in the apostle's letters, that the chief sense in which the term πνεῦμα is used by him, is that of the Divine power or influence given to him, or dwelling in him, whereby he is enabled to live unto God, or specially qualified for God's service. . . In all instances it denotes an element or factor not belonging to man as such, but originating apart from him, coming to him, and maintained in him as a Divine gift."

Dr. Dickson's view describes exactly the position of Edwards. Saving grace is a Divine gift, and the possession of it separates the possessor from those who are merely natural. It is not a question of less or more, but the separation is absolute, and those who are not in a state of salvation do not partake in the Divine nature. This is commonplace Evangelical truth, but soon we find Edwards developing the doctrine in his own way. "The first effect of the power of God is to give the heart a Divine taste or sense; to cause it to have a relish of the loveliness and sweetness of the supreme excellency of the Divine nature; and indeed this is all the immediate effect of the Divine power that there is, that is all that the Spirit needs to do, in order to a production of all good effects in the soul. If God by an immediate act of His, gives the soul a relish of the excellency of His own nature, other things will follow of themselves without any further act of the Divine power than only what is necessary to uphold the nature of the faculties of the soul." In other words, the communications of Divine grace to a man who has received from God that relish or taste for the excellency of the Divine nature, are given in a way which may be described as natural. It needed a special Divine act to open the eyes to the light of God, and to have a taste for His excellency; but the opened eyes turned naturally to the light, and the heart delights to feed on the excellency of the living God. Thus, with Edwards, all grace is resolved into love, and all moral excellence in the creature is resolved into love to God. One of his propositions is that "that principle in the soul of the saints, which is the grand Christian virtue, and which is the soul and essence of all grace, is a principle of Divine love." It is this which radically distinguishes them from the unconverted, and lifts them up above common human nature. They have received it by a direct act of God's Spirit. This leads Edwards on to connect the principles of love and grace with the personal operations of the Holy Spirit. He shows that, as the Son of God is spoken of as the wisdom, understanding, and Logos of God, so the Spirit of God is spoken of as the love of God, and may, with equal foundation and propriety, be called the personal love of God. I quote the following striking passage :—

"We often read in Scripture of the Father loving the Son, and the Son loving the Father, yet we never once read of the Father or the Son loving the Holy Spirit, and the Spirit loving either of them. It is because the Holy Spirit is the Divine love itself, the love of the Father and the Son. Hence it is also to be accounted for, that we very often read of the love of the Father and the Son to men, and particularly their love to the saints; but we never read of the Holy Ghost loving them, for the Holy Ghost is that love of God and Christ that is breathed forth primarily towards each other, and flows out secondarily towards the creature. This also will account for it, that the apostle Paul so often wishes grace, mercy, and peace from God the Father, and from the Lord Jesus Christ, in the beginning of his Epistles, without ever mentioning the Holy Ghost, because the Holy Ghost is himself the love and grace of God the Father and the Lord Jesus Christ. He is the Deity—wholly breathed forth in infinite, substantial, intelligent love: from the Father and the Son, first towards each other, and secondarily freely flowing out to the creature, and so standing forth a personal subsistence."—(*Grace*, p. 47.)

All saving grace is summed up in love; and the Spirit of God is the Divine love in a personal subsistence. And therefore the whole duty of a regenerated man is to love. A regenerated man is, however, a spiritual man, and here Edwards' view coincides with the view which Dr. Dickson has reached, from an exhaustive study of the Epistles of Paul. Spiritual men are those in whom the Spirit of God dwells. For Edwards says that the Scriptures do not call grace spiritual, but spirit; and spirit is none other than the Holy Spirit. So that true "saving grace is none other than that very love of God—that is, God in one of the persons of the Trinity—uniting Himself to the soul of a creature, as a vital principle, dwelling there, and exerting Himself by the faculties of the soul of man, in His own proper nature, after the manner of a principle of nature."

The treatise on *Grace* is of unspeakable importance for the right apprehension of Edwards' view of the doctrines of grace. It enables us to understand the teaching of the treatise on *The Religious Affections*. This treatise bears the marks of the occasion which induced Edwards to write it. In connection with the revivals of religion at Northampton, and the spurious imitations of true religion which were then manifest, Edwards was led to ask the question, What is the nature of true religion? and what is the distinguishing note of that virtue which is acceptable in the sight of God?—and his answer leads to a discussion of the nature of the affections, their place in religion, by what signs affections that are gracious may be distinguished from those which are not; and what are the distinguishing marks of affections which are truly gracious and holy. The statement in both treatises is clear, and in both it is made plain that gracious affections are the result of Divine grace. But in the treatise on

Grace we are led further back, and gracious affections are seen not to be accidental and arbitrary, but rooted in the Divine nature, and are the result of the abiding desire of God to communicate Himself to His creatures. We do not know which of these treatises was first written, but, in any event, they each supplement the other. The Holy Spirit is the personal love of God, in personal form subsisting, and is ever seeking to make men partakers of the Divine nature, to dwell in them, and to be one with them. If, in some respects, the theology of Edwards seems to lead to arbitrary sovereignty as the one essential note of God, that arises only when we limit his view to certain aspects of it. But when we penetrate into the essential conception, we find enthroned in the central position the ruling thought, God is love. And His wrath is only the other side of His love. The sovereignty of God means ultimately the sovereignty of one whose nature is love. Thus, with Edwards, as with Reformed theology in general, the articulate and final expression of the sovereignty of God is, God is love.

Thus gracious affections are implanted in us by the communication of the Holy Spirit, who gives Himself to us, and dwells in us. This is their origin; as to their nature, they are love in its diversified operations. They have as their object the excellence of the Divine character. Writing to meet the pressure of a practical need, Edwards is minute and particular in his description of the way and manner in which we may discriminate between true religious affections and those which are spurious. But the result he reaches agrees with the result obtained in the calmer, more theological treatise; as the essential nature of God is, God is love, so the essential glory of religious affections is contained in the words, all true religious affection and all virtue is love.

In the treatise on *The Nature of True Virtue*, Edwards, with that predilection of his for the use of abstract terms, has defined virtue as love to being in general. It becomes plain in the issue that more concrete terms would have expressed his meaning better. He has consequently been misunderstood, and his view of virtue has been pressed to issues which have made it agree with the view of Spinoza. Still, when we seek to understand what Edwards really means by being in general, we find that it is not quite the same as the universal substance of Spinoza. No doubt he sometimes speaks of God as the universal substance. But then we must harmonise that statement with the more definite statements in other works of his. It is only fair to interpret his general statements by his more specific doctrines, and his definition of virtue as the love of being in general will bear to be translated into the concrete language of Scripture: "Thou shalt love the Lord thy God, with all thy heart, with all thy soul, and with all thy mind, and thy neighbour as thyself." This more concrete meaning satisfies all the conditions of the case, answers all the demands of Edwards' argument, and is free from many implications which may be evolved from the highly abstract language which he uses. This appears more clearly in his work on *God's*

Chief End in Creation. Here he sets himself to answer the questions, "Is the end of creation the happiness of the creature ? or is it the manifestation of the glory of God ?" Edwards' solution of the problem is this. He refuses to put these two as alternatives. They are not alternative. Both are ultimate, and both are, in fact, one and the same thing. The creation, looked at as a whole, and in the final outcome, is the manifestation of the glory of God, and is also the highest blessedness of the creature. There is in God, according to Edwards, a disposition to manifest the fulness of His glory and power. When, therefore, He resolved to make the world and to make man, He desired to communicate to them the fulness of Himself. He delighteth to communicate Himself to men, and this communication of Himself to His creatures is delightful to God, on its own account, and not merely in relation to the further end of manifesting forth His glory. "God communicates Himself to the understanding of the creature in giving him the knowledge of His glory; and to the will of the creature, in giving him holiness, consisting primarily in the love of God; and in giving the creature happiness, chiefly consisting in joy in God. These are the sum of that emanation of Divine fulness called in Scripture the glory of God."

Stress is laid by Edwards continually on this original property of the Divine nature to communicate Himself to His creatures. God delighteth in mercy. To communicate good to the creature is in itself well-pleasing to God. It is also pointed out by Edwards that while God delights in exercising goodness and showing mercy, on the other hand, in the execution of wrath, "God proceeds to execute wrath with backwardness and reluctance; the misery of the creature being not agreeable to Him on its own account." Though the exercise of justice is a work which must be done, it is work in which God takes no delight. From this point of view, we can enter with deepest sympathy into the passion and the terror with which Edwards preached the terrors of the Lord, and the awful consequences of sin unrepented of. Edwards had a deep sympathy with the wounded feeling of Divine love, which has sought to bless men, and was rejected by them. He had sympathy also with the reluctance and backwardness with which God proceeded to do "His strange work." And the ferocity which sometimes appals us, and the burning intensity which scorches us in his sermons, are but the expression of the horror of sin which Edwards felt, and of the desire within his heart that all hindrances which prevented God from communicating Himself to his creatures might be taken out of the way. Thus, on reflection, we shall find that Edwards' preaching of the terrors of the Lord is quite consistent with— nay, is part of his central conception, God is love.

In his *History of Redemption* and in his sermons on Justification, we have Edwards' views of many great and cardinal doctrines. The *History of Redemption* is only the first rough outline of the great work which was in the thought of Edwards at the time of his death. But the first draft is a work of extraordinary power. In it almost all his thoughts on Divine things have met, and are in the process of being formed into a unity. God's works and God's ways, all theology, and all history are shown forth as culminating in the redemption that is in Christ. It is a theodicy, a vindication of the ways of God to man; it is a philosophy of history, which shows that through the ages "one increasing purpose runs." It is a wonderful work to have been written while the historical method was yet in its infancy, and the historical material at his command so scanty. As, however, the method of severe scientific exegesis has justified the conclusions which Evangelical insight reached without their help, so it may be said that the historical method has largely justified the main conclusions reached by Edwards in the *History of Redemption*. All previous history was a preparation for the coming of Christ, and all subsequent history has been moulded by His influence. We may have to shift some of the material used by Edwards from one period to another, or otherwise alter the relative adjustment of topics; but the main outline and the central thought of it will remain, for it is based on the due recognition of the Lord Jesus Christ as the uniting principle, the aim and goal of universal history.

Had time permitted, we might have dwelt on Edwards' view of the atonement made by Christ, on the relative order and place of the decrees, on justification, and on other kindred topics. In truth, there is room for much to be said, which might not be without interest and edification. But we must be content with the statement that his treatment of these doctrines is in substantial agreement with that of Calvinistic divines generally. We say, in substantial agreement; for Edwards cannot write on any topic without raising important questions, or setting old doctrines in new light, and placing them in fresh points of view. If there has been any doctrine which has engaged the attention of divines from the time of the Reformation downwards, it has been the doctrine of Justification by Faith alone. All systematic treatises on theology have dealt with it, and separate works, not a few, have expounded it. But Edwards cannot handle even a well-worn subject like this without raising a number of questions untouched before, all of them lying within the statement of the doctrine as set forth, say in the Shorter Catechism. He does not doubt that our sins are pardoned and we are accepted as righteous in the sight of God only for the righteousness of Christ imputed to us and received by faith alone. Not questioning the truth of imputation, he yet asks why and how is the righteousness of Christ imputed, and the answer is as follows:

"God does not give those that believe an union with or an interest in the Saviour as a reward for faith, but only because faith is the soul's active uniting with Christ, or is the very act of unition, on their part. God sees fit, that in order to an union being established between two intelligent active beings or persons, so as that they should be looked upon as one, there should be the mutual act of both, that each should receive other, as actively joining themselves one to another. God, in requiring this in order to an union with Christ as one of His people, treats men as reasonable creatures, capable of act and choice; and hence sees it fit that they only who are one with Christ by their own act should be looked at as one in law. What is real in the

union between Christ and His people is the foundation of what is legal ; that is, it is something really in them, and between them, uniting them, that is the ground of the suitableness of their being accounted as one by the Judge. And if there be any act or qualification in believers of that uniting nature, that it is meet on that account the Judge should look upon them and accept them as one, no wonder that, upon the account of the same act or qualification, He should accept the satisfaction and merit of the one for the other, as if these were their own satisfaction and merit."
—(*Works*, i. p. 626.)

In the same series of sermons he touches on a number of questions concerning the Atonement, the active and passive obedience of Christ, the relation of the sins committed after justification to the declarative sentence of justification; and, as his manner is, while holding fast the faith once delivered to the saints, he ever seeks to apprehend it in all its bearings and relations. Thus it is with his treatment of any particular doctrine; he compels us to think, and will not permit us to go away with a mere abstract general statement of doctrine. He forces us to examine it in all the phases of its operations.

While laying out for himself new works for years of toil, while his thoughts were occupied with the purpose of setting forth the truth of God " to the greatest advantage, in the brightest light, and in the most striking manner," the end swiftly came— " God's finger touched him, and he slept." His earthly work was done. In any view of it, a great work it was. It is something for which we may be thankful, that Scotland in the person of Dr. Erskine, was among the first to recognise his greatness and his power, that his works from the beginning have had a place among the works read by the godly people of Scotland, in former years. Along with the works of Boston you will find detached volumes of the works of Edwards in the treasured and well-read books, which our fathers were wont to read in the far-off villages and withdrawn glens of Scotland. I have met grey-haired farmers, weavers, and others, who could enter with intelligence into discussions on various points in the works of Edwards, whose intelligence was fed, and whose hearts were kindled by the mighty religious emotion of the great New England divine. These men are now gone, and others have risen in their room who are not accustomed to think thoughts so great, nor feel the pulse of so mighty an emotion. But neither would we have been what we are, nor would Scotland have accomplished her work, had not our sires in castle and in hut pondered on the ways of God to man, and learned wisdom and strength at the feet of the fathers who make the great Evangelical Succession.

JOHN WESLEY.

By the Rev. J. H. WILSON, D.D., Edinburgh.

ON the night of the 9th February 1709, the rectory of Epworth, in the fens of Lincolnshire, was set fire to by the rough people of the parish, who bore no kindly feeling to the minister, Samuel Wesley. With difficulty all the family, save one, made their escape from the burning house, and when the father, hearing a child's cry from the attic, attempted to rescue the one who had been left, he found the stair burned away and all access debarred. By one friendly helper standing on the shoulders of another, the child was rescued just before the roof fell in, and a precious life was almost miraculously saved. That child was John Wesley, then about six years of age, whose mind was deeply impressed by this remarkable providence at the time, and who regarded and spoke of himself through life as, in a very peculiar sense, "a brand plucked from the burning"! He had these words engraved on his seal, and when half a century later he thought himself dying, and wrote his own epitaph, he wished them carved on his tombstone. His father's words had a more weighty significance than, at the time, he had any idea of, when he said on that memorable night, "Come, neighbours, let us kneel down. Let us give God thanks. He has given me all my eight children. Let the house go. *I am rich enough!*" Had that young life perished, a mighty and world-wide influence for good had been lost.

John Wesley was born at Epworth on the 17th June 1703. He was the fourth son and tenth child in a family of nineteen. His parents, Samuel Wesley, rector of the parish of Epworth, and Susannah Annesley, were both descended from godly Puritan forefathers, and had the advantage of Puritan training and teaching, though both had, in early life, conformed to the Church of England, and become warmly attached to it. The father, in the discharge of his ecclesiastical duties, and in the prosecution of his literary pursuits, found occasion for frequent and lengthened absences in London, and the entire care and training of their large family devolved upon the mother. She was a woman of remarkable character and gifts, who made the upbringing of her children the great work of her life, and laid the foundations, in a more than ordinary degree, of the life and character and work of her afterwards famous sons. Her methodical training moulded the habits and developed the powers of her children, and she has come to be familiarly recognised as not only the "Mother of the Wesleys," but the "Mother of Methodism."

The first and most important school which Wesley attended, was the school—for such it was in the strictest sense—conducted by his mother in the rectory. There he had the benefit of all that systematic and painstaking teaching and discipline could do for him, from the age of five till he was between ten and eleven. His spirit and behaviour were such, that, when but eight years old, he was admitted by his father to the Lord's Table. His mother's practice of devoting a portion of time every week, to personal conversation about the things of God, with each of her children separately, had great influence in directing their thoughts and developing and stimulating their spiritual nature, and young Wesley made touching reference to this in after years.

In his eleventh year he was sent to the Charter-House School, in London, where he remained for six or seven years. There he applied himself resolutely to his studies, so as to secure the cordial approval of the head of the school. He had to submit to very serious hardships at the hands of the older boys, by whom he was relegated to the companionship of the younger scholars, with an important twofold effect, in the way of training him for the work of his after life—accustoming him to the bearing of privations uncomplainingly, on the one hand, and, on the other, to the habit of exercising control over those associated with him. Besides his classical studies, in which he made great proficiency, his elder brother, Samuel, speaks of him as "learning Hebrew as fast as he can." His school life was not favourable to his spiritual progress, though he still kept up the form of religion. He says, "What I now hoped to be saved by was—

1. Not being so bad as other people; 2. Having still a kindness for religion; and 3. Reading the Bible, going to church, and saying my prayers."

In this state of mind he went, in 1720, to Oxford, where he was elected to a studentship at Christ Church College. In 1726 he was elected Fellow of Lincoln's, and a few months later, in his twenty-fourth year, he was chosen Greek Lecturer and "Moderator of the Classes"—a position which indicated the high place he had taken as a student, and gave him the very kind of practice that helped to fit him for other fields of conflict where his regulating hand was to be powerfully felt. He specially distinguished himself as a logician and a classical scholar, studies which he continued to cultivate long after his student days were over. In 1727 he took his degree of Master of Arts.

During the earlier part of his University career his religion seems to have been of the same formal character as when he left the Charter House. He was startled by the irreligiousness and even immorality of many of those who were in training for the Christian ministry; and when he came to think of taking deacon's orders in the Church of England, which he did in 1725, he had to face the great question of his own state in the sight of God. As before, he found a faithful counsellor in his mother. She had written to him: "I heartily wish you would now enter upon a strict examination of yourself, that you may know whether you have a reasonable hope of salvation by Christ. If you have, the satisfaction of knowing it will abundantly reward your pains; if you have not, you will find a more reasonable occasion for tears than can be met with in a tragedy. This matter deserves great consideration by all, but especially by those designed for the ministry; who ought, above all others, to make their calling and election sure, lest, after they have preached to others, they themselves should be cast away."

It was about this time that he began the earnest study of Thomas à Kempis' *Imitation of Christ*, and Jeremy Taylor's *Rules for Holy Living and Dying*, and, some time afterwards, William Law's *Serious Call to a Devout Life*. These became very much his spiritual guides. They wakened up his conscience, and he sought to deal with his heart and to frame his life according to their teaching. Doubtless there must have been a purpose in his being guided to these authors at such a time; and they may have done their part, in that transition period of his life, in preparing him for the great work that lay before him. And yet, one cannot but regret that he did not, at this critical time, meet with some more simple and direct evangelical teaching, in book or living friend, which might have guided him to the sinner's one resting-place, saved him long years of painful soul-struggle, and given the world sooner the benefit of those labours which it so urgently needed.

Not now, nor till long after, was the great discovery made to him of a full, free, and immediate salvation through faith in Christ. Amid all his earnestness, his views were entirely legal. His aim was to attain salvation by devoutness and self-denial, by holy living and deeds of charity, to which he gave himself with all the ardour of his nature. And while these books might have helped him at a later stage, they but served, in the state of mind in which he then was, as with others in the same state of mind now, to furnish rules for a life which had not yet begun, and to stimulate the soul to higher and intenser efforts, where the motive power was awanting, instead of leading to the life itself. He himself comes back upon this bitterly in after years, and speaks of it as "laying a foundation beneath the Foundation."

In the latter part of 1727 he returned to Epworth, at his father's request, to aid him in his days of failing strength, and for two years he acted as curate. There he gave himself largely to the reading of mystic authors, regarding which he says at a later date, "I think the rock on which I had the nearest made shipwreck of the faith, was the writings of the mystics." His labours bore no visible fruit; and gave no foreshadowing of the spiritual power that was afterwards to accompany them. When urged to settle down permanently in the parish and get the succession to the living, he could not forego the attractions of Oxford, alike from regard to the work he might do there, and the help he might get.

On returning to Oxford he found that a very important step had been taken. His brother Charles, who was his junior by four years and a half, was an undergraduate of Christ Church. He had become an earnest and diligent student, alive to the reality of divine things. During John's absence at Epworth, he had gathered several younger students around him, and formed them into a kind of club, partly for purposes of self-improvement, literary and religious, and partly for the helping of others. In connection with this, the name *Methodist* came into use, as describing the men who originated the great movement to which this term came to be permanently applied. It had been in use, before the times of Nonconformity, as marking out one of the sects of the day, which was characterised by its plain preaching and plainness of dress and manners. Towards the close of the previous century, the name had also been applied to some of the Nonconformists who differed from their brethren on the subject of Justification, and adopted what was called the *New Method*. Charles Wesley thus explains the application of the name to himself: "He had lost his first year at college in diversions; the next, he set himself to study; diligence led him into serious thinking; he was wont to go to the weekly sacrament, persuading two or three students to accompany him; he observed the practice of study prescribed by the statutes of the University, and *this* gained him the harmless name of *Methodist*."

John Wesley joined this band of students, which had come to be known by the name of the "Holy Club," and his age and abilities at once placed him at its head. Besides the reading of the Greek New Testament and the classics, and the study of theology, the object of the society was declared to be—" to converse with young students, visit the prisons, instruct some poor families, take care of a school and a parish workhouse, rescue younger members of the University from bad company, and encourage them in a sober, studious life." It was a remarkable association of young men, all of kindred spirit—including James Hervey (afterwards well known by his *Meditations*) and George Whitefield,—stinting themselves so as to give all they could to others, abounding in philanthropic labours, practising the severest austerities, and being subjected, in consequence, to serious persecution. It is difficult to believe that they should have persevered for years in such Christian labours and such trying crossbearing, and in such blamelessness of life, without having some root of true godliness in them; and yet several of them afterwards spoke of this as a time of spiritual bondage and darkness, out of which they emerged, after severe mental conflict, into the full light and liberty and rest of faith in Christ.

In 1735 old Mr. Wesley died, and the house at Epworth was broken up. Shortly after, a proposal was made to Wesley that he should go as "missioner" to Georgia, in the Southern States of America, to minister to a body of British settlers and to preach the Gospel to the Red Indians When his mother was consulted about the project, though she was then in the first months of her widowhood and without a permanent home, in a noble spirit of self-denial, she answered, "Had I twenty sons, I should rejoice if they were all so engaged, though I should never see them more." Wesley's state of mind, at this time, may be gathered from what he says: "My chief motive, to which all the rest are subordinate, is the hope of saving my own soul. I hope to learn the true sense of the Gospel of Christ by preaching it to the heathen."

His experience in Georgia was in the last degree humbling, and yet in its issue was not a little profitable, in its bearing on the crisis of his life. His outward voyage was eventful, as bringing him in contact with the Moravian Brethren, to whom he afterwards owed so much. He could not but see and feel that they had something which he utterly wanted. Their calm confidence and fearlessness, during a terrific storm, in marked contrast to the bearing of the English passengers on board, and the mild answer of one of them, " Our women and children are not afraid to die," deeply impressed him — an impression which the kindly and faithful dealing of their pastor with him still further deepened, as convincing him that he still wanted a true faith in Christ. And yet all through the voyage he laboured indefatigably from morning till night, for the good of those on board, learning German, that he might be able to speak to a body of German emigrants (as on his arrival he learned Spanish, that he might be able to help some Spanish Jews who came in his way), and leaving no moment unoccupied.

In Georgia he came out as the full-blown Ritualist and High Churchman, enjoining confession and fasting, re-baptizing the children of dissenters, and refusing to admit to the Lord's Supper or to bury, any who had not received Episcopal baptism. We find him afterwards saying, "Can High Church bigotry go further than this? And how well have I since been beaten with mine own staff!" He stirred up the people against him, not by his faithfulness, but by his excessive and ill-directed zeal. His ministry there, as at Epworth, was very much a failure, and the account which he gives of it, in the one case, applies to both: "From 1725-29 saw no fruit of my labours. It could not be, for I neither laid the foundation of repentance nor of preaching the Gospel. 1729-34, laying a deeper foundation of repentance, saw a little fruit—but only a little, for *I did not preach faith in the blood of the Covenant.*"

Humbled and self-emptied by the result of his American expedition, he returned to England in 1738. He had a stormy passage, and was led by his fear of death to doubt his having any interest in Christ at all, and to feel that all that had been, must go for nothing. He was thus prepared for what was the great event of his life.

Scarcely had he reached the shores of England when he met Peter Böhler, a devoted Moravian brother, who, from the moment of meeting them, took the warmest personal interest in the two brothers, John and Charles. He saw the state of mind in which they were, opened up to them the real nature and object of saving faith, and pressed Christ as a personal Saviour on their immediate acceptance. John, in his Journal, notes February 7th, 1738—the day on which he first met Böhler—as "a day much to be remembered." Separately, the one at Oxford, the other in London, the two brothers were being driven out of their formal and self-righteous religion, and were earnestly seeking the way of life.

At length John got the news that, on the 21st May, Charles had found rest to his soul, what he had begun to learn from Böhler, being completed by a brazier with whom he lodged,—"a poor ignorant mechanic who knows nothing but Christ, yet by knowing Him, knows and discerns all things."

John received the scriptural doctrine of faith as taught by Böhler, after much conversation and searching of the Word, but it was not till some time later, on the 24th May 1738, that he finally surrendered himself to Christ. This is so important, that it must be given at length and in his own words. His experience, throughout this whole period of anxiety and suspense, strikes us as wonderfully like that of Luther at the same stage. He says, " I continued preaching and following after, and trusting in, that righteousness whereby no flesh can be justified. Being ignorant of the righteousness of Christ, which, by a living faith within, bringeth salvation to every one that believeth, I sought to establish my own righteousness, and so laboured in the fire all my days." After describing his conversations with Böhler and others, he says, "They added with one mouth, that this faith was the gift—the free gift of God; and that He would surely bestow it on every soul who earnestly and perseveringly sought it. I was now thoroughly convinced; and by the grace of God I resolved to seek it unto the end—(1) by absolutely renouncing *my own* works or righteousness, on which I had really grounded my hope of salvation, though I knew it not, from my youth up; (2) by adding to the constant use of all the other means of grace a continual prayer for this very thing, justifying, saving faith, a full reliance on the blood of Christ shed for me; a trust in Him as *my* Christ, as *my* sole justification, sanctification, and redemption.

"I continued then to seek it (though with strange indifference, dulness, and coldness, and unusually frequent relapses into sin) till Wednesday, May 24th. . . . In the evening I went very unwillingly to a society in Aldersgate Street, where one was reading Luther's preface to the Epistle to the Romans. About a quarter before nine, while he was describing the change which God works on the heart through faith in Christ, I felt my heart strangely warmed. I felt I did trust in Christ, Christ alone, for salvation; and an assurance was given me that He had taken away *my* sins, even *mine*, and saved *me* from the law of sin and death. . . . I then testified openly to all there what I now first felt in my heart."

Charles's account of it is: "Towards ten, my brother was brought in triumph by a troop of friends, and declared, 'I believe.' We sang the hymn with great joy, and parted with prayer."

Thus, after having been tempest-tossed on a sea of uncertainty for ten years, this vessel reached the haven of rest. There will be various opinions as to what the experience of these years amounted to, and what was the real character of this change. Wesley himself always spoke of this as the time of his new birth, his conversion, his justification. At one time indeed, he makes this distinction, that before, he had "only the faith of a *servant*—now, that of *a son*." But anon we find him declaring explicitly, "I knew that I had not faith, unless the faith of a devil, the faith of Judas, that speculative, notional, airy shadow, which lives in the head, not in the heart. But what is this to the living, justifying faith, the faith that cleanses from sin?"[1]

Some may be inclined to regard the change as a mere re-quickening, what has come to be spoken of in certain quarters as "second conversion," or as "the higher Christian life." In any case, this much is certain, that henceforth Wesley was a new man, that this was the great era in his history, and formed a new point of departure, alike in his life and in his work. If his life is to be divided into two great parts, this is unquestionably the dividing-line.

His first step, after this, was to visit Herrnhut, in Saxony, the headquarters of the Moravian Brethren, to study more closely their character and manner of life, their teaching and organisation. There he met the devoted Christian David, whose conversation and clear and full evangelical preaching he much enjoyed. "The right foundation," said he, "is not your contrition, not *your* righteousness, nothing of *your own*, nothing that is wrought *in you* by the

[1] "I did go thus far for many years, as many of this place can testify; using diligence to eschew all evil, and to have a conscience void of offence; redeeming the time; buying up every opportunity of doing good to all men; constantly and carefully using all the public and all the private means of grace; endeavouring after a steady seriousness of behaviour, at all times, and in all places; and God is my record, before whom I stand, doing all this in sincerity; having a real design to serve God; a hearty desire to do His will in all things; to please Him who had called me to 'fight the good fight,' and to 'lay hold of eternal life.' Yet my own conscience beareth me witness in the Holy Ghost, that all this time I was but *almost a Christian.*"— *Sermon II.*

Holy Ghost; but it is something *without* you,—the righteousness and blood of Christ." From him he got a further impulse for the proclamation of the new-found truth. To Count Zinzendorf, however, the head of the settlement, Wesley was less drawn; the community was too little aggressive for the ardent Englishman, and though he learned much and borrowed much from their system of organisation, and always regarded them with respect and gratitude, he kept on a separate line of his own, and finally separated from them in London, when, some time after, serious error began to show itself among them.

And now the great work of Wesley's life began. He had before him a large and inviting field for a spirit like his. We cannot enter into details regarding the state of England at that time. A very dark picture might be drawn, without at all over-colouring, of the state of things alike among the upper and lower classes, the clergy and the people. The peasantry were ignorant and degraded, coarse in their tastes, and in many cases almost brutal in their enjoyments. In the large centres of population there had been a great falling away from the means of grace, and where there was not positive unbelief, and hatred of everything that had the appearance of godliness, there was a dead formality, and an utter want of intelligent acquaintance with the vital doctrines of Christianity. The Reformation in England had only been partial. The masses of the people had never been thoroughly leavened with a knowledge of evangelical truth. And though both in the Church of England and in the ranks of nonconformity there were bright lights, the lustre of which has not been dimmed to this day, the ministry of the Word had largely fallen into a state of spiritual torpor, Socinian views had crept in where once there was orthodoxy, and the lives of many were as defective as their teaching. Vice in the upper classes was winked at, while it was utterly unheeded among the lower. Socially, morally, and spiritually, there was much which earnest men could not but mourn over, and which called loudly for help.

That was what met Wesley's gaze, wherever he turned his eye. He had long sought and laboured for the moral elevation of his country. But he had wanted alike the right lever, the fulcrum on which to rest it, and the spiritual power to move it. Now he had all the three. He had the promise of God as a great reality, he had the true doctrine that had met his own need and brought light and life to him, and he was himself full of faith and of the Holy Ghost. He had large views of the possibilities of the case,—of what *might*, *should*, *must* be done. He had no idea of starting a new sect. He was a loyal Churchman, and continued so to the last, in spite of all that was fitted to weaken his attachment to the Church of his early love. He aimed at a new Reformation—a Revival of the Church of England —the awakening of it out of its slumber—the reviving among its ministers and people of the true doctrine and of spiritual life. He had no new doctrine to propound. He wanted but to disentomb and re-animate the doctrine of the Apostles and the

Reformers. He had now got something to preach to the people that he knew would do them good. His great themes were few in number, simple in their character, and vital in their importance— Depravity, the New Birth, Faith, and Holiness: the natural and utter depravity of man, the consequent need of a supernatural work of regeneration by the Spirit of God, justification by faith alone, the scripturalness of instantaneous conversion, the possibility of men knowing that they are saved, not only by the fruits of the new life, but by the inward witness of the Spirit, and as the result of all, holiness of life. Or, as he himself put it—"repentance, faith, and holiness; the first, the *way* to religion; the second, the *gate* of it; the third, *religion* itself." After his own experience he was clear and emphatic on the subject of *faith:* "Christian faith," said he, "is not only an assent to the whole Gospel of Christ, but also a full reliance on the blood of Christ, a trust in the merits of His life, death, and resurrection; a recumbency upon Him as our atonement and our life, as given for us, and living in us."

With this message he was prepared to go over the length and breadth of England, and he did so, without intermission, from the time of what he believed to be his new birth till his death; from the thirty-fifth year of his age till his eighty-eighth —as one of his biographers has called it—"a grand monotony of holy toil." And the results, direct and indirect, were such, that the time from 1739 till 1791, might well be spoken of, as the "Revival of the Eighteenth Century."

1. Let us look at Wesley as a *Preacher*.—His great work was his *preaching*. He was the great Itinerant Preacher of his day. He preached everywhere,—in town and country, in all parts of England, repeating these visits once a year till the very year of his death, in North and South Wales, in Ireland, Scotland, and the Channel Islands. He preached all the days of the week,—one might almost say, all the hours of the day. His habit was to rise at four in the morning—this he did for sixty years—to preach at five, and as a rule, three or four times daily, often with long journeys between his services. In this respect, Whitefield was the only man who could be compared with him, Whitefield having preached 18,000 sermons in the course of thirty-four years, or ten a week, and Wesley 42,400 in fifty-three years, from the time of his return from Georgia, or fifteen a week. He defended his practice of itinerating, in the memorable words, "*I look upon all the world as my parish;* thus far, I mean, that in whatever part of it I am, I judge it meet, right, and my bounden duty to declare unto all that are willing to hear, the glad tidings of salvation;" or, as he said when he was summoned to appear before the Bishop at Bristol, "My lord, my business on earth is to do what good I can. Woe is me, if I preach not the Gospel wherever I am, in the habitable world!"

He kept up his habits of study to the last. He accustomed himself to reading while travelling on horseback, and continued the practice for forty years, in this way going the whole round of literature. He thus preserved a freshness and variety in his preaching which few evangelists have succeeded, for any length of time, in doing.

Like others of his fellow-labourers, he did not deal in mere abstract statements of truth, or make mere general appeals. He *individualised*. He pointed his weapon, as a good soldier does, not indiscriminately at a multitude, but at *a man*, so that each hearer felt as if *he* alone were in view, as if he were the one man who was being spoken to. And so it was *now* and *here*. To those who knew the way of salvation more or less, and had thoughts of closing with Christ, and to those who never had an earnest thought before, the offer was, of a *present* salvation—the call was, to *present* decision. Thus he says: "Who art thou that now seest and feelest both thine inward and outward ungodliness? *Thou* art the man! I want *thee* for my Lord; I challenge *thee* for a child of God by faith. The Lord hath need of *thee*. Thou who feelest thou art just fit for hell, art just fit to advance His glory,—the glory of His free grace, justifying the ungodly, and him that worketh not. Oh, come quickly. Believe in the Lord Jesus: and *thou*, even *thou*, art reconciled to God."

He took a great step in advance, when, yielding to Whitefield's urgent solicitations, and following his example, he ventured on *Field Preaching*. It cost him no little effort, as one who, as he says, "had all his life been so tenacious of every point relating to decency and order, that he should have thought saving of souls almost a sin, if it had not been done in a Church!" It was an immense addition to his power, rendering him independent of Church accommodation, extending vastly the number and variety of his hearers, compelling him to use the language of the people, and throwing him back upon God. In this as in other work, his courage, tact, and self-possession were extraordinary, looking a mob in the face, planting his chair in the midst of it, taking the leader by the hand, and turning him into a friend and helper!

What his preaching was, his published sermons remain to tell. His discourses on the Sermon on the Mount are striking examples of practical exposition and appeal.

2. Wesley as an *Organiser.*—His system of organisation has been the wonder and admiration of Christendom; in its efficiency and completeness, rivalling that of the Church of Rome. In this respect he differed utterly from Whitefield, who was the simple preacher of the gospel, and had no turn for organisation, and no thought of it. Wesley had no finished scheme carved out from the first, and filled up by degrees. He moved when the emergency came, and followed the leading of God's Word and providence and the teaching of experience. He saw the importance of conserving the results of his work, and keeping the converts together for their mutual help and edification. This was the object which he had in view in the *Societies* which he established wherever he went. They were just such as might be formed now, in any congregation or district, after a time of revival, for mutual encouragement and instruction, for promoting helpful fellowship, and stimulating to Christian activity. The *Classes* were subdivisions under the Society, each composed of about twelve

persons, meeting once a week for praise and prayer and religious oversight, presided over by exhorters or class-leaders, men of established character and experience, who have been compared to non-commissioned officers in the army. Then there were the *itinerant* and *local preachers;* who held the ground which Wesley had gained, and who, as a class, were called into existence by the very necessity of the case. When an interest was awakened and souls were saved, in localities where the ministry of the Word was utterly unhelpful, or where there was no provision of any kind to meet the spiritual needs of the people, while there was much to hinder and discourage, it was necessary to send lay preachers to share the work with Wesley himself, who, though almost ubiquitous, could not by any means meet the demands made on him. These preachers were afterwards arranged in *circuits*, which at the time of Wesley's death numbered a hundred and fifteen in the United Kingdom, by means of which the work was kept going on in a permanent and systematic way. And, finally, there was the *Conference*, where his clerical brethren and itinerant helpers met to consider the past and take counsel as to the future.

It was with great hesitation that Wesley ventured to sanction *lay preaching*. He had hurried to London for the purpose of stopping it, when his mother, who had heard the first offender preach, said to her son, " Take care what you do with respect to that young man, for he is as surely called of God to preach, as you are. *Examine what have been the fruits of his preaching, and hear him also yourself.*" He took the advice, and had his objections removed. He afterwards defended his action in the matter on these grounds: "It is true that in *ordinary* cases both an *inward* and an *outward* call are requisite; but we apprehend there is something far from ordinary in the present case; and upon the calmest view of things, we think that they who are only called of God and not of man have *more* right to preach, than they who are only called of man and not of God. Now, that many of the clergy, though called of man, are not called of God to preach His Gospel, is undeniable, first, because they themselves utterly disclaim, nay, and ridicule the inward call; second, because they do not know what the Gospel is, and of consequence, they *do not* and *cannot* preach it."

Wesley took great pains to instruct and guide his preachers, above all things urging them to prayer and study, and charging them to preach the need of the new birth, and salvation by faith, and to seek the conversion of men to God. Some of them were very remarkable men, with a singular experience and special gifts, and their work was productive of great results. One of them says of himself: "I am but a *brown bread* preacher, that seek to help all I can to heaven, in the best manner I can." Wesley's three tests for such men were *piety, gifts*, and *usefulness*, taking them on probation, at first for one year, and subsequently for four years.

One of the secrets of the success of Methodism, making it the pioneer of all the Churches, has been *its organisation,* which has only in small part been described, its giving *the people* so large a place in the active service of the Church, and especially its system of *itinerant preaching*, which has carried it everywhere, to the utmost limits of civilisation, where no other agencies could exist.

Isaac Taylor,[1] who saw the weak points in Wesley and Methodism, and did not spare them, says, " His organisation is the most efficiently expansive Christian institute which modern times have seen. It stands alone without a parallel in the field of Church history. That 'Society,' which was the product of the founder's mind, claims to be considered as one of the most remarkable experiments in ecclesiastical science that has ever been carried forward," with " results which find no parallel, even in the exciting times of the Reformation or since, especially as regards *the untaught masses of the people*, non-attendants on public worship—the millions that circulate every Sunday around church and chapel."

What I call special attention to here is, that all this was carried on *within the Church*, and never needed to have gone out of it. I have not been speaking of the Methodist *Church* in its separate condition, but of Methodism within the Church of England. If the Church had been wise, all this elaborate machinery and evangelistic power might have continued within it, and been a source of strength and spiritual life to it. Never was there greater infatuation than when the Church closed its pulpits against Wesley and his coadjutors, excluding the great evangelist from the church of his early years, (and even from the Communion table, as not being

[1] *Wesley and Methodism.*

"fit" to be admitted!) so that once and again he had to preach to his old parishioners from his father's grave! The very classes which the Church of England is now so anxious to gain and to hold were thus alienated from its communion. Men like the Kingswood colliers and the Cornish miners, whose conversion and altered life would have made them an honour and strength to any Church, were actually debarred from the Lord's Supper, because they came in such numbers that they exhausted the patience of the clergy! What might that Church not have been to-day, with all this life and spiritual energy within its pale, as might have been, if the people could have found there the teaching and sympathy which they were at length compelled to seek elsewhere!

It is interesting to know that, in the Scottish Church, in the dark times of Moderatism, there were similar "Praying Societies," which maintained the life of the godly people, these afterwards forming twenty-five congregations of the Secession Church.

3. Wesley as *a Writer.*—Amid his incessant labours otherwise, Wesley found time both for study and for writing. At that time there was great want of a healthy and interesting popular literature. He found the people to whom his ministry was useful in special need of good reading, both secular and religious; and forthwith he set himself to supply this want. From 1738, it is said, there was scarcely a year, for fifty years, in which he did not issue from the press some new work, large or small. He was the precursor of such men as Charles Knight and William and Robert Chambers, in bringing informa-

tion on almost every subject, in a cheap and attractive form, within the reach of the masses; and he anticipated the Tract Societies of later times by the large issue and circulation of publications in a tract form. He prepared numerous abridgments and translations, in poetry, history, philosophy, and biography, as well as grammars, dictionaries, and other useful works. His principal original works were his Sermons, Notes on the New Testament with a revised translation, and Extracts from his Journals. These last contained graphic descriptions of his labours, in all parts of the country, which were read everywhere with the deepest interest, and did much to increase his influence and spiritual power. He published the *Christian Library* in fifty volumes, consisting of extracts from the writings of the older divines. In 1773 he issued an edition of his works in twenty-three volumes. And not the least in importance, were his brother Charles's Hymns, which, with others of his own, had an extraordinary popularity, and came to be a very special means of grace to multitudes. It would be difficult to estimate the number of his separate publications. They have been variously reckoned at between 200 and 400, which his preachers circulated everywhere, the proceeds helping to carry on his other work, and to maintain his large charities.

4. Wesley as a *Philanthropist*.—His whole work was an outburst of genuine philanthropy. From early life the prisons were his special care, till even *they* were shut against him. He took up the cause of the poor wherever he went, devising the means of

employment for them on a large scale, and otherwise seeing to their support in times of scarcity. He established schools and libraries. He anticipated the work of modern Temperance Societies, practising temperance himself, and promoting it among his people. His denunciations, in his public sermons, of the making and selling of drink, were scathing and terrible in the extreme. He carried on what would now be called Medical Mission work among the sick poor. The last letter he wrote, was one to Mr. Wilberforce, encouraging him in his great work of Emancipation. His personal liberality was without limit. His rule was "to *save* all he could, and *give* all he could. His practice at Oxford is so well known, as hardly to need mention:—living on £28 a year, he gave £2 out of £30 of income; after his income increased to £60, £90, and £120, he still lived on £28, and gave the balance; and thereafter, in proportion. His reply to the "Accountant-General for Household Plate," who had demanded a return of his plate from him, cannot be omitted: "I have two silver teaspoons at London, and two at Bristol. This is all the plate which I have at present; and I shall not buy any more, while so many around me want bread."

Whitefield was equally large-hearted and self-forgetful, and the infection spread, down to the humblest of the people. In one case, where the giving was large, inquiry was made as to whether the people were rich; the answer was, "No; but all of us who are single persons have agreed together, to give *both ourselves and all we have* to God.

5. Wesley as a *Controversialist.*—It was not his

way to meddle much with controversy. But he had to deal with errors that crept in among the Moravian Brethren and among the people of his own societies, and he did so with a firm hand. His most serious dispute, however, was with his special friend and fellow-worker, Whitefield, leading to a painful separation, though ultimately, so far as personal friendship was concerned, the breach was healed. Wesley left the controversy, on his side (the Arminian), in the hands of his friend Fletcher of Madeley, while Toplady, Berridge, and others championed the Calvinistic cause.

Wesley's teaching may, in the general, be said to be *Arminian*, as opposed to *Calvinistic*, and yet he was, most emphatically, an *Evangelical* Arminian. While denying the doctrines of Election and of the Perseverance of the Saints, he differed from other Arminians (as Arminius himself did), in holding firmly the orthodox view of human depravity, the work of the Spirit in regeneration and sanctification, the nature of the atonement, and justification by faith. We shall have difficulty in finding anywhere, stronger statements as to the depravity of human nature, than we have in Wesley's Sermons. And while he gave prominence to the doctrine of Perfection, there are many passages in his sermons which ill agree with this view, and make it, as has been said, a very "imperfect perfection" indeed.[1] It is also true, as Principal Cunningham, one of the greatest Calvinistic authorities of recent times, says, that "much of what is often classed under the general name of *Arminianism* contains a much larger amount

[1] See Sermon *On Sin in Believers*.

of error, and a much smaller amount of truth, than the writings of Arminius and Wesley exhibit." At the same time, Wesley's representations of Calvinistic teaching cannot be accepted as a fair statement of the views of its recognised exponents, least of all, of evangelical men in the Scottish Church; while he held views on man's free will, which these have always regarded as inconsistent with the sovereignty of God in the salvation of men.

Referring to Dr. Cunningham's *Historical Theology* for a full discussion of the subject, I think it well to quote a single sentence from that work as to what Calvinism really is: "The salvation of sinners is to be ascribed to the sovereign mercy of God; man can do nothing effectual, in the exercise of his own natural powers, for escaping from his natural condition of guilt and depravity, and must be indebted for this wholly to the free grace of God, the vicarious work of Christ, and the efficacious agency of the Spirit. Now Calvinism is really nothing but just giving a distinct and definite expression and embodiment to these great principles, applying clear and precise ideas of them to each branch of the scheme of salvation."

There can be no doubt that Wesley's views on this subject, were a serious bar in the way of his success in Scotland, where he found a different state of things, indeed, from what he had to do with in England, but where he never got the welcome that greeted Whitefield, and never reaped such fruit. Wesley said of the Scotch: "They *hear* much, they *know* everything, and *feel* nothing!"

I must say a word about *Wesley's associates* in his great work, as helping largely to make it what it was. The names of several ministers of the English Church who, at that time, preached with great spiritual power the same evangelical doctrines, are familiar to all—the saintly Fletcher of Madeley, Romaine, Venn, Grimshaw, Berridge, and others. But by far the most outstanding of his fellow-helpers were Charles Wesley and George Whitefield. Charles Wesley was more cautious and conservative than his brother, and besides actively co-operating with him, was invaluable to him as his counsellor and friend. His greatest service, however, was as the writer of those Hymns which were one of the mainstays of the movement at the time, and have been handed down as a most precious legacy to the Church.

Whitefield, less intellectual and scholarly than the Wesleys, excelled them both as an orator; and after passing through a very similar spiritual struggle, emerged into the same clear light, and devoted himself with burning zeal to the service of Him who had saved him. We learn the spirit of the man from such utterances as these: "When the bishop laid his hands on my head, if my vile heart doth not deceive me, I offered my whole spirit and soul and body to the service of God's sanctuary. . . . I gave myself up to be a martyr for Him who hung upon the cross for me; I have thrown myself blindfold, and, I trust, without reserve, into His Almighty hands." He speaks of being "constrained to throw himself on the ground, and offer his soul as *a blank in God's hands*, to write on it what He pleased." Wesley, urging him to go to America, said, "Do you ask me what you shall have?—Food to eat, and raiment to put on; a house to lay your head in, such as your Lord had not; and a crown of glory that fadeth not away." Whereupon, he says, "my heart leaped within me, and responded to the call."

Some have spoken as if Whitefield's Calvinism had prevented his doing a similar work to Wesley's, leaving nothing permanent behind him. It should be remembered, however, that he and Wesley were entirely different men. As we have seen, he was the preacher and evangelist, not the organiser and administrator. Besides his great work in England and America, he made his mark in Scotland as Wesley never did. He helped to turn the tide in favour of evangelism in the Scottish Church, and to lay the foundations of what became a great spiritual movement, the benefits of which we still enjoy. And, along with the Countess of Huntingdon and others, he did much to leaven the Church of England with evangelical views and Christian life, so that though he did not found a new Church, he helped eminently to revive the old. He was emphatically one of the founders of Methodism, and besides the direct winning of souls, in which he was greatly honoured, he acted a leading part in the revival of religion both within the Established Church and outside of it. With men of this stamp heading the movement, it was not strange that it made such rapid progress.

It would be difficult at all adequately to estimate

the *results* of Wesley's life and labours, as the leader in this great movement. Many of these were of an indirect kind, and though of the very first magnitude, cannot be calculated. There was the arrest put on the progress of vice and unbelief. There was the revival of religion among the masses of the people, bringing back the belief in a living and divine Saviour (which, in many quarters, had died out), persuading men that sin and atonement, and faith and the life to come, were great realities; elevating the lower classes morally and spiritually, and through them influencing the upper, and producing like effects among these. There was the revival of the ministry, in life and doctrine, alike among Episcopalians and Nonconformists, so that they again became a power for spiritual good where before they had been a hindrance. There was the furnishing of a practical illustration of the three great means of reviving the Church and blessing the world—the *preaching of the doctrines of grace*, the opening of the door for *Christian fellowship*, and the calling into exercise of the *gifts of the people*. Even the extreme views, as some may regard them, of Wesley, on the subject of Assurance and the Witness of the Spirit, served a purpose, as a rebound from the opposite extreme. Extravagances and excrescences were almost inevitable in such a work; and yet it is not too much to say that England has felt the beneficial influence of it ever since.[1]

[1] Macaulay says: "Wesley conducted one of the most wonderful moral revolutions the world ever saw. His eloquence and his piercing logic would have made him an eminent literary man, and his genius for government was not inferior to that of Richelieu."

The history of Methodism since Wesley's death has been remarkable. America has been its greatest field. There, one of its offshoots, the Methodist Episcopal Church, is said to be the largest Protestant Church on that great continent, which, I suppose, means the largest Protestant Church in the world. It seems to be the most defensible form of Episcopacy, rejecting Apostolic Succession, and "founded on the principle of bishops and presbyters being of the same degree—a more extended office only being assigned to the former." Mr. Green states that the Churches belonging to the great Methodist family, number between *twenty-three and twenty-five millions of adherents*—"a fact unparalleled in modern ecclesiastical history." The Foreign Missions carried on by the same Churches, in all parts of the world, have a more numerous body of adherents and a larger annual income, than those of any other Church.

If anything would shame us into activity and self-denying devotedness, it should be the study of such a life and such labours as Wesley's. At every point, it puts one to the blush. What, to him, were the mere "odds and ends" of work, cast into the shade what most of us reckon our main occupation. Even before he had come to apprehend the grace of Christ in its fullest sense, we cannot but be impressed with his untiring assiduity, in furnishing himself with the needed equipment for his ministry, and in the actual discharge of it. He turned his many and varied gifts to the utmost possible account. He did what all Christian workers should do,—tried all the ways of it, exercised a holy versatility, left no stone unturned, by which he might get a hearing for his message and win men to God. No difficulty discouraged him : no danger daunted him.

We need men like Wesley still. Different as the times now are, there is ample room for such workers and such work. Amid the prevalence of unbelief, worldliness, neglect of divine ordinances, intemperance, and immorality, a Wesley would be a good gift of God to us to-day, shaping himself to the altered times and circumstances, not paying a flying visit, like Mr. Moody, but going over the same ground again and again, and helping the Churches to conserve the fruits of his labours.

But it would be a far greater gain if we were *all* to aim at being *Wesleys*, to the extent, at least, of having our lives as well filled up as his was, and devoting ourselves with as great singleness of aim and earnestness of purpose to the serving of God and the saving of men. It were well that our ministers and candidates for the ministry should make a study of the life and labours of this apostolic man. It would rebuke. It would suggest. It would stimulate. It would show what even one man, thoroughly consecrated, might, with God's blessing, accomplish. Some of the things which he did, may seem not desirable to be repeated in our time. Some things were such as could only be done by himself. But after making the largest deductions on that score, there still remains enough for men of like spirit, and with more ordinary gifts and abilities, to aspire to and to do. Can we think of such large numbers of our fellow-countrymen, in town and country, being left to perish? And if not, when and how is the work of reclamation to be overtaken? There is surely something to be learned by the Churches, from that master of organisation, and from the movement in which he was the leading actor. We have a sufficient agency, in the ministry and among the people, to do all that needs to be done, if each man were doing his utmost and best, adopting the best methods, and falling back, for the power, on the Spirit of God.[1]

It only remains to say, as regards Wesley himself, that he continued his labours undiminished to extreme old age. On his 86th birthday, he says he "found it difficult to preach oftener than twice a day!" He went all his ordinary rounds of duty to the last. His prayer had been, "Lord, let me not live to be useless!" and the prayer was answered to the full. On the 18th February 1791, he preached at Chelsea from the text, "The king's business requireth haste." On the following Wednesday he preached his last sermon on "Seek ye the Lord while He may be found." Some of his sayings, during his last illness, were—

"I the chief of sinners am,
But Jesus died for me!"

"There is no way into the holiest, but by the blood

[1] Wesley's being able to overtake such an amount of work throughout his long life—preaching, travelling, reading, overseeing, dealing with individuals, keeping up an immense correspondence—has been attributed to his "inflexible temperance and unexampled economy of time;" and Isaac Taylor says, "A perfect management of his time, his untiring energy, and his self-command, made it easy for him to accomplish tranquilly a vast and various daily work."

of Jesus;" "The best of all is, God is with us;" "He giveth His servants rest;" "I'll praise—I'll praise!" "He is all—He is all!" On the 2d March 1791, he fell asleep, in the 88th year of his age and 65th of his ministry. The verse which he gave out, almost uniformly, to be sung, at the close of his latest meetings, was a literal description of the end :—

> "O that, without a lingering groan,
> I may the welcome word receive,
> My body with my charge lay down,
> AND CEASE AT ONCE TO WORK AND LIVE!"

Note.—Southey, in his great biography, has immortalised Wesley, but he failed to appreciate his motives and the secret of his power. The "Observations" of Richard Watson should be read as an explanation and corrective of Southey, and in the edition which I have used (Bohn's *Standard Library*), the two are given together. While consulting the Journals and numerous biographies of Wesley, I have had frequent recourse to Mr. Green's admirable little volume (Cassell's) and M. Lelièvre's, as being easy of reference. These give a most graphic view of Wesley's life and labours.

J. H. W.

WILLIAM CAREY.

By GEORGE SMITH, C.I.E., LL.D.

WILLIAM CAREY'S TEXTS.

" Look unto Abraham your father . . .
For I called him alone, and blessed him, and increased him.
For the Lord shall comfort Zion : He will comfort all her waste places ;
And He will make her wilderness like Eden,
And her desert like the garden of the Lord ;
Joy and gladness shall be found therein, thanksgiving, and the voice of melody."
Isaiah li. 2, 3.

" Enlarge the place of thy tent,
And let them stretch forth the curtains of thine habitations:
Spare not, lengthen thy cords, and strengthen thy stakes :
For thou shalt break forth on the right hand and on the left ;
And thy seed shall inherit the Gentiles,
And make the desolate cities to be inhabited."
Isaiah liv. 2, 3.

COWPER IN 1782.

" But, above all, in her own light arrayed,
See Mercy's grand apocalypse displayed !
The sacred book no longer suffers wrong,
Bound in the fetters of an unknown tongue,
But speaks with plainness art could never mend,
What simplest minds can soonest comprehend.
God gives the word, the preachers throng around,
Live from his lips and spread the glorious sound :
That sound bespeaks Salvation on her way,
The triumph of a life-restoring day ;
'Tis heard where England's Eastern glory shines,
And in the gulfs of her Cornubian mines.
And still it spreads.
*   *   *   *

Paul's love of Christ, and steadiness unbribed,
Were copied close in him, and well transcribed ;
He followed Paul ; his zeal a kindred flame,
His apostolic charity the same ;
Like him crossed cheerfully tempestuous seas,
Forsaking country, kindred, friends and ease ;
Like him he laboured, and like him, content
To bear it, suffered shame where'er he went."—*Hope*.

WILLIAM CAREY.

By GEORGE SMITH, C.I.E., LL.D., Edinburgh.

TWO events make the year 1783 memorable as the close of the dreariest century of Christendom and the opening of the brightest political and spiritual period in all history. These events are the Peace of Versailles, following the Independence of the United States; and the baptism of William Carey, then twenty-two years of age. The Peace of 1783 left England exhausted financially and morally. But the righteous defeat of our country by Washington made Great Britain the mother of the Christian civilisation which has covered North America; and turned its own energies into a new Indian and Colonial Empire greater even than that of the United States. That all the ruling of old empires and colonising of new lands is not only English-speaking but aggressively Christian, is due to the fact thus recorded by Dr. Ryland: "October 5th, 1783, I baptized in the river Nen, a little beyond Dr. Doddridge's meeting-house, a poor journeyman shoemaker, little thinking that before nine years had elapsed he would prove the first instrument of forming a society for sending missionaries from England to preach the Gospel to the heathen." So, still, in the midst of our modern progress and godlessness, the

All-wise Sovereign of men chooses the weak things of the world, even as when His Son was born into a carpenter's home.

In 1783 the Evangelical Church had more nearly died out of Europe than in the tenth century, when men cried for the Day of Judgment to end the misery of the race, or in the fifteenth, when Luther came out of a miner's hut and a Scottish cloister. The few Moravian Brethren had fired John Wesley, and the New England Edwards had inspired George Whitefield; in Scotland the "Marrow" men had fought under Boston in the General Assembly, and the Erskines had seceded from it; so that some place the Evangelical Revival between 1730 and 1740. But by 1783 Methodism had "subsided" for a time, to use the language of Isaac Taylor, its ablest historian. The light that was in all the reformed lands at that time was slowly becoming darkness. And how great was that darkness, made ever denser by the Rationalism of Luther's land, the Arianism of the Church of England, and the Socinian "moderatism" of the Church of Scotland! The natural fruit was seen in the lives of a generation represented by George IV., who, as Prince of Wales, came of age and received a separate establishment in 1783. The Church, the Universities, society high and low, were all alike. The Archbishop of Canterbury, Secker, publicly bewailed that his Church had lost many of the people "by not preaching in a manner sufficiently evangelical." The Bishop of St. David's questioned the right of one people to send their religion to any other. Dissent was little better. Isaac Watts wrote: "There is a general decay of vital religion in the hearts and lives of men." When the great lawyer Blackstone removed from Oxford, he sought out every eminent preacher in London, and this is his startling statement made of 1780: "I did not hear a single discourse that had more Christianity in it than the writings of Cicero; I never could discover, from what I heard, whether the preacher was a follower of Confucius, or of Mahomet, or of Christ." In Europe the French Revolution was at hand, suppressing belief in God altogether for eleven years, and forming a fanatical mission against Christ, so frightful, that Tocqueville terms it a Western Mohammedanism. Cowper had pictured it the year before, in his *Table Talk*.

The fire of Foreign Missions burning in the heart of William Carey changed all that. That village shoemaker was used by the Spirit of God to become (1) himself the first Englishman who went out of Christendom as a missionary; and (2) the man who put missionary work, its duty and its dignity, in the van of all the spiritual and philanthropic movements which it at the same time did most to originate. For the peace of 1783 introduced on the one side geographical discovery, colony-founding, the French Revolution, English political and fiscal reform; on the other, the abolition of the slave-trade and slavery, the improvement of prisons and humanising of prisoners, the care for the poor on rational principles, the establishment of education on national lines, the spread of Sunday-schools, the translation of the Bible into every language. And the third (3) merit of the founder of modern missions is, that while, in his humility, he first sought to go to the cannibals of the Pacific, whom Captain Cook had just revealed to Europe, he so educated himself that God sent him to India, to the very front and forlorn hope of the fight against idolatry. This was at a time when the public life of England was being corrupted by Nabob influence, against which Burke protested and Pitt legislated, and India itself was being denied all the Truth of the West, scientific and spiritual, by the Brahmanised Englishmen who ruled it. Carey was the first English missionary in the modern sense of the word. Carey's mission revived Protestant Christendom, and pointed the way to modern philanthropy. Carey was the first and greatest apostle of India.

But he did and he became all this, in his modest saintliness—always a John, and yet never a Boanerges—directly as the outcome of ten years of united prayer. An evangelical writer of the Church of England has recently remarked, in the only missionary periodical[1] worthy of the subject in our language, that the missionary idea first took practical shape amongst the Baptists, a body then enjoying far less of social position than they do now, because they are "almost the furthest removed from any help that could be derived from national *prestige* or State countenance." Most true, but the greater spiritual freedom and evangelical faith of William Carey and a few Baptists of the Midland counties, were the

[1] *Church Missionary Intelligencer* for December 1883.

direct offspring of what they called hearty and persevering prayer. In 1784 the Northamptonshire Association (or quasi-presbytery) of Baptist ministers and messengers, meeting at Nottingham, sent forth to the people the first invitation to united prayer, which is as truly the foundation of modern missions as Carey was their founder. Sutcliff of Olney, who first led Carey to become a minister, himself suggested, and Ryland of Northampton, who had baptized Carey the year before, wrote the appeal, solemnly exhorting all to spend one hour in the first Monday of every month in prayer, wrestling with God for the effusion of His Holy Spirit. The now historic document contains this passage with its emphatic italics: "Let the whole interest of the Redeemer be affectionately remembered, and *the spread of the Gospel to the most distant parts of the habitable globe be the object of your most fervent requests.* We shall rejoice if *any other Christian societies* of our own or other denominations will join with us, and we do now invite them most cordially to join heart and hand in the attempt." These obscure men had the true note of Evangelicalism as given by the Lord, charity to all, catholicity, universality of aim, and petition, and labour. The difference between them all and Carey was that they prayed, while only Andrew Fuller went the length of writing; Carey prayed and wrote and gave himself.

Let us study the Man, and then estimate his work in England and in India.

At a point fifty-six miles north-west of London, over ground rising from the old Roman road to

Chester known as the Watling Street, straggles the village of Paulerspury, so called from the knightly family of the Paveleys. Here, in a two-storied cottage and garden, now supplanted by meaner structures, dwelt the Careys, from father to son, all through the Civil War at least, and doubtless further back, while the oaks of Whittlebury Forest still provided sport for Edward IV. The beeches which give Buckinghamshire its name, and which Hooker loved, are close to the south; on the east are the lazy streams and fat meadows of Olney and Bedford. In conditions, physical and social, precisely similar to those which surrounded John Bunyan in the not distant Elstowe, William Carey was born on the 17th August 1761. His grandfather and father were successively the village schoolmaster and clerk of the church, then a fine example of the early English style. In its decaying nave and aisles, and around its altar-tombs and knightly effigies, young Carey became proud of his connection with the Church of England, and learned also to be familiar with the Bible which he was to translate into all the languages of Southern Asia. His father, who was a weaver for a time, having married again, the boy was really educated by his grandmother, a woman of high Christian character, and by his uncle Peter, a gardener, who, childless himself, developed in the lad that love of Nature which made him the first agricultural improver and the second botanist in Bengal. Thus early, as in John Eliot's case, did God through him teach the Church, that he who would be a successful missionary should master and apply all the best knowledge of his time if he is in the full sense of the phrase to bring nations to the birth. The boy grew up gentle and loving, as he carried one of his three sisters about, noticing every plant and insect and bird, or playing with the villagers, with whom he was a favourite. The father gave him a little room to himself, which he filled with natural history preparations of his own, and with drawings and paintings, of which he was fond. His vices were those of the youth Bunyan, whose *Pilgrim* he read with eagerness, as he read every book that came in his way. He was fond of bell-ringing, he was sometimes guilty of lying, swearing and filthy talk, and it was an act of dishonesty in which his master detected him that led to his conversion at the age of fourteen. Being unfitted for out-door work, he had thus early been apprenticed to a shoemaker in the hamlet of Hackleton. There, when a journeyman and still under twenty, he married the sister of his employer, who had died, and he supported the widow also.

Thomas Scott, the commentator, used to visit his master, and was attracted by the intelligence of the journeyman. Carey owed the beginning of his conversion to Scott's preaching, but the talk of a dissenting fellow-journeyman, and especially a sermon by Chater of Olney on the blessedness of bearing reproach for Christ, led the youth to evangelical faith and obedience. The only pride which this humblest of great men ever felt was thus cast out of him. Law and other mystics deepened his spiritual longings, and the *Helps to Zion's Travellers*, written by the father of the eloquent Robert Hall, who was to be one of Carey's successors in Leicester, completed the change. The Spirit of God caused the first English Missionary to believe and rejoice in what the Reigning Christ had taught Saul, when He called the proud Jew to go forth to the Gentiles. No message has ever yet in all history transformed individuals and lifted whole races to the higher life short of the evangelical—that of His free grace God became Man in Christ Jesus to reconcile the world unto Himself. The Nestorian heresy in the east, the Arian in the west, every message which does not hold forth Christ, "the only wise God, our Saviour," falls short of the glad tidings of great joy which are for all people. Carey not only broke through all delusions as to the person and work of Christ which had smitten the Churches of England and Scotland with a blight, but through a more subtle heresy, the spurious orthodoxy which called itself Calvinism, and yet used the fact of God's sovereignty as a reason for declaring the inability of sinners to accept the Gospel and for declining to take the trouble to offer it to them. This false Predestinarianism did more to kill the Church at home and paralyse the few who would have covered the earth with it, than all the other heresies together. Carey, who had become a preacher at eighteen, while still a shoemaker ever struggling on the margin of destitution, when suddenly called to supply the place of an absent minister, preached the fulness and freeness of the Gospel with a force which knit to him the heart of Andrew Fuller, who was present. Fuller's

Gospel Worthy of All Acceptation soon after theologically dispelled the heresy in England as Boston and the Fathers of the Secession had begun to do in Scotland. Thus was the first Foreign Mission Secretary prepared, as well as the first English Missionary.

William Carey had been, above all things, a reader of such books of travel as he could find, and had especially revelled in the narratives of Cook's three voyages in the South Seas. As he sat in the little shed, still standing, at the back of his well-kept garden in Hackleton, plying his craft and teaching the children whom he gathered around him, he would pause and point to a rude map of the world which he had made of sheets of paper pasted together and attached to the wall. The spiritual light which by eighteen had fully shone into his darkness now lit up all the past knowledge of history and geography, of men and manners, of beliefs and religions, of statistics and nature, which he had been persistently arranging in his well-ordered mind and marvellous memory. There, on the dirty but well drawn map, the rough-handed shoemaker had entered all that he could learn regarding the population and religion of every land. Once his talk had been of stirring adventure, and strange people, and new customs. Now, night and day, he thought, and to his own family and friends he spoke, only of the fact —as old as Abraham, as pitiful as Christ painted it, as real in its bearing on man's responsibility—that darkness still covered the earth and gross darkness the people, that the nearly eighteen Christian centuries had brought only one-eighth of the whole human race within the influence of the Christ. Bunyan's picture of the man burdened with his own sins was nothing to the reality of this gentle soul's groaning under the sense of the duty neglected by the whole of Christendom. Even his natural modesty could not keep silence. As Thomas Scott passed from Olney to Northampton he would look in upon what he used to call Carey's "College," and admire the learning and the enthusiasm of the cobbler. There was in Olney about this time another man whom Carey must have often seen, as he meditatively walked, or pleasantly chatted by the way; but there is no evidence that he knew Cowper, so like-minded with himself, so sympathetic with all cultured dissenters, the poet of the Slave and the oppressed Hindoo, the eulogist of Whitefield, of Howard and the Moravians. The English Cowper and the Scottish James Montgomery were the poets of the dawn of the Missionary Reformation.

Carey turned for sympathy and aid rather to the Baptist ministers and deacons who had been praying for action every month since 1784, for "the spread of the Gospel to the most distant parts of the habitable globe." But if the Eleven knew so little of the nature of the kingdom after three years' close converse with the Master Himself as to ask Him petulantly, just before the Ascension, of the immediate restoration of the glory to Israel, we must not expect more of the Northamptonshire preachers. True, the Spirit had come, and had shown the Church "greater works" than those of its Incarnate Head, but one man like Carey may seem a far larger response to the prayer of those days than they deserved. The Son of Man had come to His Church in these Isles in "all power" and grace, and had He found faith on the earth? Only in humble Paulerspury, in a weaver's cottage; or in little Hackleton, on a cobbler's stall. It is pathetic to read how, when this Jeremiah of Modern Missions, his heart breaking with the love he had to his race, proposed as a subject of discussion in a ministers' meeting the question of their duty to the heathen, the chief of them, who had invited proposals, thundered out, "Sit down, young man; when God desires to convert the heathen, He'll do it without you or me." Not Sutcliff, not Ryland, not even Andrew Fuller had faith, according to their own confession, to believe in Carey's mission, adopting the sneer of the Old Testament doubter— "If the Lord would make windows in heaven, might this thing be?" The difference was that Carey had eyes to see the open windows, had felt the first droppings of the rain. Now at Hackleton, then at Piddington and Earls' Barton, again at Moulton, and finally at Leicester, his cry was, "Woe is me if I preach not the Gospel to the heathen!"

For eight years Carey was scouted, or—worse—politely put off by his brother ministers. His youth, obscurity, poverty, and exceeding humility, were all against him in their eyes. A layman came to the rescue, whose plain name deserves a place in the record of Mission worthies. The Baptist minister, schoolmaster, and shoemaker then of Moulton, had taught himself six languages besides his own, Latin, Greek, Hebrew, French, Dutch, and Italian. He had that linguistic gift which was soon to make famous the name of Mezzofanti, the librarian of Bologna. He had reduced to the proportions of a small volume the results of his geographical and statistical studies, first set forth on his map. In 1790, when in Birmingham, he met Thomas Potts, a retired haberdasher who had made a fortune in trade with the United States. There was in the room a lad who afterwards became known as Medley, the portrait painter, and to him we owe the report of the talk which followed.

Potts.—" Pray, friend Carey, what is it you have got into your head about missions? I understand you introduce the subject on all occasions."

Carey.—" Why, I think, Sir, it is highly important that something should be done for the heathen."

Potts.—" But how can it be done, and who will do it?"

Carey.—" Why, if you ask who, I have made up my mind, if a few friends can be found who will send me out, and support me for twelve months after my arrival, I will engage to go wherever providence shall open a door."

Potts.—" But where would you go? Have you thought of that, friend Carey?"

Carey.—" Yes, I certainly have. Were I to follow my inclination, and had the means at command, the islands of the South Seas would be the scene of my labours, and I would commence at Otaheite. If any society will send me out, and land me there, and allow me the means of subsistence for one year, I am ready and willing to go."

Potts.—" Why, friend Carey, the thought is new, and the religious public are not prepared for such undertakings."

Carey.—" No, I am aware of that; but I have written a piece on the state of the heathen world, which, if it were published, might probably awaken an interest on this subject."

Potts.—" Why don't you publish it?"

Carey.—" For the best of all reasons, I have not the means."

Potts.—" We will have it published, by all means. I had rather bear the expense of printing it myself, than the public should be deprived of the opportunity of considering so important a subject."

The conversation is now historical. The ten pounds of Deacon Potts was the first contribution to Modern Missions, and, you will note, it was given to use the Press in the great enterprise. I know not in all prose literature, outside of that which is the work of the imagination like Bunyan's allegory, any book so remarkable as this production, written by a young Northamptonshire shoemaker, on such a subject and at a period when colonisation, trade, and science were hardly born, in the modern sense. But one copy exists, in the possession of Dr. Underhill, late Secretary of the Baptist Mission. It was published at Leicester in 1792, and re-published there in 1822, under the title of *An Enquiry into the Obligations of Christians to the Means for the Conversion of the Heathens, in which the Religious State of the Different Nations of the World, the Success of Former Undertakings, and the Practicability of Further Under-*

takings, are considered, by WILLIAM CAREY. So wide is the grasp of spiritual principles, so graphic the sketch of missionary development and obstruction, from the giving of the Lord's commission down to the effort of "the late Mr. Wesley" in the West Indies, and so masterly the survey of the state of the world in the decade 1783-1792, that if the statistics were brought up to date and the *Enquiry* re-published, it would be pronounced worthy of the first literary ability in the present day. Still better would it be to publish a Survey of the World in 1783 and in 1883 side by side, that men might know what they owe on every side of progress, secular as well as spiritual, to William Carey.

His praying, his talking, and his preaching, being thus completed by his publishing, the faith of the weaker brethren was braced to action at last. In the same year, 1792, on the 30th May, Carey preached in Nottingham, on the spot whence nine years before the invitation to prayer had sounded out, a sermon of which Dr. Ryland said: "If all the people had lifted up their voice and wept, as the children of Israel did at Bochim, I should not have wondered at the effect; it would only have seemed proportionate to the cause, so clearly did he prove the criminality of our supineness in the cause of God." The preacher went for the text, in which to lay deep and broad the foundation of Missions, to the evangelical prophet, to the last twenty-six chapters of Isaiah, in which the missionary triumph springs from the travail of the Man of Sorrows, who shall see a seed and shall be satisfied; centres round the marred visage and the wounded form of Him who shall sprinkle many nations. From the picture in Isaiah liv. 2, 3, of the little tent of a nomadic tribe breaking out into the boundless canopy of the City of God, Carey handed down to the Church ever since the two pregnant maxims which are all that remain of that sermon: "1. Expect great things from God. 2. Attempt great things for God."

Retiring to the house (still standing) of a godly widow, as if to secure, unconsciously, that woman should take *her* place in the enterprise now as at its beginning in Galilee and Calvary, the Mount of Ascension and the Pentecostal upper room, twelve ministers contributed £13, 2s. 6d., and signed the resolutions which thus began: "(1) Desirous of making an effort for the propagation of the Gospel among the heathen, agreeably to what is recommended in brother Carey's late publication on that subject, we do solemnly agree to act in society together for that purpose. (2.) As in the present divided state of Christendom it seems that each denomination, by exerting itself separately, is most likely to accomplish the great ends of a Mission, it is agreed that this society be called 'The Particular (Calvinistic) Baptist Society for Propagating the Gospel among the Heathen.'" Membership was secured by a subscription of ten pounds at once, or ten shillings and sixpence annually. The committee consisted of the Rev. John Ryland, Reynold Hogg (Treasurer), William Carey, John Sutcliff, and Andrew Fuller (Secretary). A layman almost immediately succeeded Mr. Hogg as treasurer. Thus did the true Calvinism of Calvin vindicate itself, as the first theological school to preach the evangel of grace to all sinners. Thus did these despised Baptists teach the lesson of toleration and catholicity. With the modesty of gentlemen of Christ's school, they went on to declare that, failing a mission of their own, they would help the Moravian, Presbyterian, or other missions then existing. Alas! all that Presbyterians did then was to send to Brainerd's successor among the American Indians a dole from the Scottish Propagation Society, and to seat in its Moderator's chair the minister who had denounced missions to the heathen as "highly preposterous."

To these men, dimly feeling their way amid the darkness of the Church which had nearly lost its hold of the Master's hand, and had altogether forgotten His last words, the world and its heathenism looked like a blank unexplored mine, at the mouth of the pit of which they stood. As Carey alone offered to go down if they would hold the rope, they seemed to themselves to take an oath to him that they would never let the rope go. So Andrew Fuller afterwards described the scene, when, in his study at Kettering on the 10th January 1793, Carey agreed to go to India. On the 26th March thereafter, a "holy convocation" was held in the chapel at Leicester, where the Secretary gave the solemn charge which sent the father of modern missions forth to the millions of Hindostan. Thus Carey had led England to become a missionary land once more, had placed us in the van of the civilising races of history. How was India prepared to receive him?

England had not long before sent a Clive to found the Empire of British India, and a Warren Hastings to consolidate it, both from old squire families of the neighbouring counties. But from the very heart of the people God early called Carey to Christianise it, and from a village in the Grampians He, in due time, sent Alexander Duff to receive from the aged missionary's own mouth the apostolic missionary succession. But for the work represented by Carey and Duff, even men of the world will admit that the empire of Clive and Hastings would have had no more of the salt of life and growth in it than the world-empires which Daniel had seen in vision. Two men were unconsciously used to prepare India for William Carey. Charles Grant, a poor boy of Inverness, had found his way out to Bengal in the Civil Service, soon after Hastings. He had seen thirteen millions of human beings swept away by the most terrific famine of modern times—that of 1770. He had learned, amid the responsibilities and the solitude of an Indian career, the power of Christ. From that hour he did not cease for half a century, in India, in Parliament, in the Court of Directors of the East India Company, and in the Press, to plead that the Christian missionary and schoolmaster should be sent to the Hindoos. He it was who stirred up Wilberforce and even Pitt, Simeon and Sir James Stephen, and the galaxy of evangelical philanthropists who triumphed at last in the charter and the reforms of 1833. And when he passed away he left behind him two sons to continue his work, Lord Glenelg, who administered the Colonies, and died in 1866, and Sir Robert Grant, the Governor of Bombay whose hymns we delight to sing in our churches and families. At the time when the twelve country ministers were founding the Baptist Missionary Society at Kettering, Charles Grant was writing those *Observations on the State of Society among the Asiatic Subjects of Great Britain, particularly with respect to Morals, and on the means of improving it,* which contain the germs of all Indian progress since the House of Commons published the work in 1813. Charles Grant had formed at Malda a scheme for bringing out, chiefly at his own cost, eight missionaries, who were to qualify themselves for overthrowing Brahmanism by study at Benares, but even Simeon failed to find one Church of England clergyman willing to go. He had there become the centre of a small Christian circle of godly civilians and indigo-planters' families, through whom, all unwittingly, he was providing a home for Carey. Thirty years after this he wrote: "I had formed the design of a mission to Bengal; Providence reserved that honour for the Baptists."

The second man who drew Carey to India was the surgeon of an East Indiaman and his first colleague. John Thomas, erratic enthusiast and first medical missionary, found his way to the Christian community at Malda, whom he alternately edified by his zeal and outraged by his fanatical eccentricity. He was to Dissent and to Carey what John Newton, once slave-trader, became to the Church of England and to Cowper. The circumstance of his having returned home from one of his long voyages at the very time when his fellow-Baptists were considering to what land they should send their first agent, led to the selection not only of India, but of Bengal, as the scene of the Mission. Carey had thought of Tahiti, and then of Western Africa; the same wise and loving Providence who had given India to us in trust, sent there the man He had already trained as if to teach England how He would have that trust discharged. Christ sent forth His disciples two and two, so Thomas was united with Carey, the medical man with the preacher, the scholar, the teacher, the giver of the Word of God, as Luke with Paul. "We have not gone about this business in a hurry," wrote Fuller, when asking Thomas if he were willing to unite with the Society. "We have been praying for it by monthly prayer-meetings for these eight or nine years, and now we wish to do something more than pray. We have solemnly bound ourselves to God and one another at least to make an effort, by individual subscriptions and congregational collections." "You see," he wrote to Ryland, "things of great consequence are in train." Yes, as one passes from the tombs of Carey and his associates amid the dust of three generations of their native Christians in Serampore to the grave of Andrew Fuller behind his church at Kettering, and surveys the results of that year's work, even man can see the grandeur of the consequences which every year is unrolling before our eyes, and only eternity will fully reveal.

When, after having been ejected from an East Indiaman of that Company which has since perished as the victim of its blinded policy, and having been carried in a vessel of Denmark which had sent out the first Protestant Mission to South India, and was to give them an asylum till their death, Carey and his companion landed quietly at Calcutta, what did they find? We reserve for the central event of history, the grand Greek phrase which, in all the inspired as well as philosophic wealth of its meaning, the missionary apostle applies to the state of the Church and the world, when Christ came born of a woman—"the Fulness of the Time" (Gal. iv. 4). But the same apostle writes of "the dispensation of the fulness of the times" (Eph. i. 10). If ever that came in our national history, since we ourselves received the gospel, it came then, when all these events we have described conspired to send Carey forth, and to receive him, that he might begin in the heart of Hindooism, which is itself the very kernel of idolatry, the work of gathering together in Christ all things which the sin of ages had separated, and is still striving to keep apart from the One Fulness.

When, after touching at Balasore, Carey arrived at Calcutta on the 11th November 1793, India was in the same extreme of social and political hopelessness, apparently, as the Europe which he had left. The English had legally obtained the sovereignty twenty-eight years before, but they had continued to administer the country through corrupt native officials. Nor were the Company's own servants free from rapacity. Famine had desolated vast tracts. Lord Cornwallis, the Governor-General after Warren Hastings, had described agriculture and internal trade as in a state of rapid decay. His first step had been to create real property in land by making "Zameendars" proprietors or rent-collectors at a fixed rate for ten years. This decennial settlement had just been made perpetual before Carey landed. The peasant-proprietors had thus been handed over to the exactions of the large rent-receivers, in opposition to the opinion of the new Governor-General, Sir John Shore, who, when Lord Teignmouth, became the first President of the Bible Society. A permanent settlement of the land-tax with the people, on a system of corn rents, might have made the now seventy millions of Bengalees the most hopeful race of all Asia. But this settlement doomed them to something like praedial serfdom, which the Government to-day is trying to correct, unrelieved by education and intensified by the power of the money-lender using our own civil courts. The seventy millions now are paying thirteen millions sterling of rent to 20,000 big landlords, who contribute only one-fourth of this vast sum to the public treasury. Nor had the judicial reforms introduced at the same time begun to tell. Only one Christian missionary had been seen north of Madras, the Swede Kiernander, whom Clive had brought to Calcutta to do chaplain's work. Not a Brahman had been baptized; not one of Kiernander's casteless converts had propagated the faith; not five converts from caste could be found in all Hindostan proper. The millions possessed not a page of the Bible or of a Christian book in their mother tongue. Their rich and nervous and sweet vernaculars had no literary form or works. From Calcutta across the breadth of Eastern, Central, and Northern India, which had been then thirty years under our sovereign rule, at least a hundred millions of our new subjects walked in what was far more a land of the shadow of death than the evangelical prophet's Galilee of the nations (Isaiah ix.). But now, for the first time—inscrutable mystery—in all their far-reaching history with its Aryan literature, it could be said, "upon them hath the light shined." From this time began the messengers of Jesus to preach and to say—"Repent ye, for the kingdom of heaven is at hand." And ever since, multitudes have rejoiced in the light. In a sense peculiar to Bengalee and Burman, Hindostanee and Sikh, Panjabee and Afghan, Maratha and Goojaratee, Muhammadan and Parsee, there has been fulfilled the prophecy, written when as yet their Aryan ancestors were flocking south from the uplands of Iran, and were chanting the nature hymns of the Vedas :—

> "Thou hast multiplied the nation, Thou hast increased its joy;
> Thou hast broken the yoke of his burden and the staff of his shoulder.
> The rod of his oppressor.
> For unto us a Child is born, unto us a Son is given,
> Of the increase of His government and peace there shall be no end."

The sun-rising was amid clouds, nevertheless, as it was to Syria in Abraham's days; and to Abraham's experience Carey in his early years of solitude ever turned. The Society, frowned on at first by the leading Baptist ministers of London, and encouraged only by John Newton, had raised a few hundred pounds required for the passage of two missionaries and their families, and also for their support for one year. The latter sum was so invested, according to the necessity of those pre-banking days, that it was lost. Carey and his family had only starvation before them, and he was indebted to a native for a roof to shelter them. Toilsomely walking in the sun, in the streets of Calcutta, as no European above beggary ever dares to do, again at Nuddea and then at Bandel, he found no help but in God. The worthy chaplain, David Brown, who was afterwards his friend till death, received him as a stranger, and did not offer the dust-laden pedestrian a glass of water. He applied too late for an appointment requiring botanical knowledge. He resolved to turn to the jungle, there build a hut or two, and till the ground as no white man can do in the tropics with impunity. Meanwhile, assisted by an old convert of Thomas, he preached daily in the streets and markets of the capital, he disputed quietly with Muhammadans, he worked at the language, he enjoyed much communion with God. His wife had reluctantly accompanied him, and she became a prey to the mania which ultimately carried her off. They had four children. His wife's sister was with them. All these things were against him. His first gleam of earthly hope was when he sailed eastward to farm a plot of tiger-haunted ground, and a neighbouring official made the whole party his guests with Anglo-Indian hospitality. After months of hardship and exposure which might have strangled any lesser enterprise in the birth, Carey was invited to Malda, to become an assistant indigo planter under Charles Grant's friend, Mr. Udny. There for the next six years he prepared himself for the Gospel triumphs which, from the opening days of this century, have been identified with Serampore.

The twelve village preachers whom the people's prayer and Carey's faith had roused to attempt the conversion to Christ of seven-eighths of the whole human race with £13, 2s. 6d. in their treasury thus began the organisation of modern missions. Outside of the Gospels and the Acts of the Apostles they had only one precedent, the Moravian. From the first Carey had adopted the plan that he, and all missionaries, should be self-supporting after the first year's experience in a heathen land, and should form a brotherhood with a common purse. Hence the whole sum allowed to Carey and Thomas, their wives and children, was £200. Carey was to work with his hands, as the Lord Himself did at Nazareth, as Paul did all his life. Thomas had his profession, and he knew the language of the people well. By an oversight the books for Bible translation, tools and seeds ordered by Carey on his arrival, were not sent for two years. He had no sooner escaped from the six months' destitution and exposure into the position of a manufacturer of indigo on Rs. 200 a month—then equivalent to £300 a year —than he wrote to the Society that he would not require even the meagre support they had promised him, but would like to see it devoted to a mission to Africa, which was at once done. The heroism was Abraham's, as was the trial of faith. From his personal income he established his mission, first among the ninety native subordinates on the factory, then in two hundred villages in which he regularly itinerated, then all over the two counties of Dinajpore and Malda, which now have a population equal to that of Scotland at that period, and soon in the neighbouring state of Bhootan on the Himalayan slopes, from which he hoped to push into Tibet, one of the few lands still shut against the Gospel. He preached in Bengalee once every day and more frequently on Sunday; he founded a church which required ministrations in English, and he won the gratitude of the leading civilians of the Company. He established schools for the people and projected a college where Sanskrit and Persian should be taught, and the students should be boarded after the simple fashion of the Brahmanical *Tols*. He studied and wrote with scientific accuracy on the varied natural history of the district, its men, its beasts, its plants, its agriculture, its communications. Above all he so learned the language that in three years he translated the New Testament, and in six years nearly the whole Bible into Bengalee, of which he wrote the rudiments of a grammar and dictionary.

If it be asked how all this was honestly possible for one who was a grower and manufacturer of indigo, the answer is, that William Carey worked and prayed fifteen hours a day. His economy of time was not less remarkable than his power of memory and his linguistic gift. All the time he was what the East India Company officially termed an "interloper," on sufferance. Under a regulation as barbarous as that of the Chinese rulers of Tibet, and as rigorously applied to keep out Christian missionaries, Carey had a five years' passport as an indigo planter, without which he too would have been deported. Even up till the charter of 1833, our own missionaries, John Wilson and Alexander Duff, had to procure such a document, not only for themselves, but for the young ladies they were about to marry.

Carey's first letters and journals, especially those from Dinajpore, set the little evangelical world of England and Scotland on fire. They are modest, and seem even cold enough to us who read them now in the *Periodical Accounts*, for he had not one purely native convert to tell of. But to the spiritual discernment of that time they were redolent of lively faith and most reasonable hope. They fell upon hearts in every Church prepared by the Spirit, and longing for the life which service begets from faith. They led directly and immediately to the creation of the great London, the Scottish, the Glasgow, and the Church Missionary Societies, and after a time to the formation of the Bible Society. Nowhere did they produce a more profound impression than in Scotland. Presbyterian ministers in England, like David Bogue, had been the founders, and like Love, the first secretary of the catholic London Missionary Society. But in Scotland, which soon established two missionary societies of its own, the letters of Carey called forth the most splendid home act of self-denial which the history of the Church records, and second only to the self-surrender of Carey and his associates.

Robert Haldane sold Airthrey, the beautiful estate in the shadow of the Ochils, which he had been adorning for ten years. Going to his friends Pitt and Dundas, this Scottish gentleman declared his determination to take out with him, at his own cost, three ministers of the Church of Scotland, one printer, and several catechists, in order to set up a mission in the very centre of Hindooism, at Benares. Bogue, then forty-seven, and Innes and Greville Ewing, famous young preachers of Edinburgh under thirty, were to be the missionaries, and John Ritchie, the printer, was to superintend the press, "aided by catechists, city missionaries, and schoolmasters." The energetic John Campbell was to be the first catechist. To this mission, on a gigantic scale for these days, after all the expenses of establishing it at Benares, Robert Haldane devoted £35,500 in case of his death. The East India Company reprobated the enterprise, as they had three years before got Dundas to strike out of the charter of 1793 Wilberforce's "pious clauses," under which such a mission would have been legalised. For another twenty years, at least, the taunt of Burke was to remain true of our empire in India: "With us no pride erects stately monuments which repair the mischiefs which pride has produced, and which adorn a country out of its own spoils. England has erected no churches, no hospitals, no palaces, no schools. Every other conqueror of every other description has left some monument, either of state or beneficence behind him!" Yes, for up to that time it was a German, sent out by the Danes, who had built the only church and schools for the natives, and one of these in a Hindoo Rajah's palace. Schwartz was already dying when his apostolic successor, Carey, wrote to him a pathetic letter which it fell to Guericke to answer.

The epistles of the more outspoken Thomas, and of Fountain, who had been sent out as their first colleague, had an effect of a different kind on the anti-evangelical world of England. In an unhappy hour, for which Francis Jeffrey afterwards expressed his deep regret to Dr. Marshman, the *Edinburgh Review* published a sarcastic attack on the Baptist Mission, by the Rev. Sydney Smith. This the author fortunately republished in his collected works, so that all succeeding generations are enabled to convict him of malicious blindness, as they see in the ever-growing development of the missions founded by Carey the salt of modern progress. The attack seemed so outrageous even then, however, to the conductors of the *Quarterly Review*, that its first number for 1809 contained an article on Sanskrit Grammars, in which an eulogy is passed on Dr. Carey's philological labours on grounds of pure scholarship; and another, in which the poet Southey tells the story of the Baptist Mission, and advocates the duty and the policy of missions to India in the language of a statesman, and with the faith of a Christian. What said the *Quarterly*, then just established, and ever since identified with the principles of the Erastian Church of which Sydney Smith was a canon, and of a Conservative State? "There is ability and there is learning in the Church of England, but its age of fermentation has long been over, and that zeal which for this work is the most needful is, we fear, possessed only by the Methodists." Happily that is no longer true, but it is still necessary to remind that non-evangelical half of the Church of England, which has so often told the Christians of India and the heathens of Africa and Madagascar that true Christianity cannot reach them save through a fictitious "grace of orders," of what their own Southey said, with his layman's love of fair play and truth: "We are neither blind to what is erroneous in their doctrine or ludicrous in their phraseology; but the anti-missionaries . . . keep out of sight their love of men and their zeal for God, their self-devotement, their indefatigable industry, and their unequalled learning. . . . In fourteen years these low-born, low-bred mechanics have done more towards spreading the knowledge of the Scriptures among the heathen than has been accomplished or even attempted by all the princes and potentates of the world—and all the Universities and Establishments into the bargain. . . . Do not think to supersede the Baptist Missionaries till you can provide from your own Church such men as these; and, it may be added, such women as their wives." Bishops Selwyn and Patteson among the dead, and Caldwell among the living, have done something to redeem this reproach, but it is by walking in the footsteps of Carey.

Thus far we have surveyed the Evangelical Preparation, rather than the missionary triumphs of William Carey, for two reasons. It is important that you should watch how Protestant Christendom came to see its Missionary Reformation some three centuries after it had begun to pass through the doctrinal and biblical Reformation of Luther. And, after having for sixteen years lived, day by day, in Carey's study, in his home, in his garden, beside his college, and amid his converts' children, where all the localities were very much as he left them on his death, I cannot here without emotion dwell on details which should find a more appropriate place of record. But his life and work of the third of a century at Serampore may thus be generalised :—

When, in 1799, four colleagues and their families, of whom Marshman and Ward deserve an eulogy second only to himself, were sent out in an American ship, they found toleration for the religion of England only under the Danish flag at Serampore, then governed by Colonel Bie, a friend of Schwartz. They were there joined by Carey, with his mastery of the language, his knowledge of the people and climate, his translation of the New Testament, his grammars, his unique missionary experience. Serampore, which has still 25,000 inhabitants, was then a river-port with large trade which the English officials were glad to use for remitting home their savings. Here, opposite the summer-palace which the new Governor-General, the Duke of Wellington's great brother, was beginning to build on the north side of the Hoogli at Barrackpore, the missionaries bought a house, enlarged and added to it a chapel, with a noble park which soon became a Botanic Garden. They deliberately formed a Brotherhood which stands out in the annals of modern Missions as those of Iona and Lindisfarne, Banchor and Lerina, Monte Casino and Corbie in the similarly dark days of Europe. As the three grew old, they added to their number Dr. Marshman's accomplished son, and two ripe young scholars and missionaries from the Universities of Edinburgh and Glasgow, Mack and Leechman. Save occasional grants for buildings and Bible translation, they received no support from the Baptist Society, of which they continued the loyal agents and loving friends all through the secretaryship of Andrew Fuller, who died in 1815. They vested the whole of the property which they accumulated in the Society, but wisely reserved its control to themselves as trustees.

They lived at first under one roof, ate at one table, always had one purse, and reckoned nothing to be their own or their children's save, in time, the small annuity provided for widows and aged parents dependent upon them alone. For once, at least, since the days of Barnabas and Stephen they realised, in loving harmony yet full personal independence, the apostolic ideal. From the first streak of dawn in the eastern sky, which is marked by gunfire in every cantonment, to near midnight, these three men, two of their wives, and their associates, worked for India in a way which more than doubled the efficiency and results of each worker.

Private prayer and meditation on the Scriptures, preaching and teaching in the Bengalee and English, and intercourse with native converts and inquirers, were common to all. Carey was pre-eminently the scholar, who translated and superintended the translation of the Bible into forty Indian languages and dialects; and he was the Professor of three languages in the College of Fort William, where he trained the young English civilians, and so influenced many that they established or aided missions in their own stations afterwards. Dr. Marshman was also the scholar, for he was the first translator of the Bible into Chinese, and the first who printed it with metal types; but he was the organiser, the man of business, the writer, and he kept a large school for Eurasian boys. Ward, printer and editor, was master of the mighty press, with its typefoundry and paper factory, sending forth "more than 212,000 volumes of the Divine Word in forty different languages" before Carey passed away, besides countless English and Bengalee books, tracts, magazines, and newspapers. Mack and Leechman were untiring professors in the college. John Marshman, C.S.I., who has lately passed away, so that we may speak of his good deeds with the more freedom that they have not yet found a chronicler, was the teaching and literary member of the staff. His school-books in English and Bengalee, his lawbooks, his Biography of the Three Giants, his splendid gifts to the natives of India, and above all his conversion of the once quarterly and monthly into the weekly *Friend of India*, which ceased only in 1875, mark him out as the most worthy member of the Brotherhood next to the Three. The accounts I myself have handled prove that these men contributed to the cause of God from their own earnings ninety thousand pounds, and the Three left their children penniless.

The secret of a self-sacrifice unparalleled in the whole history of the Church, and offered to the Lord with an unconsciousness of anything like heroism, which gives it immortal bloom, was found in Carey's childlike soul. It was perpetuated in a spiritual covenant which the three missionary heroes and their families entered into, and to which they adhered till death. On Monday, 7th October 1805, they drew up and signed a "Form of Agreement respecting the Great Principles upon which the Brethren of the Mission at Serampore think it their duty to act in the work of Instructing the Heathen." This agreement was read publicly, at every station, at the three annual meetings on the first Lord's day in January, in May, and in October. The remarkable document, which covers twelve printed octavo pages, expounds in lofty and catholic language these points upon which "we think it right to fix our serious and abiding attention." (1.) It is absolutely necessary that we set an infinite value upon immortal souls. (2.) That we gain all information of the snares and delusions in which these heathens are held. (3.) That we abstain from those things which would increase their prejudices against the Gospel. (4.) That we watch all opportunities of doing good. (5.) That we keep to the example of Paul, and make the great subject of our preaching Christ the Crucified. (6.) That the natives should have an entire confidence in us, and feel quite at home in our company. (7.) That we build up and watch over the souls that may be gathered. (8.) That we form our native brethren to usefulness, fostering every kind of genius and cherishing every gift and grace in them, especially advising the native churches to choose their pastors and deacons from amongst their own countrymen. (9.) That we labour with all our might in forwarding translations of the sacred Scriptures in the languages of India, and that we establish native free schools, and recommend their establishment to other Europeans. (10.) That we be constant in prayer and the cultivation of personal religion, to fit us for the discharge of these laborious and unutterably important labours. "Let us often look at Brainerd, in the woods of America, pouring out his very soul before God for the perishing heathen without whose salvation nothing could make him happy." (11.) "Let us give ourselves up unreservedly to this glorious cause. Let us never think that our time, our gifts, our strength, our families, or even the clothes we wear, are our own. Let us sanctify them all to God and His cause. Oh that He may sanctify us for His work! ... No private family ever enjoyed a greater portion of happiness than we have done since we resolved to have all things in common. If we are enabled to persevere, we may hope that multitudes of converted souls would have reason to bless God to all eternity for sending His Gospel into this country." That Agreement embodies the divine principles of all evangelical missions since. It is a manual to be daily pondered by all missionary men and women, and every Church and society which sends them forth. Its heroism of humble faith reveals the secret of the success with which the Spirit of God then visited, and has ever since followed the Brotherhood of Serampore.

Carey lived till 1834. The evangelical missionary became the friend of the Irish Lord Wellesley, the "glorious little man," who said that he valued his good opinion more than any honour he had received; of the Scottish Marquis of Hastings, who, after a visit to Serampore in 1815, recorded his admiration of the enterprise of the missionaries, and especially of their Bible translations; of the English Lord William Bentinck, who, in 1829, for ever abolished that burning of widows which the missionary had first denounced thirty years before. Carey lived to see nearly all the heathen crimes he had attacked put down in British India; all the intolerance from which he had suffered, stopped; all the social and philanthropic reforms he had advocated, adopted, all the eternal principles for which he had given his life, triumphant both in India and England, in spite of the East India Company at its worst. Strong in faith, irresistible in the might of his humility, he transformed public opinion by informing it, and used the Christian consciousness in England and in India to make Missions abroad and at home what they are at this day. It was the story of his life, as told in Simeon's rooms at Cambridge, that drew Henry

Martyn to work and pray by his side in the deserted pagoda of Aldeen. It was the influence of his faith that sent Judson to Burma. It was the knowledge of his deeds that fixed on him the reverent gaze of the young John Wilson of Bombay, who pronounced him the most honoured and most successful missionary since the time of the Apostles. It was the blessing of the old man, entering his seventieth year, that nerved the young Alexander Duff to take up the falling mantle of the saint who had been the means of bringing the first Brahman to Christ, and of creating the first College (in 1819) for the training of Brahmans and outcasts alike to be ministers of Christ to their countrymen. The pilgrims of Protestantism, from Europe and America, go to Serampore to see the tombs, the chapel, the Christian settlement, the college, the library of Carey and his associates, the Bibles, grammars, and dictionaries they produced in forty languages. Their work has long since left that centre to cover Southern Asia. Their Bibles are found in every tongue, from Calcutta to Kandahar, from Bombay to Peking. Their first convert of 1800, a carpenter of caste, and their first Brahman disciple of 1803, have grown into a native Protestant community of 600,000 souls at this day, increasing at the rate of eighty per cent. every decade, and of Christians of every kind, in India, there are now two millions. This is only the beginning of the "great things" which Carey expected, and therefore attempted for God, when "hearty and persevering" prayer for them began a hundred years ago.

Since Carey went to Bengal, and even in the one lifetime of seventy years since the India charter of 1813, the earth has become to its Christian inhabitants like a new world. The one British Empire has grown till it contains nearly one-fourth of the whole human race, or 315 millions who increase by 25 millions every decade. It has an annual revenue of 185 millions sterling, and an external trade worth 1000 millions a year! It has given a language and a literature to so many more millions, and these the multiplying races, that English is the written or spoken tongue of nearly half humankind. Great Britain spans the Old World and the New, reaching from furthest Burma and China on one side of the Pacific round the globe to most distant Columbia on the other. She mediates between East and West. She stretches from a hoary past more remote than any that history records outside of Judaism, to a future which only Christian faith dares to estimate. That it is to Great Britain such a leadership of the race has been given, is due—every Bible-student must believe—to Christianity. That our country was guided, by no will of its own, to be aggressively Christian, a century ago, is owing to one above all other men, to William Carey.

That the work of evangelical or missionary Christianity has only begun, in spite of all this— so long as the Gospel claims but one-fourth of the race, and is actively sent forth, or earnestly prayed for, by only one-fourth of the members of the Catholic Church—is the confession of our own faithlessness with which it becomes us to close this study of the greatest and meekest missionary of Christ since Paul.

Carey, childlike in his humility, is the most striking illustration in all Hagiology, Protestant or Romanist, of the Lord's declaration to the Twelve, when He had set a little child in the midst of them, " Whosoever shall humble himself as this little child, the same is greatest in the kingdom of heaven " (Matt. xviii. 4). Yet we, ninety years after he went forth with the Gospel to Hindostan, may venture to place him where the Church History of the future is even more likely to keep him—amid the seven uncrowned kings of men, who have made Christian England what it is under God to its own people and to half the human race. These are Chaucer, the Father of English Verse; Wiclif, the Father of the Evangelical Reformation in all lands; Hooker, the Father of English Prose; Shakespeare, the Father of English Literature; Milton, the Father of the English Epic; Bunyan, the Father of English Allegory; Carey, the Father of English Missions.

ALEXANDRE RODOLPHE VINET.

By the REV. R. J. SANDEMAN, Edinburgh.

ALEXANDRE RODOLPHE VINET was born on the 17th of June 1797, at Ouchy, on the lake of Geneva, near Lausanne, the chief town of the Canton de Vaud. The inn there where Lord Byron wrote "The Prisoner of Chillon," " thus adding one more deathless association to the already immortalised beauties of the lake," is in summer a great resort of English tourists. Of these pilgrims not one in a hundred knows that in the square tower which dominates the village the greatest light of modern French Protestantism was born. To most of them the name of Vinet is unknown. His family, which came originally from Switzerland, had been settled in France for several generations. In a moment of irritation with a freak of Swiss democracy, he spoke of himself as belonging to France already by language, almost by birth, by literary habitudes and by the keenest joys of his intelligence, and as upon the point of claiming French Citizenship. Yet of the Canton de Vaud he could say: "I have loved this land of my fathers, this home of my childhood; its interests and its honour have been ever dear to my heart."

Marc Vinet, his father, was a man of great talent and elevated character. Brought up according to the strict Huguenot tradition, he was extremely conscientious, severe alike to himself and to others. Starting in life as a schoolmaster at twenty louis per annum, he passed through many vicissitudes of fortune, and at last succeeded in obtaining a petty government appointment which he held till his death. Very affectionate, but devoid of imagination and sympathy, he was a stern and exacting father, especially to Alexandre, whose slow development vexed him, and whose excessive sensitiveness he could not understand. He made himself a terror to the timid, morbidly sensitive child, who trembled when he heard his father's footsteps on the stair as he came home to meals. At the sight of his father the child cried, promised not to cry, but cried still. Alexandre had an unfailing refuge in his mother, who was a woman of strong common sense and "goodness itself," and a solace in books, with which a friendly bookseller freely supplied him; but the severity of his father cast a shadow upon his childhood. Even after he entered college, at a students' festivity where he was acting the part of cup-bearer, the sudden view of his father's profile in an obscure corner caused a thrill of terror which he never through life forgot. The stern discipline was too much for the tender sensitive nature. It aggravated if it did not create an extraordinary nervous weakness, which he deplored but could never overcome. As he grew older, however, he discovered that this severity was only a mistaken form of affection.

Of his father he himself says: "The severity of his judgment was equal to his love for me: affection carried him into severity, just as it carries others into indulgence." Vinet on his removal to Basle corresponded regularly with his father by letter. This correspondence is beautifully frank and singularly full and minute in its reference to the incidents of daily life. It is the free familiar converse of two souls who have nothing to conceal from one another, and whose interests are identical. Parental love, as exacting as ever, criticises freely, and seeks to make its object perfect in everything from moral conduct down to the niceties of French style and penmanship. Filial love, having cast out fear, speaks with perfect freedom. Vinet, when his father died, was overwhelmed with grief, and in a letter to a friend wrote: "My well-beloved father has been so long the light of my judgment and the point of view of all my relations, that I seem now to be in an unnatural state; the spring of my life is broken; I have lost my way in the world, and it is only when I raise my eyes to heaven that I find anything immutable, sure, eternal."

In the Academy of Lausanne which he entered in his thirteenth year the teaching power was at a very low ebb. No lofty intellectual ideal was held up to awake enthusiasm; and the youth, wearied of the mill-round of tasks that seemed to lead to nothing, gave themselves up to social dissipation and desultory reading. Vinet found employment chiefly in the study of French literature and in literary composition, writing verses with amazing facility. With overflowing spirits and unfailing good humour he was the life of the college reunions. He entered with the keenest relish into every innocent pleasure of student life.

Vinet made choice of the ministerial profession, in compliance with his father's desire, without constraint, with a serious purpose, but without anything that indicated a marked vocation. His highest ambition was a quiet life of benevolence in a country parsonage. Most of the clergy, while their creed was orthodox and their outward conduct correct, manifested little of the evangelical spirit. In their sermons they affected a literary in contradistinction to a Biblical style, and for the most part confined themselves to an inculcation of the moral duties. Vinet afterwards said of the preaching to which he then listened: "A wooden orthodoxy sought to march straight to a tottering morality which it endeavoured to support by isolated fragments of Scripture." Every special manifestation of religious earnestness was discountenanced by the clergy. On the Sunday evenings the students acted little comedies and played cards in the parsonages with the wives and daughters of the pastors of Lausanne. Among the clergy, however, there was one outstanding individual who, through the sincerity and depth of his religious convictions and the force of his character, exercised an immense influence for good. This was Dean Curtat, one of the city ministers of Lausanne, and the acknowledged leader of the clergy of the canton. His fresh, fervid, manly preaching, which was much run after, compelled attention. It touched the conscience. It went straight to the heart. But it was not only through his preaching that Dean Curtat influenced the students. With the view of supplementing the very defective theological course of the Academy, he had a conference with them twice a week in his study, at which controverted topics were discussed, and sermons read by the students, and criticised. In these conferences the Dean was always lively and energetic. "You felt that there was concentrated fire within." The originality and force of his character gave a piquancy and charm to everything he said. While his own views of Gospel-truth were defective, he communicated an evangelical direction and impulse to many, which carried them far beyond the point which he himself had reached. When the great Religious Revival visited the Canton de Vaud, Dean Curtat regarded it with suspicion, and became its bitterest opponent. But its chief supporters were the young ministers whose religious life had been kindled at his conferences. They attributed to his influence the origin of the whole movement. One of them said of him : " He put our fingers upon the latch, but he did not open the door to us."

Vinet has warmly acknowledged his obligations to Dean Curtat. He was not, however, during his College career awakened to a true and independent religious life. The most striking feature of his character was moral earnestness, combined with exquisite tenderness. His large, massive, bodily frame, with its fine nervous organisation, represented the remarkable union of strength and refinement in his personality. He is described as a big, broad-chested, ungainly, coarse-featured youth, who, when he smiled or spoke, revealed a feminine delicacy. Madame de Montholieu, at the close of a conversation in which he had taken part, after he left the room, asked : "Who is that ugly young man that becomes beautiful when he speaks?" To the earnestness and sincerity of his character one of his fellow-students, and most intimate friends, bears testimony: "As far back," he says, "as my recollections go, I saw in Vinet an inborn need of truth, of rectitude, of frankness, of clearness. Thus, when still very young, he was scandalised at the oath which the members of the Grand Council, of whom many were notorious unbelievers, were obliged to take on assuming their functions, as also at the oath required of catechumens before admission to the Lord's Table; and in general in all relations, among friends and acquaintances, he was always afraid lest the word should go beyond the thought."

While Vinet was pursuing his studies, M. Charles Monnard, in the course of his candidature for the vacant professorship of French Literature in the Academy of Lausanne, held, according to ancient custom, a public disputation. The young Vinet came forward to break a lance with the Professor as the champion of the Classical against the Romantic School. In this appearance he acquitted himself with such remarkable ability that, chiefly through the influence of Monnard, he obtained the post of Master of the French Language and Literature in the Gymnasium at Basle. He threw himself enthusiastically into the work of teaching. He laboured with untiring energy, giving lessons publicly and privately from twenty-nine to thirty-two hours a week. He says: "The interest of the studies to which I devote myself, and, above all, the affection of my pupils, make me love the post where Providence has placed me." He was a born educator. Even the French Grammar became in his hands an instrument of intellectual discipline and moral influence. In addition to his Mastership he received the appointment of Extraordinary Professor in the University. Two years after his removal to Basle, he paid a brief visit to Lausanne, where, on completing his examinations, he was admitted to the Christian ministry. He was at the same time united in marriage to his cousin, Mademoiselle de Rottaz, who proved to him a singular blessing. I cannot follow his career at Basle in detail. Besides teaching five or six hours a day, he preached frequently, delivered courses of lectures, and wrote articles for various periodicals which were read with admiration by the most eminent men of the day. It was in the humble position of French Master in a German school, with a salary of about £100 a year, that Vinet, by the force of his genius, seconded by his indomitable industry, gained a foremost place among the Christian thinkers of Europe.

At the University town of Basle Vinet came, for the first time, into contact with the bold inquiring spirit of German scientific theology. His traditional opinions on many points were shaken. He felt an imperative need of independent views. His father, alarmed for his orthodoxy, earnestly warned him against the presumption of setting up his own opinions, the opinions of a youth of twenty, against the doctrine of the Church. Vinet, in a letter to M. Leresche, said that with all his heart he hated the domination of ecclesiastical authority. In this mood, he saw even in the earnest Biblical piety of the friends of the well-known Basle Missionary Institute only a blind and servile faith. Of the Missionary Society he spoke with contempt as an English importation "maintained, some thought, primarily for political ends;" and of its supporters, he said: "These people are always furious against reason, always preaching blind faith, servile submission; the law of Christ is a law of light, and the apostles were not pietists."

The process of independent inquiry gave rise to a conflict and confusion in his understanding, through which in regard to many things he fell a prey to the most painful scepticism. But the consciousness that essential vital truth was so enshrined in his heart as to be unassailable kept him tranquil. In a letter to Professor Monnard, speaking of the investigation in which he was engaged, he says: "When in this conflict there are sacred truths, which are in some degree imperilled, they are treasured and preserved by *feeling*. I rejoice to be able to say to you that for me there are several which have nothing to fear from the investigation, because they have taken refuge in my heart. Of this sort are religion and patriotism, and why should I support them by proofs? If God has deposited them in my heart as a sacred asylum, while he will defend them against myself, would it not be a great absurdity to assail them, or to bolster them up by outside supports? Must one not in many cases trust feeling as well as reason?" Yet the faith of Vinet at this time was but the faith of tradition and custom. It was not the individual appropriating faith that receives Christ as the light of the intelligence and the life of the heart.

The wave of the great Revival of Religion, which passed over Europe in the beginning of the present century, had reached the Canton de Vaud. There evangelical truth, though never expressly denied, had been long ignored in the preaching of the Church. In the year 1820, twenty-five candidates for the office of schoolmaster were being examined upon their religious principles. The examiners put to each the question: "Upon what foundation does the Christian's hope of eternal salvation rest?" Only one of them pronounced the name of Jesus Christ in his answer. In view of this state of matters, a Roman Catholic Canon of Valais said that the religion of Calvin would have become extinct in the Canton de Vaud had it not been for the Methodists.

Vinet was at first more repelled than attracted by the promoters of the Revival. Dean Curtat, who was hostile to the movement, had written a violent pamphlet against conventicles. At a conventicle held under the auspices of Cæsar Malan of Geneva, known as "the Cæsar of the Swiss Revival," prayer was offered for the opponent of the Revival, that God would give him light and love. The prayer appeared in an account of the conventicle published with great imprudence by Malan. Vinet, in a little brochure, expressed his indignation against this public insult, as he regarded it, to his beloved master. He denounced the doctrine of the Revival as "new, sectarian, and a curious mixture of pride and humility." Some years later, after he had identified himself with the cause of Evangelism, an opponent made a handle of these words against him. Vinet at once retracted them, saying that he had "judged ignorantly, rashly, and wrongly."

Sometime in the course of the summer of 1823, there took place a great and decisive change in his views. At what precise date or in what form the Heavenly Vision appeared, he never told, either because he was fastidiously averse to such disclosures, or because he was unable clearly to read his his own experience. "The first indication," his biographer says, "of a religious life really independent, "and with marked features of individuality, followed the distress occasioned by the death of his father, and the excruciating attacks of a malady, brought on by an accidental injury, which entailed life-long suffering." "Rome," says Vinet, "might be more easily built than a man converted in a single day. Such a prodigy is possible with God, but in a thousand, in ten thousand cases to one, we may safely predict he will not perform it." The spiritual process in his case extended through many months; but of its special character and progressive stages we know nothing. The grand result however was a solemn vow of service embodied in a poem which he composed in August 1823. Not with the rapture of a Charles Wesley, but in his own subdued and humble fashion, he says: " Lord, cast thine eyes upon the tardy offering which my timorous piety brings to thine altar." His life henceforward, in the spirit of that vow, was a thankoffering most humbly but most unreservedly laid upon the altar.

The public question that first stirred the soul of Vinet to its depths, and called forth all his energies, was the question of Religious Liberty. It had become a burning question in his native canton. Vinet was no mere man of letters, content to display his genius in the region of high literature. He was no mystic, nursing pious feeling without seeking or caring to act upon the world around him. He was, above everything else, a Christian philanthropist, keenly alive to the deepest needs and miseries of men. He was a Christian patriot.

In the Canton de Vaud, the advancing cause of Evangelism was met by a storm of persecution. The people generally were in that state of self-satisfied ignorance to which the light of the Gospel is a disturbance and an offence. The Evangelical preachers, who presumed to address honourable citizens as "sinners," and to declare the salvation of members of the Church impossible without regeneration, were reviled as intolerant fanatics, mobbed, insulted, and assailed with brutal violence. The magistrates too often, instead of punishing disturbers of the peace, struck the unoffending victims. The legislature, yielding to popular clamour, passed a law on the 20th May 1824, forbidding conventicles, under penalty of fine and imprisonment. The passing of this law was hailed by the people with savage demonstrations of joy. The inhabitants of Fech came in a triumphal procession to Aubonne, headed by a man holding a hatchet, which he swung round his head, and, striking sparks from the pavement, he exclaimed that he would "do for the Methodists." The effect of this atrocious enactment was that a house where a religious meeting was suspected was subjected to a visit from the police; if the inhabitants should happen to be occupied with bottles, glasses, and cards, their innocence was established, but if they were found with Bibles, or, as sometimes happened, upon their knees, they were arrested as culprits. The repressive enactment did not put an end to the conventicles; but it drove them and their supporters outside the National Church; it called into existence the first Dissenting Church in the Canton de Vaud. The old story of the multiplication of believers through persecution was repeated. The Dissenters flourished amazingly under a law which forbade their existence. Vinet was deeply moved by the state of matters in his native canton. He wrote to his friend Monnard that he was constantly dreaming about liberty of conscience, which till then he had scarcely thought of, but which had become his favourite idea. A scathing exposure of the tyrannical government, which he inserted in a journal, involved him in a public prosecution, which ended in his being subjected to a fine, and suspended for two years from his clerical functions. "Voltaire had pled for liberty of conscience in the name of religious indifference. Vinet does so in the name of Christian faith." What he always places in the foreground is, *first*, that Christ expressly forbids the employment of force in religion, and, *second*, that it is of the very essence of the Christian faith that it should be adopted freely. The principle, of course, for which Vinet contended was liberty of worship. Liberty of thinking is as much beyond the control of governments as the ebb and flow of the tides or the circulation of the blood. Even the principle of liberty of worship, however, was generally conceded with this restriction, that it must be withheld by the magistrate when he judged it to be dangerous to the public peace. Upon this principle the meetings of the Salvation Army have been lately prohibited in Switzerland. The liberty of worship, however, which a magistrate unfavourable to religion may withdraw whenever he considers it dangerous to the public peace, is, as all history shows, a very precarious possession. The principle, which Vinet expounded with unwearied reiteration and extraordinary eloquence, is that liberty of worship is the indefeasible right of every human being, in the exercise of which he is entitled to legal protection.

The cause of religious liberty is not safe in the hands of men who are indifferent to religion. Those who do not value it will not contend for it, and it cannot be maintained without a struggle. Those who support it merely in the interest of political liberalism too readily, as we have often seen, oppose it in the same interest. But, until religious men apprehend that liberty is of the very essence of religion, and are willing to grant impartially to all the same freedom which they claim for themselves, they are still really upon the side of persecution.

Very early the idea of the separation of Church and State occurred to Vinet as the only satisfactory solution of the religious difficulties. In a letter to M. Leresche, written in February 1824, he attributes all the troubles of the Canton de Vaud to what he calls " the specious but false principle of a State Religion." He says: " The existing relations between civil society and the Kingdom of Heaven appear to me, I avow it, adulterous and fatal." This idea of the relation between Church and State, to the exposition of which he devoted all his energies, struck him suddenly, he says, like a ray of light. His biographer recalls a similar passage in the life of Rousseau, when, sitting under an oak, in a moment of ecstasy and sudden illumination, the great ideas that form the substance of his principal works flashed into his mind.[1] There is, however, a striking difference between the vision of Vinet and that of Rousseau. Rousseau had a dream of imaginative genius, to which he at once surrendered himself with joyful enthusiasm. Vinet had a stern vision of conscience, of which he at first struggled hard to rid himself, and to which he yielded only when conquered. His inspiration originated in that passionate thirst for truth and justice which is, perhaps, his chief characteristic. In a conversation with a friend, so far back as 1816, upon the relation of Church and

[1] Rambert: *Alexandre Vinet*, tom. ii. 98.

State, he said: "We must find a means of being equitable to every one." He was haunted by a conviction that the existing arrangements were unjust.

In his Prize Essay, entitled, *Mémoire en Faveur de la Liberté des Cultes*, published in 1826, and more fully in a later work,[1] Vinet has advocated the separation of Church and State. In his view, State and Church differ entirely in their origin, sphere, and function, and can never be united without injury to both. The State originates in necessity, the Church in liberty. The State necessarily embraces all who are born or come to live within a certain territory. The Church is a purely voluntary association, to which no man can belong save by his own free choice, or longer than he chooses. Again, the State is a civil institution, whose function is to minister to secular needs. The Church is a religious society, whose function is to further the spiritual interests of men. State and Church lie in two different spheres of human life, the secular and the spiritual respectively. Their union is adulterous and fatal. Their separation is demanded by their very nature.

Vinet is a thorough-going and uncompromising theorist. The view of the so-called "irreligious godless state," which our religious voluntaries are so eager to disclaim and their opponents so anxious to fix upon them, Vinet boldly avows. He holds that

[1] *Essai sur la manifestation des convictions religieuses et sur la séparation de l'Eglise et de l'Etat envisagée comme conséquence nécessaire et comme garantie du principe.* Paris, 1842.

the State *qua* State has and ought to have no religion. He goes the length of saying what seems a paradox : that society, and the State as the representative of society, has no conscience; for he says : If society collectively has a conscience, the individual can have none. In regard to the theory, I remark, *First :* It entirely breaks down in its application to legislation. Legislation cannot be confined within the sphere of material needs. It must take into account the moral well-being of society. Vinet admits this. He affirms that there is a social morality which the State is bound to protect, and on which it reposes. This social morality of a community, however, springs from and is inseparably bound up with its religion. In fact when Vinet makes the admission that social morality should have state-protection, his Christian heart opens a door for Christian legislation which his theory taken in its rigour excludes. *Second :* What led Vinet so rigorously to confine the State to the secular sphere was simply his deep regard for the interests of religion. The spectacle of a State asserting control over religion, with brutal violence and with lamentable results, was under his eye. The frightful evil kindled in his generous soul a noble indignation. The logical instinct, acting under the stimulus of strong passion, carried him in oblivion of certain facts to an extreme theory. But, in advocating his views, he is never merely the cold logician. He concludes his principal work on the separation of Church and State with a prayer which breathes the fervid Christian spirit that characterises all his writing on this subject. "Vouchsafe, O

Father of Spirits! to infuse more of the spirit of love into the souls of those who shall read than has been manifested by the writer; ... touch the hearts of my readers with those very truths which have too little affected my own. Nevertheless, O God! I feel at this moment that they do influence me, and that I do love them. I am conscious of a desire to act for thee and for my brethren; some desire for thy glory, some love for souls seems to awake within me. Ah! continue it, Lord, and make me altogether what I ought to be as a teacher of others. Great master of assemblies, thou seest the evil for which in much weakness I have essayed to find a remedy. Have compassion, O God, and fulfil my desires! Bless the efforts of the society to which I present this work; and grant that others also who are seeking to promote the cause of truth in the spirit of charity may be sustained by thy powerful spirit. 'Not unto us, O Lord, not unto us, but unto thy name give glory!'"

Like some clergymen of the Church of England, Vinet did not then feel constrained by his theoretical voluntaryism to withdraw from the National Church. The severance of Church and State was to him then an ideal and not a dogma. He was deeply attached to the Church of his fathers. But he says: "I love in her rather what she may become, than what she has been; I love in her one of the provinces of the territory of the invisible Church. I love in her that which our fathers have loved in her, an asylum for souls weary and heavy laden, a hospice for travellers on the way to eternity, a thread of attachment cast by the hand of the Lord upon my earthly country. I love in her something more ancient than all our past; I would say, I love what she still has in her of the Church of Christ, or rather it is the Church of Christ that I love in her."

The Church of the Canton de Vaud, which reckons the great reformer, Theodore Beza, among her founders, had by the tyrannical domination of the State been reduced almost to a nullity. She was the merest shadow of a Church. She had no power of self-government. There was properly no Church at all. There was only a religion of the State. As Dean Curtat, the most eminent representative of the clergy, said : "In our happy country, Church and State are one whole." The laity had no share in the management of the Church. It was "a mere clerical machine, controlled by the government." At the Reformation, when the Canton de Vaud was a dependency of Berne, the infallible Pope had been supplanted by an infallible government, whose direction in religion the people accepted with servile submission. A Swiss clergyman relates, that a Vaudois peasant said to him what no Scotch peasant could have said, that there was no danger of his becoming a Methodist, unless indeed he were ordered to do so by the government.

But, just as in Scotland before our "Ten Years' Conflict," the religious life, awakened by the revival in the National Church of the Canton de Vaud, became impatient of the barriers that hindered its free development. The ministers of the Establishment saw the freedom which dissenting churches now legally tolerated enjoyed, and desired that their own church should possess the same liberty. Vinet heartily sympathised with this growing desire for spiritual independence. The severance of Church and State was evidently a distant ideal. He hoped, however, that the Church even in union with the State might attain to a measure of freedom. He laboured as a journalist, with untiring energy and zeal, to foster and direct the craving after Church independence. He believed that the Church, when she attained perfect freedom, would, like a fruit fully ripe, fall of her own accord from her position of state-dependence. His programme was first spiritual independence, and then separation of Church and State. His anticipation was not fulfilled. But the character of the men who succeeded to the reins of government after the Revolution of 1830 made him at first very hopeful. Among them were statesmen of enlightened views and elevated aims, who were favourably disposed to religion. Some of them were even considered Methodists. In 1837 Vinet, who by his writings had gained a European reputation, was called to the vacant chair of Practical Theology in the Academy of Lausanne. The University of Basle made an effort to retain him by offering to institute for him a special chair of French Literature and Eloquence. Many other offers from different places were addressed to him. But his love to his native land, and especially his interest in her religious development, determined him to accept the call to Lausanne. In 1837 the government prepared the draft of a new constitution for the Church. They called together a representative assembly of the four classes of the clergy which had not met for more than a century, in order to consult them in regard to the proposed constitution. Vinet was appointed delegate of the class of Lausanne and Vevay. Among the points discussed in the assembly there were two of special importance. There was first a proposal to set aside the Helvetic Confession, the ancient symbol of the Vaudois Church. This proposal was made in a spirit of hostility to evangelism. The venerable creed was attacked because it was regarded as the flag of the Methodists. Vinet opposed the abolition of the Helvetic Confession, not because he regarded it as an adequate expression of the actual faith of the Church, but because he believed, *first*, that a creed of some sort was essential to a Church, and, *second*, that if the old creed were abolished it would probably be supplanted by a creed of a very negative and unsatisfactory character. His attitude on this question, as I understand the facts of the case, seems to have been a mistake. The setting aside of the old creed was in the circumstances a step out of the region of fiction into that of truth and reality. In the supposed interests of religion, he pleaded for the retention of a creed which no longer represented the faith of the Church. His attitude, on this occasion, seems to me a solitary inconsistency in a noble life, when the fear lest the cause of religion should fall to the ground, if one of its traditional supports were removed, prevailed over the fear of insincerity and falsehood.

The other point was the admission of the laity to a participation in the government of the Church. There were those who regarded the Church as a school in the direction of which the people should have no part. Vinet regarded the Church as a society, in order to the life and free development of which it was essential that all its members should share in the management of its affairs. At one of the meetings of the Assembly he made a powerful speech, in the course of which he said : "There is a religious life ; and there is an ecclesiastical life ; and the second is the complement of the first. . . . It is with the ecclesiastical life that we are concerned here, because it is that which we lack. I say boldly an *ecclesiastical* life, because we have a Vaudois Church to preserve, to save,—to save, do I say? Yes, gentlemen, to save." A prominent delegate, Dean Liardet, called upon Vinet to state the last consequence. This of course was separation of Church and State, which however could not well be spoken of in such an Assembly. Vinet was completely put out, stammered, and left the meeting in confusion. The conviction seems to have flashed across his mind at the moment that the free ecclesiastical life he desired was unattainable by a Church in union with the State. The Assembly did not much regret his withdrawal. Some members even regarded it as a providential deliverance ; for his speeches were at such an elevation, that they hardly ever understood them, and no one was able to make any proper reply to them. Brilliant thoughts, one says, coruscated from him, which dazzled you, but only made the darkness deeper. With all his genius he had not the talent of a debater, and so was not very helpful in an ecclesiastical assembly. Vinet from the day of his sudden withdrawal from the Assembly, it was noticed, regarded the severance of Church and State no longer merely as an ideal, but as a dogma. The new ecclesiastical constitution which expressly sanctioned the supremacy of the State received legislative sanction in 1839. Vinet regarded it as a deathblow to the liberties of the Church. He withdrew from the ministry of the National Church, and soon after resigned his Theological Professorship. He felt that it compromised his position, and was unworthy of his Christian character, for any worldly motive, to remain connected with a system of which he disapproved. He believed that convictions were given us that we might make sacrifices for them, and that this special sacrifice was required of him.

In the revolution of 1845, a radical government came into power, animated by bitter hostility to evangelical religion. The triumph of radicalism was the signal for a deplorable outburst of popular violence against the Mômiers or Methodists.[1] They

[1] The Rev. Clement de Faye of Brussels, in the *British and Foreign Evangelical Review*, July 1872, quotes from M. Guers the following account of the origin of this injurious term, which the Supreme Council of the Canton de Vaud and the Synods were not ashamed to apply to Dissenters :—

"When M. Malan was interdicted from preaching in the Canton of Geneva he began to preach from time to time at Ferney-Voltaire. On the 7th October 1818, a man who had obtained a certain literary reputation among us, J. G., published the following article

were denounced at political assemblies as the Protestant Jesuits who must be expelled as the Jesuits had been. Their prayer-meetings were dispersed by brutal mobs. They were assailed with insult and gross violence. The police either were or pretended to be unable to afford them protection. The Radical Government, ruling in the name and by the will of "the sovereign people," made no serious attempt to allay the storm of popular passion. Their leader, Henri Druey, an able and unscrupulous man with Socialist tendencies, alluded in the Grand Council to the *sauvagerie primitive* of the people, as having its good side, as indicating native force. The old law which had fallen into abeyance was revived, forbidding the pastors of the National Church to attend religious meetings held elsewhere than in the parish Church, or at other times than those appointed for public worship. "In fact this democratic Canton de Vaud framed an enactment as stringent as the act of uniformity of the Cavalier parliament of Charles II. The intolerance of the Monarchical party of that day was outdone by the intolerance of the Democratic party in our own time."[1] The Government issued an order to the clergy to read from the pulpit a manifesto in defence

in the *Feuille d'Avis* of Geneva : 'Next Sunday at Ferney-Voltaire the company of the Mômiers under the direction of the Sieur-Régentin (Malan, Minister, and Regent of Geneva College) will continue their exercises in phantasmagoria, jugglery, and simple feats of strength. The black clown will contribute by his buffooneries to make his audience laugh. Tickets to be had at the door near the lottery-office.' This ignoble joke was enough to bring the name of Mômiers into fashion among the population."

[1] *British Quarterly Review*, January 1877.

of the Revolution. This resulted in the withdrawal of 153 ministers from the National Church. On one point, which he now regarded as of cardinal importance, Vinet had no sympathy with these men. He was a voluntary; and they were State-Churchmen "to the very marrow of their bones." He nevertheless publicly congratulated and thanked them for their act of self-sacrifice as an invaluable service to the morality of the country. The Free Church of the Canton de Vaud which they founded was for him as a manifestation of the free Christian spirit, " a ray of light amid the dark shadows which licentiousness and materialism spread over the land." He became a Professor in her Theological School.

The Free Church of the Canton de Vaud, unlike her popular sister in Scotland, embraced a mere fraction of the people. She was despised and hated by the majority of the nation. The Radical Government, to gratify "the sovereign people," or the turbulent spirits who represented them, sought by the revival of persecuting laws to stamp out the Free Church. Vinet was once more called forth as a defender of the cause of religious liberty. On this subject as a writer he is at his best. Upon other matters he writes with a too manifest deliberation, with a too carefully measured step; but this theme always draws forth his heart and soul in a torrent of free, fresh, and fervid eloquence.

The Apostle of Religious Liberty, however, preached in the wilderness. The savage spirit of religious intolerance was not subdued by his powerful eloquence. At the date of Vinet's death the right of public worship was denied to the Free Church, and it was only through the multiplication of conventicles held in private houses in defiance of the law that for several years she maintained her existence. In these conventicles Vinet often officiated. A year after his death a prayer-meeting held in the house of his widow was dispersed by the police. Madame Vinet was summoned to the court to answer to a charge of misdemeanour. At the trial M. Guisan, her counsel, said :—

"There are causes which defend themselves. The presence of Madame Vinet at the bar of this tribunal for having a prayer-meeting in her house is more eloquent than all that I could say. As to her, she has the honour to be the first individual who is struck for the cause of religious liberty. Among the number of M. Vinet's titles of glory, is it not the greatest perhaps to have been one of the first apostles of liberty in the Canton de Vaud? Is not the first of the writings that have made him famous a treatise in defence of this liberty? And did he not die in some sense a martyr to it? It was fitting that his widow should be the first victim in this noble cause. The day when Madame Vinet received the summons to appear before this tribunal was the anniversary of the death of M. Vinet. The day when she appears before you is the anniversary of the day when M. Vinet was buried in the midst of a concourse of his fellow-citizens. It is not possible to see in this singular coincidence a mere result of chance; there is something in it evidently providential, and the prosecution instituted to-day will be an immense step towards the conquest of religious liberty."

Madame Vinet, Pastor Scholl, who presided, and all who had been present at the meeting, were sentenced each to a fine of 50 francs with expenses.

In a letter written a year before his death Vinet said :—" I have just spoken of my unhappy country ; unhappy it is without doubt, very unhappy; but I cannot think that a country where impiety persecutes, and where it always finds some one to persecute, is a country abandoned by God. . . . I hope that good will come out of all this. Neither the Government nor the people will in the end overturn the Free Church which is being formed, and the worship of which is now celebrated in private houses. They will expatriate some of the best citizens ; many have already gone, and the emigration increases, but there will remain a nucleus of Christians resolute and humble who at the price of some suffering will restore to Christianity and civilisation a country that has been violently torn away from them."

This prediction has been so far fulfilled. Mr. Froude says that it was not the great theologians who argued for Protestant truth but the simple peasants and humble tradesmen who died for it that established the Reformation in England. Christians " resolute and humble " have, as Vinet anticipated, at great personal sacrifice maintained the Free Church of the Canton de Vaud, and in her the cause of the Gospel and religious liberty.

Vinet has many other claims upon our regard which I can only briefly indicate. Through his rare literary talent he gained the ear of cultivated France more thoroughly than any other representative of evangelical truth. Literature, which had been his first love, was his life-long passion. In Jesus Christ he found the perfect realisation of the humane ideal which literature aims to represent. In his view, in order to be wholly Christian it was necessary to be entirely human, and " Christianity and humanity were not antitheses." In him the literary spirit and evangelical faith, commonly too much at variance, were completely reconciled. " The jotting in his commonplace book—'Religion and Literature, two liberties'—expresses the unity of his life." It was in the department of literary criticism that he gained his chief distinction. Sainte-Beuve, the first critic of the time, says of Vinet : " We have at this time a critic, sagacious, exact, and, when it is necessary, severe, who obeys in all his movements a Christian spirit of charity." With the fan of Christian criticism Vinet sought to purge the threshing-floor of French literature from the chaff of levity and profanity. His criticisms, however, are not mere assays of books; they are just and generous expositions of their authors, always from a Christian standpoint. Several writers such as Chateaubriand, Sainte-Beuve, and Béranger, whose works he reviewed, wrote letters to the critic, unknown in some cases to them by name, in which they express their deepest feelings as to a father confessor. With some of them, as Sainte-Beuve and

Emile Souvestre, he came into close relations of friendship. It has been said that if there is a serious reading public in France now it is due in great measure to the influence of Vinet. Verny, in a letter to Vinet, says of *Le Semeur*, the journal in which his articles appeared: "It is an elevated tribune raised expressly for you in the midst of Paris, from which you are able to call all France, I say intelligent and cultivated France, to the knowledge of the Gospel of God."

His preaching, which was extemporaneous, at least as regards the language, possessed charms that are not found in his printed sermons. "Vinet," says Chevannes, "was eloquent with true natural eloquence fortified and chastened by study. His language was grave, correct, and pervaded by a genuine warmth and austere grace. It effloresced in appropriate images, springing from the thought itself. Add to this a full and sonorous voice, admirably managed, bringing out by its inflexions every shade of the thought, and every intention of the orator, and you will have some idea of the charm of his preaching." Of his printed sermons, many of which have been translated into English, it has been said that "they resemble more the carefully weighed address of the Christian philosopher than the simple and direct utterances of the Christian preacher. Yet throughout many of them, especially in the volumes published after his death, there runs a deep vein of Christian experience rising at times into a rapture of devotion."[1]

[1] *North British Review*, August 1854.

Vinet was, as he always lamented, imperfectly acquainted with scientific theology. Yet Professor Astié speaks of him as "the greatest, the most fertile, the most original theologian in the French language since Calvin, and the father of a new conception of Christianity which meets the exigencies of sacred and profane science."

The theology of Vinet, which he never constructed into a system or expounded in a separate work, which lies scattered through sermons, literary criticisms, and philosophical discussions, is a distinctly original method of conceiving Christian truth, of immense significance especially for French Protestantism. It has been said that, while from the men of the Revival Vinet got religion, he gave them a theology. We know that Christian theology originated in apologetic. When the Church, under the impulse of Christian love, strove to commend the Gospel to the mind and heart of the heathen world, she herself reached a deeper and more comprehensive view of Divine truth. Every fresh theology has originated in the same way. It was through a loving effort in his apologetic to bring the cultivated semi-paganised French world of his day to Christ's feet, that Vinet reached his theology. In the method of his apology he follows Pascal, but not slavishly. He has even been accused of unwittingly attributing to Pascal his own sentiments. Pascal, the solitary student, has perhaps a profounder sense of the intellectual difficulties: Vinet, the busy worker, thinks more of the moral discords. But the fundamental idea of both is that the vanished divine light for which the human soul thirsts is found in the Gospel. "Have you ever," asks Vinet, "seen lines traced in sympathetic ink become visible when presented to the fire? The law of nature is an invisible writing in the soul, which the fire of divine love in the Gospel reveals." Again, in a very beautiful passage: "You remember the usages of ancient hospitality. Before parting from a stranger the father of the family was wont to break a clay seal on which certain characters were impressed, and giving one half to his guest he kept the other. After the lapse of years these two fragments being brought together again would, so to speak, recognise each other, and would be a medium of recognition between the two men who held them, and by the evidence they bore to the relations of former days would become the basis of new ones. Thus is it in the book of our soul; the lines there begun find their divine complement; thus our soul does not, properly speaking, discover the truth, but may be rather said to recognise it. The gospel is believed when it has ceased to be to us an external fact, and has become an internal truth, when it becomes a fact in our consciousness. Christianity is conscience raised to its highest exercise."[1]

I might show in detail how Vinet, regarding the Gospel from this point of view as meeting human need, has laid the main stress upon the subjective element in Christian doctrine. "Even in the pulpit,"

[1] Vinet's words as condensed by Pressensé in his *Contemporary Portraits*.

he says, "it is much better to treat the truths contained in religion as internal moral facts than as objective truths." In the prosecution of such a method there is evidently a danger lest the objective contents of historical revelation and of Christian doctrine should fall too much into the background or even altogether vanish. Of this Vinet himself was thoroughly aware: "I cannot enough repeat," he says, "that every truth whose subject is man has two poles, and is truth only on this condition. In every truth of this order two elements support and complement one another, which are only apparently opposed to each other. In other words the moral and the religious truth is one combined whole; and life, which is only the realised truth, has this combination and this unity for its condition." Yet Vinet has, as I said, by the method of his apologetic, been led to give chief prominence to the subjective side of Christian truth. Professor Astié, who as an able expounder of Vinet's theology, has rendered an invaluable service to the Church, maintains that Vinet in his later years renounced the Calvinistic theology of the Revival.[1] The evidence he adduces, however, in support of his assertion, is of the slenderest and most unsatisfactory kind. While Vinet disapproved of modes of statement and procedure adopted by the men of the Revival, there is no reason to think that he departed substantially from their theology. This is the view taken by M. Frederic Chevannes, who however holds that but for a constitutional timidity of character, Vinet would certainly have

[1] *Le Vinet de la Légende et celui de l'Histoire*, Paris 1882.

cast off the yoke of traditional supernaturalism.[1] But the last failing with which Vinet can be justly charged is cowardice. If he never disclaimed the traditional theology of his youth, the whole tenor of his life sufficiently proves that it could not have been because he wanted the courage of his convictions. In the very year of his death he prepared a draft of a Confession of Faith for the Free Church. It professes merely to embody the minimum of essential truth beyond which in his opinion a Church creed should not go. It is his last deliverance upon what in his view constituted the sum of saving truth. It acknowledges the "Divinity" of the Old and New Testament, and proclaims as the only means of salvation for penitent sinners faith in Jesus Christ, the Son of God, and the Son of man, the Mediator between God and man, and the Priest of the New Testament, delivered for our offences, raised again for our justification, effecting our sanctification by the Holy Spirit of God, which He conveys to us on the part of His Father, able, worthy, and resolved perfectly to save all that come unto God by Him.[2]

The work of Vinet was manifold. As a teacher

[1] *Alexandre Vinet considéré comme Apologiste et Moraliste Chrétien*, Leyde, 1883. Vinet was silent in regard to those Evangelical doctrines which did not specially appeal to his individual experience. In the opinion of Schmid (Article "Vinet," Herzog's *Real-Encyclopaedie*), who, as a foreigner, may be presumed to judge with the impartiality of posterity, Vinet did not reject any of these doctrines. It is true that in a letter to Mr. Thomas Erskine of Linlathen (25th November 1844) he expresses his dislike of the doctrine of Substitution, but he takes care to add that he is "not in a position to speak theologically against Substitution."

[2] The Free Church did not accept this creed, regarding it as too indefinite.

he exercised an extraordinary influence. Pressensé, one of his pupils, says: "I never knew any teaching so suggestive as Vinet's, any which so surely communicated to heart and mind the living spark without which all mere learning is comparatively vain." As a philosopher he is distinguished as the originator of the system known as Christian Individualism. But as a man he was far greater than his work. "The personality of Vinet," says Scherer, "is one of those that live in the memory of men as having reflected in a quite peculiar manner the image of the Master; his work has consisted less in what he has done than in what he has been." His simplicity and gentleness appear in the following extract from a letter to a little girl in a house where he had been visiting: "There remains something," he says, "of the friends that have been under our roof when they are gone: their remembrance haunts the chambers where they are no longer seen. I am sure that mine haunts you as a spectre, tall, pale, black. I hope, however, that you are not afraid of it. The only spectres of the past that are frightful are those of our faults. May they never appear to us but as suppliants bathed in tears, who take us by the hand and lead us to Jesus!" He was a true son of consolation, as the following extract from a letter to a newly-made widow shows:—

"The separation under which you groan is more apparent than real; after the breaking of visible ties, the invisible remain; the latter become even stronger; you and your husband are even more united, nearer to each other than you have ever been. You know the secret of making this union, unseen by the eye, but visible to the mind, and felt by the heart stronger and closer. It will be so the more your thoughts and sentiments continue true to the henceforth unchangeable direction which the thoughts and sentiments of your husband have taken. Recollect in what frame of mind he closed his life. Did he not humbly commit the interests of his immortal soul into the hands of a Saviour? Did he not refuse every other support than that of Jesus Christ? Did he not accept with resignation a separation which cost his heart as much as it did yours? Such are the feelings with which he passed from this world to his Father, and which make henceforth the elements of his new life; for as he died, so doubtless now he lives; and the only difference possible between the last days of his earthly life, and the days of his present life is this : that all the sentiments which he carried with him from this world,—submission, adoration, peace,—are only intensified and purified in his new existence. His love for you and the children is penetrated by this pure and divine essence. He loves you as an inhabitant of Heaven ought to love. Can you, madam, would you picture to yourself your husband with different dispositions? Do you not see him submitting to the will of God, and adoring that will even in the dispensation which separates him from what was most dear to him on earth? Ah, well, to be united to him, is it not to think, feel, and love as he does? Without sympathy there is no true union even on earth; harmony of sentiments makes communion of souls. Thus, Madam, after the extreme bitterness of the first days of mourning, when God, touched with your prayers, shall have, in the depths of your heart, sweetly subdued nature, when you shall be able with tears in your eyes, yet in sincerity, to say 'Amen' to the blow which has fallen upon you, then you will see the beginning of a better union, then your joy will be that you think and feel as he does now. You will be happy in the knowledge that your souls are in unison, and that you live the same life; nothing will interpose between his submissive soul and yours; and in the measure in which you give him up to God, God will give him back to you. The more love you have for God, the more love you will have for the friend he has given you. . . . Do not give to God less than he demands, nor to your husband more than he asks. He does not ask from you a love that would make of his dear memory an idol and a temptation. He does not wish to be so loved; he would be a bond between God and you, and not a barrier. His life edified you, I know; but his death is a part of his life, and the most living part of it, the crown and the key of all. His death is a principal part of God's plan for you; it was doubtless determined beforehand as a means of grace and progress for you as well as a means for him of deliverance and glory. Honour the design of God by concurring in its accomplishment. Accept this death even without understanding it, and say to yourself with a submission full of hope, 'Except a corn of wheat fall into the ground and die, it abideth alone; but if it die it bringeth forth much fruit.' Dream no longer of anything but of changing your loss into gain, your sadness into glory, and your separation into a closer union."[1] This tender soul fought the battle for freedom against the fierce Swiss democracy without a tremor. His was very much the character Bunyan sketches in Mr. Fearing. He was never afraid of the lions upon the path of duty. "One look" [to Christ], he says, "delivers from all fear, except the fear of doing evil." The prominent characteristic of his faith was the element of aspiration. Hence he was deeply dissatisfied with himself. He was dissatisfied with the state of matters in the world and in the Church of his day. In theology, it was not his vocation to formulate the attainments of the past. In everything he was reaching forward. When death overtook him before he completed his fiftieth year, he was full of plans of work that might help to bring in a better future. "Not being permitted to travel," he wrote to a friend, "my imagination travels, and shows me at the fireside, I am persuaded, far more beautiful things than are ever beheld with the bodily eye." Outwardly a prisoner all his life through suffering and severe exactions of duty, he found his liberty in accepted dependence. He was cheered by visions of the ideal in which he believed, and which he steadily pursued. In the noble line of the Evangelical Succession, no one has commended the Gospel by a more beautiful and attractive personal character, or has more faithfully and courageously sought to apply it to every province of human thought and activity, and to every relation of society.

[1] *Lettres de Alexandre Vinet*, tome i. p. 423.

THOMAS CHALMERS.

By the REV. W. C. SMITH, D.D., Edinburgh.

THERE is no name that could more fitly wind up the "Evangelical Succession" than that of Thomas Chalmers. For he was thoroughly embued with the evangelical spirit, and convinced that its view of doctrine was the true one. He brought to its aid indeed certain philosophical instincts and habits which some of its later leaders would have thrown away as carnal weapons, but if he used the sword of Goliath it was always to defend the Ark and the Israel of God. He carried out also, with absolute trust in their power, the evangelical methods of work, its best traditions of Christian service; and if he differed from the English portion of this great school in their views of the Church's independence, it was only because he believed that we in Scotland had an earlier and more catholic doctrine on that head, which had been endeared to us by the long struggles of a martyr-history. On the whole, then, no man of late years more fully embodied the higher thought and nobler qualities of the party than he did. A theologian who had no rancour, a churchman who was no schemer, a philanthropist as sagacious as he was benevolent, and an orator whose splendid eloquence was ever at the service of any righteous cause, he yet retained, amid the blaze of an unequalled popularity, the perfect simplicity and humility of Christian character, and turned from the buzz of applauding multitudes to work in lanes and closes where they wist not what manner of man he was. Pity that he who would have so lovingly described him to you to-night had to drop his pen just as his memories and his studies were clearly bodying forth the idea of the man whom he had known so well, and held in such honour! Late in the day, I have been asked to fill the place vacant by the death of Sir Henry Moncreiff. I do so with shrinking, but yet with the feeling, that if love and reverence and warmest sympathy can give one some insight into a great man's nature, in these qualities at any rate I come not behind even him who would otherwise so much more fittingly have discharged this duty to night.

I do not mean to enter into the story of his life at any length. It ought to be familiar to you all, for it has been told with singular grace and beauty in a biography which should rank on your bookshelves among their most cherished treasures. Yet the literature of the day is so abundant, and the fresh currents of thought are so pressing, that unhappily many great books have but short lives, being smothered by the crowd and crush of their successors. It may be well, therefore, to tell at least as much of the story as will perhaps lead you to read it for yourselves. For we have drifted, whether for better or for worse, a great way off from the point at which we stood in Chalmers's day; and the young especially might be all the better for knowing what was thought and said in those years, and what manner of men they were who then led the way.

Thomas Chalmers was born on 17th March 1780 at Anstruther in Fife, where his father was a substantial burgher, and sometime provost. From the parish school there the boy went to St. Andrews University at an absurdly early age, as the custom then was. At College he distinguished himself in Mathematics and Chemistry and what other science was taught, but he did not take to classical literature, which was a pity, for that has long been the weak point of our Scottish divines. We are all fain to be philosophers, and not very careful to be scholars. Yet the preacher should be something of both, if he would do his work thoroughly. In due time he was licensed to preach, and after acting as assistant for a short time at Cavers, was presented to the parish of Kilmany, whose little grey kirk stands in a quiet rural valley, not very notable for anything but its connection with him. Settled to preach the gospel there, he had yet pretty much to learn what the gospel was which would do any good to those Fifeshire lairds and farmers and cottars. A theology indeed he had, clear, logical, compact; for he had been schooled by Principal Hill, whose lectures, still known to students as a system of lucid and sensible Calvinism, retained their hold on his convictions as long as he lived. But one may have a theology of a sort, and yet have little or no gospel,—no feeling that one is burdened with a message from God, and that he is straitened till it be delivered. As yet the "cure of souls" sat somewhat lightly on Chalmers. He thought that a parish minister could do all that was necessary for his people, and have plenty of time over for quite other affairs. "Pluralities" therefore seemed to him highly desirable institutions, and his first publication was a strenuous defence of them. We have some examples of the kind of work which he did in those days for the poor Kilmany folk; and they are alike curious and interesting. They treat of such themes as "Courtesy," and in general of the class of minor moralities, very good in their own way: but the singular thing is, that he handles them with all the fervid eloquence which he afterwards devoted to the very highest concerns. His logic works at the same white heat of conviction when he is insisting on good manners, as it did when he came to proclaim the grace of God that bringeth salvation. He is the same man in both; but in the one case it is a noble and fitting passion of eloquence, in the other the vehemence seems a little out of place. So things went on for a while, his parishioners liking him, and wondering at him, but not much the better for him, till he was stricken with a fever, and brought to the gates of death. From that sick-bed he rose like one "who had been caught up into the third heavens," and who had seen and heard that which "made all things new" to him. It was as marked a point of "conversion" as that of Paul, or Luther, or Colonel Gardiner. Preparatory stages there may have been; very likely there were. But all we know is that, in the still hours of convalescence, he thoughtfully read Wilberforce's *View of Practical Christianity,* and that he came from that sick room a changed man, with another idea of life, and its work and its hopes. Now his fervid eloquence had a fitting theme, and men's hearts were moved by it to their very depths. Of late years, Scotch preaching, even the evangelical kind, had not sought much help from the art of the orator. It had been sound, judicious, earnest; but rather carefully shunned the whole field of imagination and passion. People were pleased with it, but not greatly moved by it. The intellect was satisfied, but the heart was not much stirred. Now, however, genius once more laid its offering on the altar, and the flame and the fragrance of it drew wondering pilgrims from all the country round. The little grey kirk was thronged, Sunday after Sunday, with entranced and breathless hearers. People looked forward to their Sabbath as the supreme day of the week. Nor was that all. Prayer-meetings, Sunday Schools, Bible Societies, Missionary Societies, all kinds of pious and benevolent agencies spring up, so that never was such a busy little place as sleepy Kilmany now became. And it was all because one young man had been touched with the inspiring consecration of things unseen and eternal.

Of course the tidings soon got abroad that there was a new prophet in Fife, and Kilmany could not hope to keep him always to itself, any more than Capernaum could keep his Master long ago. Such forces do not belong to villages: all great powers must find a fitting sphere, otherwise some of their strength will be wasted. Glasgow greatly wanted just such a man then, and did not rest till she had got him. That great city was at that time, in 1815, moving to the front, and taking its place as the commercial capital of Scotland in an age when the commercial promised to be the most energetic life of the country. Wealth was rapidly growing there, and it was of infinite moment that a voice should be lifted up on behalf of the imperishable treasures, which should be powerful enough to assert their higher claims against those of this world. The Church in Glasgow must not become second to the Exchange, if that city was to flourish in the spirit of its ancient motto. Thither therefore Chalmers went, nominally as Minister of the Tron parish, but really as God's messenger to the whole prosperous community. And soon its merchant princes and its cunning handicraftsmen were held fast in the spell of such an eloquence as they never had heard before. It seemed for the time to transport the speaker, even to transform and glorify his ordinarily heavy countenance so that it "shone like the sun for brightness." The torrent of passionate persuasion carried the hearer completely away. One could not criticise it—could not analyse the source of its power—could only be swept along with it, glad now and then of a momentary pause, to draw a full breath and relieve the overwrought feeling. And yet it was not merely emotional; it was full of solid thinking, laying down, as a rule, some broad principle, and applying and illustrating it in a variety of practical details, which carried conviction to all. Many were awakened by it to a new life of which the fruits may yet be seen. Many more were moved by it to acts of liberal generosity such as became their prosperous condition. A lively interest was stirred up in the social and religious state of the town. Controversies of course sprang up here and there as he went on his victorious way,—small theological squabbles about an occasional sermon—poor-law pamphleteering about his parochial ideas—ominous voluntary storm arising for his Church extension scheme—and finally great wrestle about patronage, passing ere long into deeper issues as to spiritual independence, which finally seemed to overthrow the whole work of his life, but yet only completed it in the Disruption of 1843. All that was inevitable. An earnest man has always a deal of fighting to do; and the more earnest he is, the more he must be a man of war, longing for peace, and finding it not. In due time Chalmers passed from the Tron Church, where his eloquence had its chief triumphs, to St. John's, where his parochial ideas were put to the test, and found their greatest sphere of action. By this time his work in Glasgow appeared to be substantially done, and, wearied with its tremendous strain, he retired to a philosophical chair in St. Andrews, where he hoped to find a period of lettered ease, and met only uncongenial dulness and petty quarrels. Finally he came to Edinburgh University, where he had the making of Scotland's future ministry, and the shaping of her Church history to carry on. There in May 1847, at his house in Morningside, he suddenly fell on sleep, and rests in the Grange Cemetery after the gigantic labours of a life of noble and beautiful service.

So much for the general outline of the story; and now by way of filling it up I will look—
1. At his Literary work.
2. His work as a Social Philanthropic Reformer.
3. His Ecclesiastical ideas and labours.

1. As to his contributions to the Theological literature of his day :—The first of these was the Article on Christianity, contributed to Brewster's Edinburgh Cyclopædia while Chalmers was still minister of Kilmany, and afterwards expanded into a volume on Christian Evidences. It must be admitted that this work is not quite satisfactory. It rests too much on the mere external evidence, and even that it does not sift very carefully. It assumes that we know too little of God's character to be able, in any measure, to test a message professing to come from Him, and that consequently all we have to do is to ascertain what the message is, which has been miraculously certified to us. If that were a sound principle, then all the reasoning of Scripture is an idle superfluity; for why appeal to reason if it is so utterly incompetent to judge? In the end Chalmers gave up this extreme position, and learned to rely far more, as the Reformers had done, on the internal evidence of the Spirit, and the harmony between the Scriptures and our higher instincts and ideas. But this work discovered an unusual power of philosophising on religious questions, and it was the first of a series of treatises dealing with the foundations of our Christian faith. In one of these he discussed the grounds and the limitations of what is called Natural Theology, expanding the argument of

Paley, so as to make it embrace not only the nice adjustments of organic matter, but also our intellectual and moral and social correlations. On these latter he shed not a little light that is incidentally of much worth and beauty, especially from an ethical point of view; but so far as the essential argument is concerned, the pith of the book is, no doubt, that part of it in which he so far rectifies the position of Paley in order to meet the subtle objection of Hume. The latter had admitted that if any one had ever seen a watch made, then the next time he came across such a piece of mechanism he would at once conclude that it had been made by a watch-maker. But the world, he urged, is "a singular effect," if it be an effect at all. We have never seen a world made, and therefore we have no reason for asserting that there is a world-maker. To this Chalmers replied that the argument did not rest on the kind of material operated upon, but on the combinations and adjustments which indicated the presence of a designing mind working to produce a certain end. Thus in a watch there are materials having different properties, and wheels having different shapes and sizes, all so arranged that they become a measurement of time; and it is in these arrangements that we perceive the proofs of design or intention. So also in the eye, *e.g.*, we find lenses of different shapes and qualities adjusted so as to throw an image on the retina; and it does not matter though the material in the one case is brass, and in the other organic substance; for the argument rests entirely on the fact, that both are so arranged as to produce a certain result which could not otherwise be attained. As the question stood in those days, assuredly Chalmers had the best of it. This was what it came to: that our reason can discern the Reason that is at work in the universe—a thought that is old at least as Plato. In another book he again encountered the great Sceptic of the last century, but on this occasion not quite so successfully, it seems to me. Hume had objected to the miracles of Scripture, that the constancy of nature is uniform, but that human testimony is variable; and consequently that no amount of human testimony could ever prove that Nature had departed from her uniform law. One feels that this is a sophism, but it is not so easy to show wherein the sophistry lies. Chalmers held that the human testimony might be of such a kind that it would be more difficult to question it than to believe in the miracle it attested. And he laboured to show that the martryrdom of the witnesses proved their sincerity, and that the circumstances of the case made it quite impossible that they could have been deceived or mistaken. It is as to this last point that there may be room to doubt whether he has altogether refuted the subtlest thinker of the last century. There can be no doubt of the sincerity of the witnesses, but the evidence is not so clear that they might not be mistaken or deceived. Of course I do not mean that absolutely, but only so far as Chalmers's work is concerned, which in this respect seems to be defective.

He was working in the same vein when he delivered his splendid series of Astronomical Discourses to the Glasgow merchants who hurried from the Exchange to hear them. The germs of their argument, indeed, are already given in his Natural Theology, and they are only expanded and further illustrated in those brilliant orations. But there is in addition a happy treatment of Voltaire's sneer at the idea, that a God who had to deal with the affairs of so vast a universe could concern himself with so puny a creature as man. The reply to that bit of cynical contempt, drawn from the revelations of the telescope and microscope, showing that to the Infinite nothing is either great or little, and that the hand which guides the majestic heavenly bodies takes equal pains to perfect the minutest organism that flutters for a brief hour in the sunlight, is as conclusively put as it is eloquently enforced.

Yet all this part of his work which has to do with Natural Theology rests, like the original argument of Paley, on too mechanical a view of the universe after all. It suggests the idea of a mind working not from within but from without, and skilfully overcoming difficulties presented by the stubborn material which itself had made. That is not the feeling which a closer study of nature produces. On the contrary, that which strikes us on more careful inquiry is, that all is plastic there, and that, at least within certain limits, it readily takes the form which the life within it needs. The power, whatever it be, is not ingeniously overcoming difficulties, but rather busily developing its resources. Hence it has come to pass that many of the careful reasonings of half a century ago are already practically out of date. We have drifted away from the ideas which then prevailed into quite a new province of thought. It is no longer a question whether the world is a singular effect or not, or whether a miracle can be proved or not. But what men are asking is, whether matter has not in itself "the promise and potency" of all life and thought, and whether the very idea of natural law does not render a miracle utterly inconceivable. Still Chalmers's work in this province did what was needed at the time. It confirmed the faith of the Church, and may be still read with profit because of its massive style and masculine sense. But the theologian to-day must work on somewhat different lines, because the problem has assumed an entirely different shape.

This kind of service, however, was in a sense outside the boards of the Bible, and important as it may be, he is doing a still weightier service who either makes the Gospel itself more clear to us, or presents it in such a light that it shall be more effectual for its spiritual purpose. It is in this last respect that Chalmers was greatest. I do not know that he did very much to enlarge or deepen the religious thought of his time. His scientific convictions, indeed, compelled him to attempt some adjustment between Genesis and Geology; but it was one which should disturb old ideas as little as possible, for all his tendencies were essentially conservative. His interpretation has not, in the end, commended itself to the world or to the Church, but it quieted the alarm of pious souls, and it showed that, without any unfair strain of the Scriptures, the new doctrines of Lyell and Phillips might readily pass into the general body of Christian thought, and cause no more disturbance than the Copernican system had done. For the rest, Chalmers's own religious life had not been a conversion from scepticism to faith, but rather from common worldliness to earnest religion. He had simply received a light from heaven which made the Gospel an intense and overmastering reality to him. Hence the familiar teachings of his father's fireside, and of Principal Hill's class-room, passed through no material change, but were simply vitalised and charged with a power, which to him they never had before. It is true that, in accordance with his whole mental habitude, *a priori* systems of theology fell into the background, and were not much accounted of. The divine decrees, therefore, supposed then to be the deepest tap-roots of Gospel, gave place in his preaching to kindlier doctrines of divine love; and theories of atonement to justify God were transformed into the method of justifying those that believed in God. On two points only did he differ from the rest of his brethren. His doctrine of Faith was essentially Sandemanian, a mere belief in the historic record; and he held, with Jonathan Edwards, a modified system of philosophical necessity. On the whole, however, his work as a Theologian was very much akin to what the Divine Spirit had done on himself. It was just a vitalising of the common Catholic truth. And this was the very thing that was needed for the time. For it is the only safety of theological speculation and critical inquiry that they shall start from a revived spiritual life. Nothing is more perilous than that questioning and doubting spirit which springs only from intellectual restlessness, without any vital interest in the matter. The pursuit of scientific theology, when there is not first of all a living religion, is commonly a wandering in dry places, seeking rest and finding none. This vitalising of received opinion, then, was very much the function which Chalmers had to perform, and perhaps there is none of his books in which you shall see more clearly the contrast between dry dogmatising and living teaching than his Exposition of the Epistle to the Romans. Some of his incidental sermons may be more striking, as, *e.g.*, that on "The Expulsive Power of a New Affection," or that on the text, "Fury is not in me," which seems to have been a special favourite of his own, if we may judge by its frequent repetition. But nowhere else shall you find the general character of his work better displayed. There is nothing very new in it. But he takes a firm grasp of truth, and brings it out into the light both of philosophy and experience, and proclaims it with a singular wealth of argument, and illustration, and emotion. He was a great power, then, in the theology of his day; yet it was chiefly, and happily, as one who compelled men to look at the things which they believed, and to recognise that they were solid realities.

II. His work as a Social and Philanthropic Reformer. He had not been long settled in Glasgow when the condition of the poor there was painfully forced on his attention. The war had just ended, and with the return of peace came the usual collapse of that strained and unwholesome activity which war commonly produces, at least in certain departments. There had been also a defective harvest, and the dearth of victual was aggravated by the pernicious corn-law which excluded foreign bread-stuffs, till they had reached what were almost famine prices. So the looms of Glasgow were silent, and the pinched weavers looked greedily into the bakers' shops, and fiercely at the houses and carriages' of the rich. There was much discontent, and hungry men took Chartism like an epidemic. Infidelity too was rampant, for they thought the Church was callous to their sufferings. Chalmers was a statesman in character and intellect, though not in office, and he had no sooner discovered the real state of the case than he determined bravely to grapple with it. You shall find his leading ideas on these social questions in his Lectures on the Christian and Civic Economy of Large Towns. Scattered, however, through various books and articles and speeches, are many carefully thought-out views on such subjects as national education, savings' banks, workmen's strikes, and corn-laws, which are only incidentally referred to in the volume of lectures. All of these are worth careful and thoughtful reading, for they are not second-hand opinions brought from the political warehouse, but the strong convictions of a strong man who had practical dealings with the poor, and who had brought to the consideration of their affairs both intense thought and experienced sagacity.

Of course, it was as a Churchman that he approached these questions, for it was through the Church that he hoped to remedy the evils connected with them. He had great faith in the sympathy, as well as the liberality of the Christian spirit, and he had no faith in poor-laws and their officials. He thought that they sapped the foundations of old Scotch thrift and self-reliance and self-respect, and that they involved no small waste of means, and injury of feelings, without real improvement of the condition of the poor. Therefore he set himself to see what could be done with the means at his disposal,—to vitalise, in short, ecclesiastical arrangements, just as he had done religious doctrines. That was the radical idea of his life—not to invent new machineries, but to put force and human heart into those which already existed. That is a true thought always. Machinery of course may be improved, but all machines are useless without the vigorous motive power. Therefore he called to his aid congenial labourers—merchants, manufacturers, gentlemen, and common folk, all who were of his own spirit, and he breathed his inspiration into them, and set them over their fifties and over their hundreds, to visit every street and lane and house and garret, and to sweeten, as he said, the breath of society by their presence. A great deal of sympathy was to make up for the want of much money. Good counsel and friendly influence were to arrest the spirit of pauperism, and to foster an almost stoical superiority to common human wants. Where help was urgently needed it was to be given, but in such a way as not to degrade the receiver. Meanwhile the great laws of social economics were to be enforced by Christian principles, as the visitor drank a cup of tea with some poor weaver or cobbler, and talked over his affairs. So successful was this experiment that he persuaded the magistrates of Glasgow to hand over a poor parish in the east end of that city, to be managed by him without interference of any poor-law officials. He was to play the part of benevolent despot, and rule supreme in St. John's district, no one meddling with his work. There he placed young Edward Irving, as a kind of fly-wheel to regulate the machine for which he himself provided the motive power; and as long as he was there to impel it, the work went on with eminent success. Chartism withered down. Infidelity lost hold of the people. There were many poor, but few paupers. St. John's was a model parish as long as Chalmers controlled and inspired its workers.

But we may not reason from premisses of genius and enthusiasm to the commonplace people by whom, after all, the world's work has mainly to be done. No sooner was Chalmers's hand withdrawn, therefore, from the wheel than the ship would not steer as it had done. It had lost the wind, and would not answer the helm any more. Soon it began to appear that "a benevolent despot" could not count on a like successor, and that the ancient provision for the poor was inadequate to meet the wants of a more complex state of society. There were large parishes in Scotland where the whole collection for the poor amounted to only a few shillings annually. There were poor widows left to maintain a family on a sixpence a week. There was a huge system of recognised beggary, every respectable household having its regular weekly visitors carrying a "pock" for their allowance of meal. I do not know if Chalmers got quite rid of these in St. John's, but they abounded everywhere else. Unless there had been a Chalmers in every parish, then the Church could not do the duty which properly belonged to the State. She might keep her own poor, and leave the State to deal with the paupers; though even that was doubtful. Certainly in the twofold battle with poverty on the one hand and pauperism on the other, the civil power was at a disadvantage as compared with the Church. For all that the former could do was to make its provision for the poor as unpleasant as possible. It must mingle some bitter ingredient with all its gifts, so that they should be a little humiliating, otherwise it would have been flooded with a deluge of mere mendicancy, while the Church could bring moral forces to bear on them which kept up their self-respect. In this way the Church has an important part to play in solving this difficult problem, for she can act on the springs of moral character to prevent poverty from lapsing into pauperism. She can, too, and I think she ought to, take entire charge of her own poor, so that none of her members should be in receipt of public charity. But Chalmers's experiment in St. John's parish, successful as it was, showed clearly that she could not properly discharge the duty which the State owes to all its subjects. Nevertheless, his bold undertaking, and all his wise words and judicious schemes in connection with social questions did no small good in rousing the Church to a better sense of her duty, as showing that she was not a mere preaching institution for teaching sound doctrine, and still less a breakwater to protect the respectable class from encroachment of those beneath them, but rather a cement binding all ranks together by the bonds of Christian sympathy and helpfulness.

III. His work as an Ecclesiastic.—As we have seen, Chalmers had a profound faith in the Church as an institution not only fitted to prepare men for eternity, but also to deal with many present affairs far more wholesomely than any other power. He held, indeed, no exclusive theory of Church organisation, and did not object to different nations working out what form of church-government most accorded with their genius; meanwhile he reckoned that Presbyterianism was, on the whole, the best, and certainly the best for Scotland. Especially, he loved that Church as it was by law established, thinking that its connection with the State helped it not a little to do its task effectually. Yet he held with equal tenacity that it must be left free to discharge its duty in its own way, and on its own responsibility to God. They were independent powers, which might be allied together, but neither must dictate any way to the other. The State might withdraw its aid if the work was not done to its mind, but it might not interfere with the Church's proceedings, or overrule its spiritual decisions. Thus their alliance might be to their mutual profit—the Church getting help in the shape of countenance and support, and the State reaping its reward in the increased intelligence and comfort and moral worth of the people. And he was fond of picturing to himself a beautiful ideal world as the result of this union, in which the machinery of civil life was well oiled and worked smoothly, and that with a most economical expenditure—for he had always an eye to thrift—because the Church through her cultured ministry and kindly eldership, went out and in among all the people, taking diligent oversight of their religious and social condition, not as representing the government that paid them, but as God's ministers for the good of all.

A great part of his life was devoted to the exposition of this idea. He did not greatly value metaphysical theories, or analogies drawn from the Hebrew theocracy, or any of the stock arguments of the common theologian. For his mind was not of their make or texture. He was rather a statesman guided by facts and high expediencies, not by mere abstract ideas. He found these two great institutions already in the world, then, both of them ordained of God, yet both also, in some measure, shaped by man. They had different functions, and the one could not do what the other could. They moved on different planes, and relied on diverse forces. They must be free, therefore, each to do its own work in its own way. But there seemed no reason why they should not enter into a treaty of mutual helpfulness, which should be for the profit of the whole people.

Now, he discovered in Glasgow a state of society which had greatly outgrown the State provision for religious instruction. It was the same in other towns, but more marked there than anywhere else. The commerce of that city had increased out of all proportion to its church accommodation. Its religion had nowise kept pace with its shops and ships. The result was what he called "an outlying field of practical heathenism," *i.e.* a great many people who never looked near the Church, because the Church never looked near them. Dissent, indeed, had done something, but it was chiefly among the well-to-do who could pay seat-rents, for as yet these communities acted like separate units, and the richer congregations gave no help to the poorer. Chalmers saw then in the growth of "practical heathenism" both a disgrace to the Church, and a danger to the common weal, and set himself to remedy the evil at once by an appeal to the Christian community, and also to the government for aid.

This was the origin of his lectures on Church Establishment; they arose from the practical necessities of Glasgow and other great towns, and the doctrine which they enforced took its shape from the same facts. There is a principle in political economy that the supply will always, sooner or later, equal the demand: that is just as certain as that water will rise to its own level if you let it alone. If people want bread, beef, clothes, houses, then bakers, butchers, tailors and carpenters will find it their interest to provide what they need. Yet there is no rule without its exceptions, and in affairs of religion and education this law is no longer applicable. There the want may be great, while the demand is less than nothing. The greater the need of these things, the less they may be sought by the people. Hence religion especially must be provided for them, and brought to them, and even pressed on their acceptance. Therefore Chalmers argued that it was the part of a wise government to send the gospel to those who certainly would not go in search of it for themselves.

I need hardly pause to show you that this theory of Church Establishments is properly a plea for home missions. There can be no doubt that the principle on which it rests is sound. If religion is not brought to such people, they will not go to it. Therefore it is some one's business to see that this is done. But the State is not a missionary society. It would be all the better for it if its citizens were also good Christians: but it is not its proper business to make them so, and, on the other hand, that is the very object for which the Church exists. It is in the Church, therefore, that the heart to do it, and the means for doing it, should alike be found; and if they are not, there must be something wrong with the Church that lets such a crop of weeds grow within her borders, and is helpless to remove them when they are there. Chalmers did appeal to Christian men for additional edifices, and he got a considerable instalment of them from their generous liberality. But it was one thing to raise funds for building, and another thing to maintain the clergy in their new cures, which were mostly in poor neighbourhoods. There was indeed plenty of wealth in the country, but there was no organisation for developing its resources, and regulating them, so that the people in Moray Place or Bath Street should be helpful to the dairymen at the Dean or the weavers of Camlachie. It was this practical question that pressed on Chalmers, and led to the great Voluntary controversy. As a matter of fact, his defence of Church Establishments arose from an overmastering desire to reclaim the spiritual wastes of our great cities. At the time, he saw no means of doing this except by aid from the State. But he was not tied to theories, and provided the living water were only brought to the desert places, he was tolerably indifferent by what channel it came.

He was not destined to accomplish his object in the way he first hoped. For his appeal raised a great storm, and while that storm was still raging, other matters of grave import had to be seen to, which at last secured the needed Church-extension, but by means of Church-disruption. On these matters I must dwell at more length, because the younger race that is growing up now is apt to forget, or even to make light of, the great struggle which forty years ago rent the Church in twain, and filled with hope or with alarm almost every household in the land.

In the beginning of the eighteenth century the reactionary statesmen of Queen Anne, disliking the free spirit of the Scottish Church, framed an Act which lodged the presentation to a benefice there, not in the congregation or its representatives, but with the landlords whose feudal notions fitted them to be the tools of the State. Hence a race of ministers grew up, who were devoted to the landed interest rather than to the people, and there had been several secessions from the Church on the part of the better and more earnest-minded of the clergy. If there was anything which Scotchmen hated more than another, it was this law of patronage; for the patrons, as a rule, had forsaken the national Church, or were grown indifferent to religion altogether, and had little or no interest in securing the services of such ministers as the people really needed. As the result of this, there had been a great falling away in the religious and moral condition of the rural population, and many pious souls had drifted away from the national shrines, and sought elsewhere the help that they were needing.

The Church could not abolish this Law. She had annually petitioned against it for many years in vain, but latterly this had been given up as a mockery. Chalmers, however, thought that she had power at any rate materially to lessen the evil. There was such a thing as a call of the people, which Presbyteries still required. It was a mere form now, yet it was an old constitutional right. What if it could be made a reality? What if Presbyteries were enjoined to ordain no man whom the people refused to call? Reasons for such refusal they might be unable to give: enough, if they simply declared they did not want him, for they did not profit by him. They might know nothing against his morals. They might be quite incompetent to judge his " literature." But they were the best of all witnesses to the fact that they did not profit by him. Hence the famous "Veto Law," which like other historic vetoes unhappily would not work. It might have done so, indeed, had all parties loyally tried to make it work. But ere long Patrons and their factors would have nothing to do with it. Then some Presbyteries refused also to recognise it, setting their own judgment above that of the General Assembly. Finally, the Supreme Court of Appeal denounced it vehemently—alas! with as little wisdom as any parish vestry. The General Assembly was powerless against the House of Lords, but at least it had still jurisdiction over those presbyters whose rebellious conduct had led to this entanglement. So the Strathbogie ministers were solemnly deposed for contempt of their ecclesiastical superiors, but reponed and enjoined to go on by the Court of Session, which threatened their ecclesiastical superiors with imprisonment in Calton Jail.

The matter, you see, had drifted far away from its original standpoint. At first, it had been simply a question of wisely modifying the act of patronage by giving force to the people's call, or to the absence of a call. But hot blood had arisen from this, and that had led to decisions which were quite in accordance with English notions, but alien from all the traditions of Scottish jurisprudence. With sorrow and great pain, the Church now got orders to do her spiritual functions at the bidding of the civil power. But there was no hesitation as to the reply she should give. The brave old spirit of our fathers came back in a full tide of manly and even martyr resolution. Not by Chalmers and his followers should the freedom of the Church be sacrificed, or any compromise made of her allegiance to her proper Head. Law in matters spiritual they would not take from Cæsar, but only from Christ. The independence of the Church was far more to them than its union with the State. They knew well that nothing is so fatal to its proper religious influence as to make it a mere department of civil government, a kind of moral police for drilling the people into orderly habits of thought. By thus becoming the tool of the State it was sure to lose the hearts of the community, and all hope of influencing them for the higher ends to which the Church is specially designed to minister. They need no more preach faith, if they themselves were found faithless. Had they drawn back in that grave crisis of our history, then, they would have done more to shock the piety of the country, and to unsettle its belief, than all the sneers and sophistries of the sceptical eighteenth century. But they showed no faltering or uncertain spirit. They tried indeed, and rightly tried, to have their claim of independence recognised by Parliament; and they moved also to have the root of all the entanglement taken away by getting lay-patronage abolished altogether, for the legalising of the veto would no longer suffice. They calmly considered too any healing measures that were proposed, and more than one respectable statesman put his hand to that work. But they found them all weak, well-meaning but futile, not touching the essential question of spiritual independence. And so at length in 1843, between four and five hundred ministers, who dearly loved the old Kirk of Scotland, left their pleasant manses and familiar pulpits, and truly went forth "not knowing whither they went."

I do not think it is good either for a Church or an individual to be always remembering "the things that are behind," fondly dwelling on past achievements. After all, every such attainment should be only a new starting-point, an encouragement to go on to yet further service. If we are fain to pause, and think how well we have done, the world meanwhile is moving on, and fresh tasks have to be undertaken, and we may chance to lose the tide of noble opportunity as we stand looking at ourselves in the fast-flowing stream. I am not sure that our dear Free Church did not, for a while, fall into this mistake, and linger over the memories of its Disruption-birth almost as if it had been the culminating point of Christian history. But latterly it is to be feared that we have swung to the opposite extreme, and that the rising generation not only knows very little about those stirring times, but has even a growing distaste to hear about them. Yet it is good for us, at fitting times, to remember the struggles and heroisms of those who have left us an inspiring example, even though we may willingly acknowledge that time has brought many changes to soften the sharp antagonisms of those past years. Such changes, no doubt, it has brought. The hard lines of demarcation, which separated parties then, have been largely obliterated by subsequent legislation—legislation, however, which substantially allows that the contention of Chalmers and his friends was right. I am glad for the historic Church of our country that even so far her ancient claims have been acknowledged, and the long grievance of patronage taken out of her way. Yet we must not forget that still there is no recognition of that spiritual independence, that right to act out what shall appear to be the will of her Lord without interference from the State, which nerved the men of the Disruption to endure the sore hardships of many a weary year. I admit the difficulty of embodying that principle in a law. Indeed, I am disposed to think that no statute could formulate a rule, to the effect that any one portion or organism of the nation is independent of the supreme power therein. I daresay that in this I differ from most of my brethren; but holding this view, it seems to me that entire separation from the State is the best guarantee of freedom from its unjust control. I do not say that even that is an absolute guarantee. But meanwhile the common law of privilege is a sufficient protection against the narrow logic which wrought the confusion of those Disruption times.

Of course, the Disruption was a step which a man like Chalmers could only have advised under the constraint of an overwhelming sense of duty, and not without exceeding pain. It was a terrible wrench to break away from an institution, to the upbuilding of which his whole life had been devoted, and which was identified in his mind with the highest well-being of the people. But it was forced upon him to break up the Church by his very love of the Church.

The results of that step were manifold, and we have not yet seen the end of them. Its first fruit, which was also its best, was seen in a deep revival of spiritual life over all the land—a beautiful and fresh spring tide, a humble and tender first love, which men looked back to in after years as a thing to be for ever remembered. It was not whipt up by any excitements, but came silently as from the depths beneath and the heights above, an unseen power enlarging our hearts, and giving us a fresh faith in the reality of things divine. It was far the healthiest and strongest revival we have seen in our day; and its origin was the self-sacrificing obedience of those true and faithful men. Moreover, the Church extension for which Chalmers had so long laboured, was now attained on a scale he could hardly ever have dreamed of. Some five hundred Free churches were at once added to the sum of ecclesiastical edifices, and if they were not all planted so as to supply the wants of neglected neighbourhoods, which, in the circumstances, could not be helped, yet very many of them were; and in due time that principle of distribution prevailed, so that every fluctuation of our industrial population is followed by the Church, which tries to keep pace with their requirements. Quite as important, in the long-run, I believe, was that organisation of Ecclesiastical Finance, which secures for unendowed Churches all the solidarity of an "Establishment." Hitherto dissenting Churches had been practically Congregational, and while some of their ministers in the richer quarters of the cities were amply provided for, those in the poorer districts were often in great straits, and many of the rural parts were, from their extreme poverty, altogether neglected, though their spiritual condition was deplorably bad. It was to remedy this state of things that Chalmers worked out the scheme of a Sustentation Fund—or common revenue to which all the people were to contribute as they were able, and from which all the clergy of the Disruption were to receive an equal dividend, and their successors a proportional one according to their congregational givings. That was the rule as at first projected by him, though it has since been considerably modified. New charges were to get back one half more than they sent to the central fund, —a plan which, it was hoped, would stimulate their liberality, and keep them from being unfairly burdensome; but the original Disruption ministers were guaranteed an equal division of the sum then left at the Church's disposal. In the latter case it was thought that the sacrifices which all had made placed them on the same level, and gave them a moral right to equality of income; and they agreed to share alike whatever was contributed for their support. That was a safe enough principle as applied to them during their lives. But as a standing rule of general application Chalmers dreaded any law of communism, and therefore all new charges, and also the successors of the Disruption ministers were placed on a different scheme, by which the principle of distribution was meant, as far as possible, to stimulate the sources of production. Along with this central fund, there might be also congregational funds to supplement the incomes of ministers as their people thought proper. For an absolutely equal dividend would, of course, result in a great inequality. Living was more costly in one place than in another. A city minister with £150 a year would be very much poorer than a country minister with the same stipend. A real equality, even if desirable, could only be produced by an apparent inequality. But what Chalmers aimed at was not equality, but independence and efficiency, without that dead level which ends in a poor mediocrity. This was one of the noblest fruits of his large-hearted sagacity. It has already, more or less, directed the financial arrangements of the disestablished Irish Church; and no doubt it will provide a model for all Churches in those days when they may have to consider in what way funds, derived from voluntary liberality, can be made to secure all the benefits of a State endowment. Not that Chalmers looked forward to any such event, or dreamed of preparing for it. On the contrary, his defence of Church Establishments probably seemed to him the most successful bit of work he had been permitted to do. For his scheme on behalf of the poor had been swallowed up in the new poor-law, and his vindication of the Church's freedom had ended in her disruption. But he had, to all appearance, triumphed over those who had assaulted the time-honoured institution of a State Church. Reverend bishops and noble lords and honourable M.P.'s and able men of letters had hailed him as a deliverer, and echoed his pleadings wherever they could make their voices heard. He and his friends, therefore, had no misgivings as to the continuance of those institutions, or the solidity of the foundations on which they were rested. All his convictions, indeed, were held with a strong tenacity, and no change of circumstances appeared to throw a shadow of doubt on their validity, least of all on this one. Accordingly, the Free Church was launched into the uncertain waters of practical Voluntaryism, but with the standard of the Establishment principle nailed to her mast. So it had been also with the other Dissenting communities at first, but the logic of events has proved in every case stronger than the resolutions of Synods and Assemblies.

In conclusion, Thomas Chalmers stands forth, I reckon, as the greatest moral force of his age, simple, massive, and grand as some structure of the early world. "Ultimus Christianorum" Carlyle called him; but we shall have to wait a while before we see the last of the Christians, though it may be also a long time ere we see another like him. As I have already hinted, not a little of his work has already suffered that touch of change which comes upon all things human; and in his case it has been perhaps more rapid and more marked than in many others who were of less weight while they lived. Some men's thoughts are almost independent of their personality, and tell as weightily when their authors have departed as they did while they were still present. Others, again, have a certain mass of character behind their ideas, which gives a vast momentum to all they say; and when their individuality is withdrawn, the thoughts they have bequeathed lose not a little of their power. So it was with Chalmers: one can see it even in his style, which is not good in a correct or classical sense, but it is the style of a great man with a marked personal character: therefore it takes a firm grip of you, and hurries you on as by an irresistible torrent; for you cannot read it in cold blood any more than you could have critically listened to his voice. And yet comparatively few of his thoughts have now much hold of men's minds. The Christian Evidences have drifted out of sight. His discussion of Hume's objections belongs to a past state of mind. His defence of Church and State ended in a rupture whose cleavage is growing daily wider. And his Christian Economy of Great Cities broke down the moment his own hand was withdrawn from the work. It would be wrong, indeed, to conclude that there was no truth in any of those views because of their apparent practical failure. On the contrary, I take leave to say that perhaps there was nothing he put his hand to, in which there was not an element of weighty truth which the world would do well to hold fast by. On the moral side he was always right in his contendings. It was right that the gospel should be brought to those who otherwise would not go to seek it, though it is the Church's clear duty to do this,—not the State's, as he thought. He was right in asserting the Church's liberty from Erastian control, and her duty to obey her own Lord alone, though it may well be doubted if any nation can give special privileges to a sect without some compromise of its proper freedom. Above

all, he was right in pressing on the community that
no legal provision for the poor could be wholesome
or safe without that kindly intercourse between the
different classes of society, and those moral influences which help to maintain the prudence and self-
respect of the poor, and to keep them from lapsing
into the careless improvidence of the unthinking
savage. It may not be possible for the Church, as
at present conditioned, to do all that he believed
she could do, and that in his hands she proved able
to do in St. John's parish; but ever more and more,
happily, men are also beginning to see that the
system which, for a while, went on multiplying
jails and poor-houses, and trusted chiefly to them
for curing our social evils, was a wretched blunder,
while the human brotherliness on which Chalmers
relied, and which it is the Church's business to
evoke and to sustain, is now felt by all thoughtful
philanthropists to be the main bulwark of society
against the terrible tide of poverty and discontent.
A very beautiful illustration of that, and of the
strong tenacity of his convictions, was that which
Chalmers presented, when, in his honoured old age,
he turned aside from the plaudits of the great and
the cultivated into the dark lane, once made horrible
by murderous deeds, and still shameful for its vice
and misery; and there gathered round him the outcasts of our city, and set up his machinery of kindly
visitors and Savings' Banks, and helps and encourage-
ments, and the ministry of a matchless eloquence in
enforcing the gospel of Christ. From that room in
the West Port a mighty influence went forth, which

has penetrated to many a dark slum and grimy close, and in its spirit we find the true idea of Chalmers's whole life—a steadfast faith in the Christian Evangel "to love one another as Christ loved us." To the end, he took a lively interest in all those affairs that had so largely occupied his busy life. New systems of philosophy were imported from Germany, and he was as keen to learn about Kant and Hegel as he had once been to study Hume and Reid. Fresh facts of science were suggesting novel lines of thought; and he continued to look at them with open vision, willing to learn, whatever the facts of nature taught. New social problems arose, and while he tested them, always by those convictions which were the result of his own large experience, he rejoiced not a little in the growing interest with which these questions were regarded by statesmen, as well as churchmen. But amid the seething waters, and wavering mists, and mingled light and shadow of human thought, one thing abided steadfast, like a green and fruitful land, with a haven of quiet rest for all the weary and heavy laden; and day by day he turned joyfully from ecclesiastical rivalries and theological quiddities, to plead with the poor and the vicious and the criminal to take refuge in its proffered peace. Carlyle truly said of this that Chalmers was doing the thing which he and other littérateurs only talked about getting done. Very beautiful—truly a divine spectacle, it was, thus to see the chief bishop of the Christian Church in his day—for so he was by universal consent,—going, like his Master, to seek and to save the lost.

THOMAS CHALMERS:

A FRAGMENT.

By the Rev. SIR HENRY WELLWOOD MONCREIFF, Bart., D.D.

"THOMAS CHALMERS:"

A FRAGMENT.

By Rev. Sir H. Wellwood Moncreiff, Bart., D.D.
Edited by the Right Hon. Lord Moncreiff.

[The late Sir Henry Moncreiff had undertaken to contribute to this series a lecture on "Chalmers." There was found among his papers a fragment which is evidently an intended commencement of his dissertation; and although the manuscript is a first draft, imperfect in many parts, it has been thought right to print it substantially as it stands, as an addition to this volume, with only such corrections as the sense plainly requires. The author explains, at the outset, the views of the character of Chalmers which he means to enforce. He says that these were chiefly his character as a Christian evangelical luminary, of marvellously expansive power, the brightness of whose perceptions and the ardour of whose aspirations gave him a commanding and beneficent sway over multitudes.

He proposes to inquire how far the effects of his brilliant working have a sure and enduring value, and whether by the combination of his mental gifts with his moral and spiritual fervour, he mightily contributed to fix the throne of the Redeemer in the hearts of men.

These are the chief features of his subject on which he expresses his intention to enlarge; but he proceeds to say that there are other views of his theme on which, although subordinate, something must be said. They are mainly the place occupied by Chalmers in theology, philosophy, and in literature; how far his published works will support his reputation; the merits of his arrangements for the Free Church; and generally his views for the advancement of mankind, and the scriptural grounds on which he rested his ecclesiastical position. It is only to a very limited extent that in the following pages he has filled up this interesting outline, but the fragment as it stands is sufficient to suggest the probable features of the intended discourse, and is characteristic of the author as it is valuable in itself.]

THOMAS CHALMERS.

THE preceding lectures in this course have been more or less biographical. But even the briefest notice of that kind must at present appear to you as worse than superfluous. It certainly is so in the case of one who in the view of many may be regarded as the immediate precursor of our existing Scottish evangelisation. The desire of literary reputation existed in his youthful ambition and threatened to rule his heart till the overmastering power of divine grace had implanted in him the true fire of the gospel. Even after that memorable era in his progress, the same desire often influenced his movements. Thus an undue multiplicity of publications has tended rather to diminish than to increase his reputation. A fresh generation, in looking at the question, What has Chalmers done? is not unnaturally led to ask, What did he effect for the advancement either of theology, philosophy, or of political economy, or any other subject of which he has treated? But there is some delusion here. Something worth while may be said in response to those questions, but the grandeur of his achievements cannot be thereby fully exhibited. Justice can be done to the splendour of his position only by the testimony of those who had heard and seen him, with the confirmation of that testimony furnished by some few specimens that may be gathered from his recorded works, of the extraordinary power and earnestness which once fascinated multitudes and carried away their minds in rapturous delight.

Through William Wilberforce there came to the pastor of Kilmany the first clear rays of the sunshine which beamed so beautifully in the life and words of that illustrious English layman. His *Practical View of Religion*, designed mainly with the view of rousing to an adequate sense of heavenly truth the people of high condition among whom he lived, was the torch in the hand of the Almighty to kindle the flame which began in 1811 to burn with unexpected brightness in the manse and in the parish of Kilmany. Seven years of an ineffective ministry, according to his own confession, had passed; and more intellectual light had discovered to him the value of the evidence powerfully exhibited by Bishop Butler in the celebrated *Analogy*. He had sympathised with the proofs adduced by Paley; but now the force of truth through the operation of the Holy Spirit had laid hold of the whole man, as it did in the case of Thomas Scott. Everything was changed; all things had become new. The parish church had hitherto been very thinly attended. But during three years that followed the change that humble tabernacle was crowded. Both the high and the low were attracted by the unwonted utterances that came from its pulpit. Hearers came largely from the surrounding districts. Men of mark came from

Dundee, from Edinburgh, and from Glasgow. A great evangelist had sprung up in the quiet rural locality, whose power of riveting men's attention and of commending Jehovah's message was unprecedented in the experience of more than one generation. Not indeed that there was no illumination elsewhere corresponding to that which had reached Kilmany. There were then in the ministry of our Church a goodly number not only of faithful and earnest pastors, but also of effective preachers. In particular, the energy and zeal of Andrew Thomson were beginning to exercise that catching influence over the upper classes of Edinburgh, which in a few years changed the whole tendencies of the city, and made it a peculiar stronghold of evangelical truth. Under his expressive and masculine persuasiveness, frivolity and carelessness of men, women, and children were changed for a deep-seated attachment to the vital truths of the Gospel, and to vigorous activity in devoted service to Christ. But there was a surpassing power in the brilliancy of Chalmers which gave to the instrument of that brilliancy the character of a star excelling in magnitude all the burning and shining lights in the spiritual atmosphere of his generation.

It has been alleged that his most valued utterances to congregated multitudes, when stripped of his peculiar phraseology, unfolded very commonplace sentiments. It is difficult for those who knew how to appreciate him while he lived, and who know now how to estimate the singular expressiveness of his recorded words, to restrain a feeling of indignation at this method of judging him. The peculiarity of his phraseology was not a mere peculiarity of language. It carried with it a peculiarity of thought, whereby the vividness of his conceptions, and the exactness of his representation, imparted an impression of reality to the principles illustrated, which produced an indescribable effect. A dull and prosaic man might amuse himself by taking to pieces the soul-inspiring sentences of such a skilled magician, and find nothing hid under that except the simple announcement of the glorious Gospel. The student bent on depth of investigation, and the results of philosophical reasonings or of scholarly research, may despise the adornment of familiar doctrine by magnificent painting with rich and soft colours, which by enchanting the imagination obtained a strong grasp of the heart. Many persons have tried to accomplish such a result in religious exhortation. The attempt has often failed through want of correct taste and mental power. Men of limited capacity may be of immense service by proclaiming the message of Christ as they have opportunity. But the genius of Chalmers invested that message with an unprecedented interest, and brought it home to vigorous and highly cultivated intellects with extraordinary impressiveness. At the same time his eloquence had charms for people of all descriptions in our congregations. The peculiarities did not hide the truths he spoke of by too ambitious thought, beyond the compass of ordinary hearers. He swayed the understanding and feeling of the common mind, while he filled with satisfaction persons of superior judgment whom he gathered round him. It is desirable to describe this brightness as not only commencing its progress, but as even reaching its highest effulgence in Kilmany. Of course its wide diffusion in Scotland and the world was realised after years of varied experience; but the coincidence is clear from his biography that the very same sermons which, afterwards addressed to highly cultivated audiences in Glasgow and Edinburgh, raised his reputation as a popular preacher to its well-known height, were the fruit of his regenerated mind when filled with the simplicity of anxious desire for the salvation and edification of a humble rustic population. He bestowed intense labour on what he wrote, not from the ambition of applause, but from the fire of evangelical zeal taking hold of his natural genius, and bringing into the service of the pulpit all the force of a high-toned and finely constituted mental organisation. Thus the people of his parish were impressed, and multitudes were attracted, not by novelties of human invention, speculation, or imagination, but by the grand proclamations of the enduring Gospel presented to them through the medium of peculiarly vivifying words and sentences. Then the practical outgoings from his moral sympathies were full of corresponding effect upon the hearts of those with whom he was either in habitual or occasional contact. The change wrought by the Holy Spirit was conspicuous in his pastoral work and in his social life. The glorious Master had fixed on an instrument of extraordinary capacity for the accomplishment of spiritual work, and He set that instrument to shine at Kilmany, not only that it might illuminate all the region around, but also that it might be seen afar off. I have endeavoured in a recent publication to associate its clearness with the radiance of devotion to the only Head and King of the Church,—but any such radiance, if genuine, must spring from the joyful embracing of Jesus Christ and Him crucified as the central object of a soul-inspiring love.

The preciousness of the Kilmany light was felt and realised by influential persons of Christian judgment in Glasgow, who desired to set it on an eminence in that commercial city for the benefit of its teeming multitudes, and he was translated to the ministry of the Tron Church. There Dr. Chalmers rose to a great position, even in view of the general public throughout the country. One effect was a large demand for his work on the evidences, which, originally published as an article in the *Edinburgh Encyclopædia*, had appeared in a separate form. As the production of one now commanding the entranced attention of multitudes it speedily acquired a widely extended circulation. The freshness of its views as to the extent of corroboration given by particular parts of Scripture to the authority of one another and the accumulation of proofs which the author set skilfully before the mind, made that circulation a remarkable event in the progress of evangelical thought. But it contained defects and errors which required correction; so that its history illustrated not only the peculiarity of a mind that was always prone to exhibit what seemed exaggeration of one side in a complex subject, but at the same time the candour and honesty of the same mind in its single-hearted prosecution of truth. In his first publication of his thoughts on the evidences of Christianity, Dr. Chalmers used language which appeared to dismiss as worthless all the internal evidence which had hitherto been founded on, and to claim recognition for the external and historical proofs exclusively. He afterwards acknowledged the rashness of the language, and explained that his objection was to the idea that the merits of Christianity must be estimated by preconceived speculations of the natural mind. In particular, he gave a high place to what he called the experimental evidences. He came to represent the external and historical proofs as chiefly useful for commanding the attention of mankind, and the experimental as alone fitted to lay hold of the convictions and sympathies of the regenerated soul. The subject of the Christian evidences is a popular one, and thus during the initial stages of his popularity in Glasgow, the estimate of his peculiar treatment of this subject was mixed up with the impression of his pulpit eloquence. The specialty of that deep treatment presented some measure of variety before it reached its maturity, along with the additions given to it by his professorial judgment.

His time was otherwise occupied in the years which immediately followed. Those years were very eventful both for him and for the Church. The occurrences in the course of them paved the way for the still greater events which followed. But his place in the evangelical succession, and the brightness of his character in the work of an evangelist, were largely due to what he executed, what he planned for the spiritual interests of Glasgow prior to 1824, and to what he eloquently urged for the promotion of similar interests throughout the country until 1827. The nature and operation, therefore, of that Glasgow ministry are, I think, by far the most interesting and valuable portion of my subject. That portion leads me to the chief result of the striking experience through which he had passed. It also furnishes the foundation of his vigorous and effective movements in the later periods of his life. His speculations upon scientific or political or economical questions, or even on ecclesiastical subjects, are of little consequence comparatively when we look at the prodigious impulse which his exertions gave to the advancement of religious truth and scriptural enlightenment in the great commercial metropolis of Scotland. There he moved the minds and hearts of men and women belonging to all the various classes of citizens. There he raised a magnificent standard for their Christian guidance, and there he set up a mark before them for Christian attainment, which was largely aimed at, while he continued his ministrations among them. The high standard and the soul-inspiring work did not cease to have effect after his removal to St. Andrews. He left behind him, by the blessing of God, a spiritual force which swayed an active community for generations afterwards, and drew the affections of posterity to the cause of Christ and the

Church. As described by a genial and zealous friend, he had brought their fathers to know and love the Gospel. Besides his preaching the cross of Christ on the Lord's Day, in which his extraordinary energy and his wonderful faculty of composition, combined with delivery which enchained attention, were exercised delightfully and profitably, he planned and followed out a series of able discourses in which he electrified an audience brought away from their business through the attractions of his eloquence, and painted in striking colours the harmony of modern astronomy with the discoveries of the Divine Word. In remarkably bold and effective language, he gave a twofold reply to the arguments against the credibility of the Christian revelation, drawn from the apparent disproportion between the magnitude of the redemption it speaks of, and the insignificant position of the planet in which we dwell amid the immensity of creation. Assuming the certainty that the orbs rolling round our sun, and even the distant luminaries in separate and untraceable orbits, were all occupied and enjoyed by intelligent beings, he suggested on the one hand that a candid inquirer could not reasonably take it for granted that the redemption proclaimed in the Gospel has no bearing on the interest or happiness of those beings; and he suggested on the other hand that the amount of loving-kindness supposed by the gospel might be so lavished on the one alienated and lost world, as in the view of an admiring universe to bring out all the more vividly the glorious consistency of the Divine mind and the excellency of operations in the Divine hand. These astronomical discourses had more to do with his rise to celebrity than any other exertions which he made.

The chief features of his Glasgow ministry, however, were those that conspicuously marked him as an evangelist to all classes in the social scale. He looked upon the masses in the lower parts of the city with a longing eye for their emancipation from vice and ungodliness. He was impressed with the feeling that as a commissioned servant of Christ in such a locality it was more his part to put himself alongside the victims whom Satan was palpably carrying to destruction than to visit assiduously the well-conducted parishioners of the congregation. He had a vivid conception of what a Church in a densely populated locality ought to be, and of the manner in which the district surrounding it ought to be cultivated by his own diligence and by the various agencies which had gathered round him. He instituted a system for carrying out his views. Along with the erection of a new place of worship, he succeeded in obtaining an arrangement by which he was enabled to use it for that kind of Church extension which he desired. At the same time he delivered congregational discourses which, whether recently composed or of Kilmany origin, exhibited the character and foundation of his evangelical zeal. He was vehemently intent on the salvation of souls. He saw the obstacles in the way from the indifference, the scepticism, and the inveterate habits of thinking, which kept many apparently wise men in a state of resistance to his plans. He saw those obstacles in addition to the natural enmity to spiritual influences which he encountered among the outcast people whom he strove to benefit. In the face of difficulties, he accomplished a success beyond what he himself perceived. The grand weapon of his warfare was the spirituality of the great message as a remedy for guilt and depravity. Not only was the doctrine of our natural depravity maintained by him as a portion of Divine truth; but the persuasive and personal consciousness of it was represented in his preaching as fundamentally essential to the exercise of saving faith, and a life of godliness. It is not enough to say that he declared that doctrine, and enforced the conviction of it as an absolute essential for the effective reception of the Gospel, but his congregational sermons cannot be duly read and considered without fixing an impression on the mind that the chief point in the bright sunshine by which the perceptions of his audiences were lighted up, lay in the vivid illustrations of what he called the disease and its remedy.

You may thus see how, as an instrument of the Holy Spirit, he brought the rays of Scriptural effulgence to expose the depravity of many whose life was unstained by any palpable departure from the rules of accurate morality, but in whom love for his God and his holiness did not supersede the love of earthly pleasure. You may see how he opened up to view the delight of fellowship with those from whom is blotted out all sin, through the blood of atonement, and through victory over sin by regenerating power. You may see also how his well-chosen words were the means of bringing home to many a heart the urgency of the call from heaven to look intently at Jesus Christ and Him crucified. Thus the danger of neglecting what God has said to us, the correspondence between the revelation of Divine law and the revelation of Divine mercy, the association of faith with repentance, the blessedness of spiritual obedience and personal meetness for heaven, singleness of aim and spiritual discernment, the truth that God is love, a moral fear of God, the shortness of human life, and the connection of faith with peace; these and other truths unfolded by the Divine Word were dealt with in a manner which forced them vividly on the mind. He illustrated the universal blindness of mankind and the universality of the Gospel offer. The ideas brought out by or suggested in the discourses representing such varieties of doctrinal and practical Christianity were undoubtedly in themselves in a sense commonplace, but they were not commonplace in the aspect of enchaining interest which the genius and skill of a specially gifted master gave to them. They attracted by a blaze of overwhelming light the sympathies of his hearers. Some of them flashed conviction across the paths of both learned and unlearned to an extent which largely helped in bringing him a reputation that has not been equalled in our age or country. That reputation extended first to Edinburgh, and to other Scottish localities, and afterwards to the British Empire, to the Continent, and to

America. The astronomical discourses began the widely spreading influence of his voice and pen, but the congregational discourses imparted strength to the movement in his favour, and enriched the character of his popularity. The fact was all the more remarkable, because while preparing to deliver what he uttered in the pulpit, he was not governed by a desire for the fame which followed him, but had his mind and heart intently set upon the rescue of an illiterate population among whom he laboured during the week. His eminence as an evangelist, and his place in the Evangelical Succession, must be estimated by the specialties which I have now imperfectly described, and not by the results which the rash criticism of a young generation of pretentious scholarship may extract from his rather too voluminous publications.

We must connect my subject more particularly with the views and efforts which Dr. Chalmers put forth respecting the right operation in large towns of evangelical exertions, and of all practical arrangements for the Christian benefit of their inhabitants. Those views and efforts cannot be separated from the ideas as to the right treatment of pauperism, or from his conviction that a public provision for meeting all the temporal wants of the poor might engender more poverty than it could heal. His first sermon in Glasgow gave the germ and pith of his contention on that subject. It contains the following remarkable sentences:—" If every shilling of the disposable wealth of the country were given to feed the poor, it would create more poverty than it provides for. It would land us in the mischief of a depraved and beggarly population. Idleness and profligacy would lay hold of the great mass. Every honourable desire after independence would be extinguished. The clamorous and undeserving poor would spread themselves over the whole of that ground which should only be occupied by the children of helplessness; and after the expenditure of millions it would be found that there was more unrelieved want and more unsoftened wretchedness than ever." Accordingly he made it a condition of his having to carry on his ministry in the new parish of St. John's that he and his kirk-session should have separate and independent power over the weekly collections at the church-door, and that the management of the poor of that parish should be left entirely in their hands. His plan was by means of a well-instructed staff of deacons to deal with all applicants for relief in such a manner as, through careful investigation in every case, to prevent unnecessary burdens on the parochial resources, to accomplish what was necessary through the instrumentality of the collections alone, and to dispense with the assessment altogether. For the success of the plan, freedom of access to the church and his ministrations by all classes within the parish was indispensable. Arrangements were made for this requirement, and it is remarkable that an adequate amount of funds was obtained for the right operation of the system in its essential parts, through the collection at the special time of worship adjusted to suit the parochial hearers. "It required," said Mr. Stow, "the mind, enthusiasm, urbanity, and childlike generous feeling of a Chalmers to argue every point, to bear with the old-fashioned prejudice and stubborn resistance to his schemes at every step. They could not but admire the man, but to knock on the head at once all their long experience by such a revolution was not to be tolerated."

It was not enough for Chalmers to explain his views in the most graphic manner when such men believed them to be quite Utopian. He must prove that they will actually succeed, or else they must not even be attempted. They were attempted. It was found easier to do the work than to convince men that it was practicable. The success of the experiment was triumphant. While Dr. Chalmers remained in Glasgow, the expenditure, having formerly been £1400 annually, was reduced to £280, while the comfort and happiness of the population were increased. Undoubtedly their financial improvement as regards relief of the poor was accompanied by vigorous movements for educational advancement and for religious instruction.

www.ingramcontent.com/pod-product-compliance
Lightning Source LLC
Chambersburg PA
CBHW022045230426
43672CB00008B/1079